Custer Legends

Lawrence A. Frost

Bowling Green University Popular Press
Bowling Green, Ohio 43403

Library of Congress Catalog Card No.: 81-82502

ISBN: 0-87972-180-4
      0-87972-181-2

Custer Legends

Books by Lawrence A. Frost

The Custer Album (Superior, 1964)
The U.S. Grant Album (Superior, 1966)
The Court-Martial of General George Armstrong Custer (University of Oklahoma Press, 1968)
The Phil Sheridan Album (Superior 1968)
The Thomas A. Edison Album (Superior, 1969)
General Custer's Libbie (Superior, 1976)
With Custer in '74 (Brigham Young University Press, 1979)
Observations on the Yellowstone Expedition of 1873 (Arthur H. Clark, 1981)
Custer Legends (Popular Press, 1981)

CONTENTS

Acknowledgments and Special Thanks

TWENTY years ago Norman Maclean, professor and head of the English Department at the University of Chicago, urged me to put into writing the tales and legends I had collected about George A. Custer's early years. Once I succumbed to his rhetoric the die was cast. One story led to another and the early years stretched into the entire Custer story. I've enjoyed every minute of each year, thanks to him.

Hugh Shick of Hollywood, California pressed me to put the legends in a form all might enjoy. I tried to.

Col. Charles Custer (USA ret.) of Las Cruces, New Mexico supported the Schick push so he is partially to blame.

Howard Berry of Milan, Michigan, Arthur Carmody of Trenton, Nebraska, John M. Carroll of Bryan, Texas, Aaron Cohen of Scottsdale, Arizona, the Custer Battlefield National Monument staff, William A. Graff of Iowa City, Iowa, Col. Herbert Hart of Arlington, Virginia, Nadya and William Henry of Ft. Larned, Kansas, Mrs. Sarah D. Jackson of the National Archives, Capt. Mike Koury of Fort Collins, Colorado, Frank Mercatante of Grand Rapids, Michigan, Dr. Jay Monaghan of Santa Barbara, California, the staffs of the Monroe County Library, the Dorsch Memorial Library and the Monroe County Historical Museum of Monroe, Michigan, R.L. Nelson of Seattle, Washington, Alexis Praus of Kalamazoo, Michigan, Lisle Reedstrom of Cedar Lake, Indiana, Joseph Rosa of Middlesex, England, Don Russell of Elmhurst, Illinois, Fr. Dominic Russo of Bridgeport, Connecticut, John Sisco of

Monroe, Michigan, Al Stedman II of Detroit, Michigan, Everett Sutton of Benkelman, Nebraska, Robert M. Utley, Chief Historian of the National Park Service and Dr. Frank Wagner, New Orleans, Louisiana, were instrumental in providing leads and useful material.

Ms. Jill Merke and Ms. Kathleen Moore read the manuscript and provided helpful suggestions.

My secretary, Mrs. Harriet Jennette, accepted the task of typing in addition to her many other responsibilities.

And my wife, Ethel, cheerfully accepted diversions from her plans and pursuits to listen to my ideas, to my fragments of writing, and to assist me in the inevitable proof reading.

I offer my thanks to all I have named and to many others who offered assistance whose names I forgot, in my eagerness, to record.

In the course of time I became the only known casualty while on the trail of Custer legends. The wound was in the form of a sprained ankle at the mouth of the Water Carriers' Ravine while in the company of Frank Mercatante. He offered me sympathy but no purple heart. In an additional act of kindness he read the entire manuscript then drew my attention to a number of errors of fact.

Lawrence A. Frost
Monroe, Michigan

Preface

LINCOLN didn't live in Monroe, Michigan. That is why this book is about Custer, for he did. The book's central theme is about Custer—and controversy. Controversy surrounded his life and followed in its wake. Since his death over a century ago the legends, myths and mysteries, like Indians on that fateful day at the Little Big Horn, encircle George Armstrong Custer.

Since this is General Custer's home town, it abounds with Custer legends. Here as elsewhere, people delight in repeating and in believing the sensational stories about him. Though many of these legends are based on the truth, a great number are exaggerations or untruths. Others are figments of the imagination.

"Custer's Last Stand" is one of the most fascinating of historical mysteries. There were no survivors left to tell what really happened to Custer's command yet countless writers have described the final moments as if they had been there. Not satisfied with that they have drawn conclusions as to General Custer's character. How they arrived at such conclusions without a study of Custer's background or numerous military successes is as much a mystery as the finale on Custer Hill.

The great interest in the Custer Story is evidenced by the quarter of a million visitors who travel to the Custer Battlefield in southeastern Montana each summer, by the 1,000 and more artists' interpretations of the Custer story, by the numerous movies and television portrayals of Custer, by the countless articles, cartoons, poems, and books featuring General Custer

3

and, finally, by the organization of the Little Big Horn
Associates over ten years ago. This organization of artists,
authors, historians, teachers and Custer buffs publish a
quarterly research journal and hold annual conferences for
purpose of research and dissemination of the truth about
Custer.

In reading this book the hostiles will charge that the truth
has been hidden or that partiality has been shown. The
friendlies will charge that I have not gone far enough to prove
that the charges made against Custer are unsupported. At
present there are several thousand books containing material
on the Custer story and nearly as many articles. Each year new
material is uncovered that provides additional understanding.
In time perhaps the hostiles and friendlies will be able to meet
on a common ground and smoke the peacepipe.

This has been a nation of hero worshippers from the very
beginning. Patriotism—a pride of belonging—is based on the
deeds, daring and heroism of men like Washington, Lincoln,
Carver, Edison, Lindbergh, Patton and the many others who
have contributed to our heritage. All had feet of clay; nearly all
had humble beginnings. These men were judged and honored
by their contemporaries and peers. Today, without completely
or objectively examining the facts that are available, people
pass judgment upon many of our heroes, and then hold them up
to ridicule. The scoffers sneer at accomplishments they
themselves are incapable of. Without thinking for themselves
they voice the thoughts of those who appear to have some
design in tearing down our American heritage and what we
call good old fashioned patriotism.

Where Custer or any other unusual American is concerned
there is only one way to pass judgment. That is to approach the
subject with an open mind. Examine both sides of each
question, each myth or legend, each episode or event. Draw
your own conclusions.

Lawrence A. Frost
Monroe, Michigan

To General Custer's Nearest Living Relative

His Grandnephew

Colonel Charles Armstrong Custer
United States Army Retired

Chapter One
Custer Slept Here

SURROUNDED today by legends, as once he was by Indians, General Armstrong Custer has become the central figure each year in an increasing number of books and articles. Those who seem to know claim that only Washington and Lincoln have had more written about him.

A fair share of this material has been written by serious students of history who produced their material from original or primary sources. The rest are offerings of hacks who rewrite and embellish previously published myths, or concoct preposterous or unfounded tales of Custer's life.

Biographers with a bent have maintained a swinging pendulum of opinion for and against Custer. Several recent authors depreciated him while an earlier one portrayed him as a combination of Sir Galahad and Joan of Arc. Others overemphasized the virtues of his surviving officers, Major Reno and Captain Benteen, then belittle Custer. Divided into two camps, Custerphobes and Custerphils—we sometimes called them hostiles and friendlies—each side keeps the pendulum swinging.

General Hugh Johnson who served as the director of the National Recovery Act under President F.D. Roosevelt, had little use for hero-sniping. In reviewing one biography that was particularly anti-Custer, he expressed the opinion that the writer had attempted to do to Custer what a Woodland Indian would scorn to consider—scalp an heroic Indian warrior found dead on the field of honor.[1]

Indian fighter General Nelson A. Miles, referring to Custer's caviling critics said: "I have no patience with those who would kick a dead lion."[2] This statement was rephrased by General Custer's grandnephew, Colonel Brice C.W. Custer, who in response to critics of the deceased General stated: "It takes a hell of a lot of guts to kick a dead lion."

Custer's home town—Monroe, Michigan—has circulated its share of unfounded tales. There it is commonly believed by many that he was born in Monroe. Though he was born in New Rumley, Ohio, it can be said he slept in Monroe.

In May, 1842, the Custer family broke up housekeeping in New Rumley and moved to Monroe. George Armstrong Custer was two and one-half years of age. Shortly after they arrived, his father Emanuel's horses were stolen. Discouraged by this reception, they remained six months to make enough money to leave, then returned to New Rumley.[3]

At the age of ten, young George traveled to Monroe to live with his half-sister, Mrs. David Reed, for two years. Anne, as he called her, sent him to the Stebbins Academy to further his education. Her husband, David, made good use of the boy, tending to the horses used in his livery business. Anne trained him to be a reliable baby sitter for her small brood.

One day when the pink-faced, towheaded lad passed the Monroe Street residence of Judge Daniel S. Bacon, a chestnut haired girl of seven who was swinging on the picket fence gate, accosted him boldly with: "Hello you Custer boy." Then realizing her social indiscretion, she panicked and ran into the house.

The Custer lad hardly knew what to make of it, for he was new in Monroe and did not know that this was Libbie Bacon, the only daughter of the Judge. He continued southward to the Reed home some one-half mile away, scarcely giving the matter another thought. Quite probably he had more pressing matters on his mind. Girls held little interest for him. More important were a number of men in the small community who had lived there during the River Raisin massacre in 1813. Most

Emanuel Custer's Wood County (Ohio) Farmhouse. On the Tontogany Creek Road, it and 120 acres of land were purchased by the General's father in March 1861. General Custer never lived here but visited it until his father moved to Monroe in the fall of 1863. Courtesy of Mrs. Rosina Williams.

Ohio honors Custer at his birthplace. Erected by the State of Ohio at New Rumley in 1932 additional improvements and a display have been added to the park in which the statue was dedicated. Courtesy of the Ohio Historical and Archaeological Society.

Custer-Bacon Residence in Monroe, Michigan. Formerly the home of Mrs. Custer's father, Judge Daniel S. Bacon.

of them would respond to his eager questions, holding him spellbound with horrible details of the Indian massacre of the whites.

The two years passed rapidly enough, then it became necessary to return to New Rumley to help his father on the farm. His father had favored George Armstrong somehow, perhaps because Autie, as he now called him, loved horses. The love for horses had developed a strong bond between the two.

Emanuel's first love was his blacksmith shop, for there he could work with many horses not just the two with which he plowed the rich, dark soil of Harrison County, or the small team he drove to church.

With Autie back from Monroe, Emanuel would allow him to plow or help in the shop when there was shoeing to be done. The lad could be depended upon when there were horses about, for Autie took a special delight in riding the newly shod horse bareback while his father estimated the effect of his handicraft on the animal.

By the time he was fourteen his sister Anne asked for him, so it was Monroe again for another two years. At the age of sixteen he returned to New Rumley to attend the McNeely Normal School at Hopedale. After securing his teacher's certificate from the Harrison County Board of School Examiners he obtained a teaching position at the Beech Point School. While there he was nominated to the United States Military Academy by Congressman John Bingham, reporting to West Point in the summer of 1857.

Monroe has been as susceptible to Custer legends as Hollywood. Hollywood often manufactures them, then offers them with tongue-in-cheek. Though Hollywood is well-equipped to dig out the truth, fantasy comes first. Monroe townspeople, no different from people in other sections of the country, sometimes believe these wild yarns because they are convincingly told by responsible, respected citizens.

The first such tale I encountered was that related by a prominent Monroe businessman who prefaced it with the statement that his grandfather "never told a lie." This remarkably truthful man had, during the Civil War, seen

Custer gallop down the sidewalk of Monroe's main street—Front Street—dead drunk, unerringly shooting insulators off the light poles with his service revolver.

Somehow this noteworthy bit of shooting has not been recorded in the press. Custer has been the frequent subject of newspaper writeups but never on the subject of his marksmanship. Wild Bill Hickok, Buffalo Bill, Little Annie Oakley and John Dillinger, though never equalling such fantastic shooting, received ample recognition for their accuracy.

The Navy Colt in use by the cavalry at that time was hardly a weapon from which to expect such accuracy when galloping, let along when the user was inebriated. The sharpshooting appears all the more remarkable when it was learned that there were neither electric light poles nor a power plant in Monroe until 1890.

Neither in his youth nor at West Point had Custer been known to drink alcoholic beverages. On one occasion, the joy of being home on leave and the pleasure of meeting old friends made him cast caution aside. On their insistence he entered one of the local saloons to have a drink for old time's sake. Being high-strung and unused to alcohol, he overindulged. It soon became evident to his tippling colleagues that he would be unable to get home without their assistance.

The two young companions steadied him between them and made their way toward the home of his half-sister, Mrs. David Reed. The first block offered little difficulty for the flagstone sidewalk was wide. As they passed Libbie Bacon's home across the street it was Custer's luck to be seen by Libbie while he was in this rubber-legged and hilarious state. Years afterward she referred to it as "that awful day."

The next six blocks were more difficult to manage for the sidewalks narrowed down to a dirt path under a bower of trees. Once on the Reed front porch his friends leaned him against the front door, pulled the bell cord, then beat a hasty retreat. When Mrs. Reed opened the front door it was a moment of shock. All her religious upbringing revolted at the sight that

Cadet George Armstrong Custer and his first weapon, a Colt-Root revolver. Ca 1859. Lawrence A. Frost collection.

greeted her. Helping her young brother into the house, she half-carried him into the downstairs bedroom, taking a Bible with her. What transpired behind that closed door has never been revealed. Never did he touch alcohol after that, maintaining an abstinence the rest of his life.

During his stay with the Reeds, Custer attended the Sunday school classes at the Monroe Methodist Church. Though his parents attended the Presbyterian Church near their home in Harrison County, they became members of the Methodist Church after they had moved to Monroe in 1863. Though Autie was deeply religious and had professed his faith in Christianity, he never became a member of any church. It did appear that he might at one point, for he was seen to attend the Presbyterian Church Sunday services regularly while he was dating Libbie Bacon.

In 1871 the Monroe Methodists had completed the construction of a fine new edifice diagonally across the street from Judge Bacon's residence. Decades later a story was circulated that General Custer, having been asked to be the principal speaker at the church dedication, had gotten as far as Toledo, but was unable to obtain transportation for the twenty remaining miles to Monroe. Any delay would have prevented him from participating in the dedication. Custer was never one to hesitate. Ordering a locomotive and private car, so the story went, he charged the bill of $10,000 to the Methodist Church.

The story didn't ring true though the alleged teller had been a man of substance on the Methodist Church Board of Trustees at the time. A query to the railroads elicited the reply that there was no record of any such transaction. The church records were equally barren. A newspaper account indicated that General Custer and his wife had arrived in Monroe on Saturday, June 3rd[4]—an entire week prior to the dedication. There had been no need for haste on his part.

General Custer did attend the dedication, but he was not one of the speakers. In a description of the Sunday, June 11 affair, the Reverend Dr. Reid of Chicago gave the dedicatory address that morning. He was followed by the Rev. B.I. Ives in a solicitation of $18,000 to cancel the remaining indebtedness.

That afternoon the Rev. Mr. Ives used all his oratorical skill in an appeal for the remaining $3,000. In a well-planned conclusion of his address, he announced that he had the promise of "a gentleman well known not only to Monroe but to the people of the whole country, for the last $500 needed."[5] Since General Custer was present it required little thought to single him out as the donor, and little effort to raise the remaining $2,500 indebtedness. In a short time his name was formally announced and the church was placed in the hands of the trustees free of all debt.

Custer, when a captain and aide on General McClellan's staff during the Civil War, was observed one evening at a Monroe inn—the Humphrey House—surrounded by a group plying him with questions. The Judge was impressed with the way he answered their questions. He asked Levi Humphrey to introduce him to the young officer, for here was an opportunity to obtain firsthand information on current military affairs.

Custer was aware that the extraordinarily attractive Bacon girl had many admirers and that she displayed a liking for some of them. Unaccustomed to losing battles, he laid siege to her heart. According to her observation he passed her house forty times a day but "is gentleman enough not to gaze into my ladies' chamber every time he passes." He escorted her everywhere and she encouraged him to do so.[7]

Near the end of January he told her that he loved her. She had to tell him that she was not in love with him. An average man would have given up at this point, but Custer was no average man. He reasoned that she cared for him more than she would admit to herself. He decided he would stir this to the surface by an act that would cause her to be jealous. He had noticed that she had displayed some irritation toward her predatory schoolmate Fannie Fifield. Fannie was ruthless in the pursuit of an eligible male. She was pretty and talented, and a natural flirt. That the male she pursued was attached to one of her friends meant little to her.[8]

An opportunity to give Libbie some feeling of anxiety arose

Elizabeth Clift Bacon. 1862. Lawrence A. Frost collection.

several days later at a house party. Libbie observed Custer flirting and holding hands with Fannie. This had the desired effect on Libbie. That Sunday he walked Libbie to church.

He and the Judge had never mentioned Libbie's name in their discussions at the Humphrey House. The rumors linking Captain Custer with his daughter were increasing. In an effort to terminate an affair he believed could only end in tragedy Judge Bacon had some Toledo friends invite Libbie to visit them. He had told her of the gossip circulating around Monroe and advised her to break up the affair.

Libbie relayed her father's wishes to Captain Custer. She told him he was never to meet her again. Nothing was said about not seeing each other. There the matter rested.

When back in Monroe, they saw each other frequently. Though he might escort Fannie Fifield to a party it was Libbie he would take to one side and talk to. On one such occasion she thoughtlessly placed her hand on his shoulder to which he responded by putting his arm around her, then asked for a kiss. With burning cheeks, she refused, saying she was not Fannie Fifield.

She was beginning to realize that he meant much more to her than she had first thought. The act of edging by her father's wishes did not seem to bother her. It was her cousin Albert Bacon's words of advice in a letter that made her recognize her duty to her family and to Captain Custer. When she talked it all over with her friend Nettie Humphrey, Nettie made her realize she was wrong in giving Custer a little hope when both knew it was hopeless to continue the affair.

Nettie had talked in a similar fashion with Captain Custer and he had agreed, painful as the conclusion was. Nettie thought the two should meet and discuss the matter in depth.

For over two hours Libbie and Custer discussed their problem at Nettie's. The conclusion she reached, and which he agreed to abide by, was that they would never go together again but that they would recognize each other as acquaintances. This he agreed to because he loved her. He refused to return the many notes she had written to him, though she asked that they be returned.

When they parted that evening she realized how much she cared for him. On the eve of her twenty-first birthday, April 8th, Custer left for New York to assist General McClellan in making out his final report. When the report was completed he was ordered to join General Pleasonton. On his arrival he was asked to join Pleasonton's staff.

Near the end of May he wrote a letter to Nettie Humphrey which, by agreement, she read to Libbie. Libbie voiced her reactions to its contents, all of which Nettie incorporated in a letter to Custer. As a self-appointed matchmaker and go-between, Nettie assisted the two to comply with the Judge's wish that the two were not to correspond. By a technicality they were able to make the best out of what appeared to be a hopeless situation. There were letters—none directly to each other—but only to Nettie.

This correspondence through Nettie was maintained until he was wounded in the leg in September of 1863. Though a disabling wound, it was minor, but it did earn him a 20-day leave to Monroe.

It was during this period that Libbie and her Boy General came to an understanding. After returning to the cavalry corps the two continued to communicate through Nettie. It was agreed that he would write a letter to the Judge expressing his feelings toward Libbie, after which Libbie was to open the discussion with her father.[9]

It was November 15th before Judge Bacon consented to talk to Libbie about the situation. It was then he made it known he approved of General Custer and that he was aware that the two were in love. Then and until his death in 1866 the Judge had nothing but respect and admiration for Custer, and Custer maintained a similar feeling for the Judge. Just a short time before his death, Judge Bacon stated that Libbie's marriage had been satisfactory to her and to himself. He could not have wished for a more respected son-in-law.

Monroe is the second oldest settlement in southern Michigan, exceeded in age only by Detroit. A distinguishing feature today is its trail of historic markers originating at the

Custer Equestrian Monument. The stories told about the Custer Monument are legion. Since so many questions have been asked, and legends created about the monument, it might be well at this point, to give its background.

In July of 1906 Mrs. Elizabeth B. Custer was informed that the Michigan Cavalry Brigade Association had adopted a resolution to ask the Michigan Legislature to erect a monument to the memory of General Custer. She was cautioned not to get her hopes too high as the obstacle to overcome was the fact that he was not a native son and had never held a commission in the State. A point in Custer's favor was the fact that he had "taken four Michigan regiments and made them into the most famous cavalry brigade of the Civil War."[10]

Monroe nurseryman Charles E. Greening had a similar idea. In a talk before the Civic Improvement Association that November 22nd, he suggested that a worthy project would be "a monument to the memory of General George Armstrong Custer."[11] There is no evidence that he had previous knowledge of the Brigade Association's action.

Under Greening's leadership a campaign was begun to interest the Michigan Legislature, the Michigan Cavalry Brigade Association following a similar simultaneous action. Each acted without knowing of the other at this point. Greening sent out 3,000 letters with petitions, one reaching the desk of Theodore Roosevelt. In acknowledging it Roosevelt wrote that General Custer "has become ... the typical representative of the American regular officer who fought for the extension of our frontier and it is eminently fitting that such a memorial as is proposed should be raised to him."[12]

There was one major difference in the bills proposed by the two contending groups. The Cavalry Brigade had indicated that it preferred that the monument be erected in Lansing on the Capitol grounds. The Monroe group wished it placed in Monroe, Custer's home town, the community in which his family resided. The Monroe City Council added weight by offering a site for the monument.

It was obvious to both groups that neither would be successful if there was disunity. Greening's committee offered to withdraw their bill and back the Brigade Association if it would amend its bill to provide that the monument be erected in Monroe.

William O. Lee of Port Huron—commander of the Michigan Cavalry Brigade Association—wrote to Mrs. Custer informing her of the circumstances and asked for her reaction. "The question arises at which point you prefer to have it located. With both bills in the field we both will fail so I favor a compromise. If possible, express your views to my committee, also the Monroe people,"[13] he added. Greening wrote similarly to Mrs. Custer and expressed the hope that there would be no friction between the two groups. Mrs. Custer responded immediately to both communications advising them she favored Monroe as the site.

In mid-June, Mrs. Custer was informed that the bill had passed both houses and was awaiting the signature of the Governor. The amount appropriated was $25,000.[14]

Governor Fred Warner immediately appointed a Custer Monument Commission of three—Col. George G. Briggs of Grand Rapids, General James H. Kidd of Ionia, and Lieutenant Frederick A. Nims of Monroe.[15]

The Monument Commission members asked Mrs. Custer to seek a sculptor for them who would design a statue she would approve of. Mrs. Custer began the long and arduous task of interviewing sculptors and viewing their models and finished works. Near the end of October the list of applicants numbered twenty.[16]

Chairman Briggs, while advising her to take all the time she needed, informed her that: "Back of you are three stalwart veterans who are loyal to their leader; who will follow the banner of their Joan of Arc to victory, and when her work is completed will see that 'no burning at the stake' takes place."[17]

In early December, Mrs. Custer had narrowed down the list of sculptors to five. A month later Briggs traveled to New York to see a model prepared by Edward Potter. After his return to Grand Rapids, a meeting of the Commission was held and the

Sighting the Enemy. Newly appointed a brigadier general though only 23 years old, Custer, on seeing General JEB Stuart's massed cavalry four miles east of Gettysburg on Jul 3, 1863, drew his saber and led his troops with "Come on you Wolverines!" Though the engagement continued all that afternoon Stuart eventually was driven from the field. Custer became a national hero. Mainly for his success as a commander of the Michigan Cavalry Brigade the State of Michigan erected this monument to him. His wife Libbie selected the moment in his life to be portrayed by the sculptor Edward C. Potter which he titled "Sighting The Enemy." Photo by Everett Payette.

contract was awarded to Potter. Both Mrs. Custer and the Commission had been impressed with Potter's experience with equestrian statues, and his ability and practical ideas, but what impressed them most was his proposal to visit the site where the statue was to be placed so that he could study the lighting and background. No other contestant had suggested such a thought.[18]

Of the sketches Potter offered, the one depicting Custer pulling his horse to a temporary halt, as if to plan a course of action while sighting the enemy, was the most impressive. "Sighting the Enemy" became the sketch of choice. The final contract called for a statue ready and in place for dedication by October 1, 1909, but the illness of Potter made it necessary to extend the date until May 1, 1910.

It had been planned to hold the unveiling ceremony on a day commemorating a battle won by the Michigan Cavalry Brigade. In the end, June 4th was selected, primarily because it was the only day President Taft could be present.[19]

On May 10th, Fred Nims announced that the 7,500 pound 34-foot-high bronze statue had been shipped from the foundry and would arrive in a few days. The town was agog. Responses to the many invitations were beginning to arrive. All were aware that visitors would more than double the populace on the big day. Twenty thousand people meant many unusual problems, but every effort was made to anticipate and prepare for them.

Many notables arrived from all parts of the country but none stirred the hearts like the arrival of Mrs. Custer. She had lived many years for this day. The thought of receptions, the dinners, the streams of visitors all but unnerved her. Other than meeting a few of her old classmates in her niece's home, she withheld from meeting any others until after the Michigan Brigade's dinner at the Armory the evening before the dedication. After General George Spaulding gave her husband a eulogy that evening he said: "We loved him but we adore her." The applause was deafening! It was what she needed most; it gave her courage to face the ordeal of the next day. Frontiersmen, scouts, newspapermen, veteran cavalrymen

There Were People Everywhere Awaiting the Arrival of Mrs. Custer and the President. It was a great day for Monroe. Gates photo. Author's collection.

and old servants got into the reception line but she could not remember any of them.

The President arrived at 9 A.M. the next morning. Some 25,000 people had poured into town to witness the event. Garlands of flags and bunting provided a festive air everywhere. Following an immense parade the ceremonies began in Loranger Square, the site of the monument. Mrs. Custer was seated near the President in the grandstand that had been erected across Washington Street. To her left was the Presbyterian Church in which she had been married, and on her right was the Court House where her father had had his law office and had held court.[20]

The ceremony proceeded smoothly enough though afterward it all seemed as if it was a dream to the General's widow. For her it was a day she would never forget. Almost thirty-five years of widowhood had been devoted to the perpetuation of his memory. An event like this made it all worthwhile.

The Custer monument was the pride and joy of the community for many years though one facet—the English— found it quite irritating to pass it each day on the way to their offices and business establishments. This segment seethed inwardly at the sight of this German farm boy who towered over them physically and historically. Mrs. Custer had thought him equal and even superior to her English forebears but not to these jealous folk. His pose truly was that "Sighting of the Enemy."

Sculptor Potter, at the unveiling ceremony, acknowledged that it would have been more natural having it face toward the town. He wanted the sunlight on the face, and since the sun traveled around the statue on its south side the greater part of the year, he asked the commissioners to head the statue south away from the downtown.

At Gettysburg it was usual to face a statue toward the enemy. In Monroe he thought it appropriate to face it south, "for," as he said, "whoever heard of Custer showing the tail of

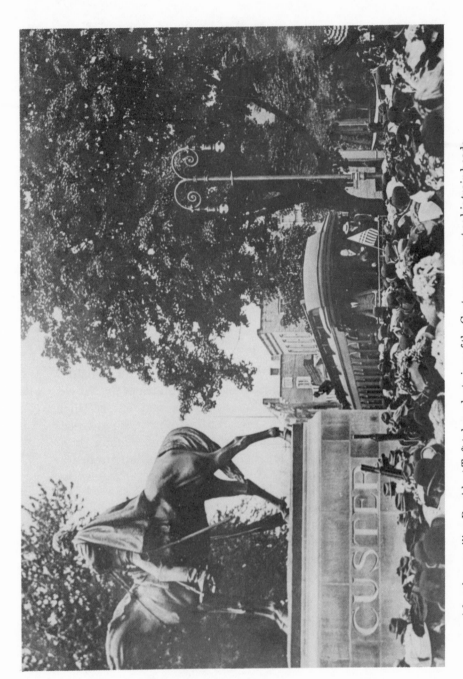

After the unveiling President Taft takes a last view of the Custer monument as his train heads west to Jackson, Michigan. June 4, 1910. Author's collection.

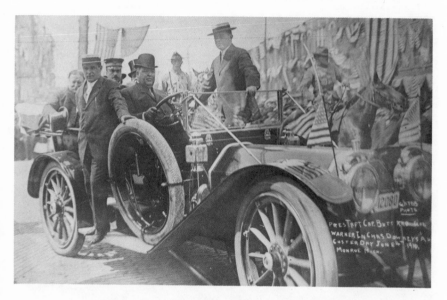

President William H. Taft Visits Monroe and Mrs. Custer. On June 4, 1910, 20,000 people came to Monroe, Michigan to see the President dedicate an equestrian monument to the memory of General George Armstrong Custer. He is seated on the extreme left. Author's collection.

Governor Fred M. Warner, President William Howard Taft and Mrs. Elizabeth Bacon Custer. It was a happy moment for all. June 4, 1910. Author's collection.

My Fellow Americans! Taft gave testimony to the heroism and patriotism of Custer and his cavalry. Mrs. Custer, dressed in black, is seated at the extreme left. June 4, 1910. Author's collection.

A Moment to Remember. Mrs. Custer, with the unveiling ribbon in hand, wonders whether it will work. President Taft and Mayor Jacob Martin on the right stand by for moral support. June 4, 1910. Author's collection.

President Taft and Governor Warner view the Custer-Bacon house in Monroe prior to the unveiling of the monument. Author's collection.

Custer Day Parade. Monroe was draped with bunting and flags in readiness for June 4, 1910. The parade that day had its ranks filled with veterans who had served in Custer's commands. Author's collection.

The Grand Stand in Loranger Square on June 4, 1910. The Custer monument stood in the center of the square facing south before an expectant audience of dignitaries that were seated in the stand built across Washington Street between the County Court House and the Presbyterian Church in which the Custers were married. Author's collection.

They Gave Until It Hurt. These five members of the Custer family died following the orders of a bureaucracy that had little interest in the welfare of the Indians. Top row, left to right: Lieut. James Calhoun and Capt. Thomas Custer. Center: Lieut. Col. George A. Custer. Bottom row, left to right: Harry Armstrong Reed and Boston Custer. All were from Monroe. Author's collection.

his horse to a Southerner?"[21]

An event occurred that gave Custer detractors an opportunity they had been awaiting for thirteen years. A driver of an automobile, while under the influence of alcohol, finding it easier to drive down the center of First Street, saw a man on horseback at the intersection of Washington Street. Unable to control his car he struck the animal and its rider, for neither seemed able to get out of his way. When the uninjured driver sobered up he was embarrassed to learn that the object of his collision was the Custer equestrian monument. The damage to it was slight. Then a rumor was circulated that the foundation was weakening from the passage of the weekly freight deliveries on the track some 100 feet away. It was soon suggested that the monument was a traffic hazard. Pressure was brought to bear upon the City Commission, they in turn requesting the State to make the necessary repairs. State Representative Denias Dawe used the opportunity to serve his constituents by requesting $3,000 for repairing—*and removing*—the monument, and the request was approved.

Before the community was aware of what had transpired, the City Commission, in an almost clandestine action, passed a resolution to move the monument onto some partially filled swamp land called Riverside Park. The Governor had added the requirement that the statue be moved into a park.

That opened a can of worms. Letters of wrath poured in from all parts of Monroe County. Mrs. Custer was informed of the odious act and her letter of objection to the Monroe *Evening News*[22] whipped the small blaze into a raging fire.

Almost everyone in the county had an opinion. Reporters interviewed many prominent citizens and the reactions were varied. They were about equally divided between leaving the monument untouched, moving it but twenty-five feet south of its location, or next to the nearby Park Hotel, or moving it to the parksite on East Front Street. Up to this point it was the male element that had been making the most noise.

On June 18th, the Monroe *Evening News* gave many distaff views. A strong majority maintained that a central location should be retained in deference to Mrs. Custer's wishes, the move to a location some twenty five feet south being highly favored. This would permit ample clearance down First Street for all drunken drivers. Apparently the argument that the foundation of the monument had been weakened by passing freight trains was being offered by the anti-Custer faction. If they could get him out of sight, he would be out of mind. The parksite was the place for him, they concluded.

Mrs. James G. Little offered some observations just a bit too logical for this element. She maintained that:

Scores of women in our city and surrounding country wish to join in a plea not to remove the Custer Monument from the center of our city. The suggestion that the foundation has been injured by the jarring of the railroad hardly seems reasonable as the residences of Mrs. Hogarth and Mrs. Phinney have stood nearly 100 years without injury. The residence of Mrs. George Armitage, very near the track, has stood 80 years or more in perfect order.[23]

It was her suggestion that the monument be moved to the south side of the intersection and the curb set back.

It appears that the distaff reaction was enough to obtain the support of Governor Groesback, for the moving of the monument was ordered stopped in deference to the wishes of Mrs. Custer.[24] There were rumors circulated that the monument might be moved to Lansing.[25]

Charles Greening, who had so actively pressed for locating the monument in Monroe, strongly opposed its being moved. He had received numerous phone calls, letters, telegrams and petitions asking that it remain where it was. Mayor James Gilmore claimed he had received many calls to the contrary, particularly from Spanish and World War I veterans. At a meeting of the monument committee the mayor had appointed, Greening and Gilmore voiced their contrary opinions, then Dr. Dawe moved that the previous action of the City Commission to move the monument be sustained. The motion passed.

The actions of Representative Dawe are inexplicable. The majority of his constituents were opposed to the move. The Governor was in accord with Mrs. Custer's wishes that it not be moved, yet Dawe took the opposite position.

On July 5th, the monument was moved to the parksite

along the River Raisin, and on July 31st there was a public announcement that the monument was completely erected. Mrs. Custer never visited Monroe after that.

In September, 1955, the Custer Monument was rededicated at its new site on the corner of Monroe Street and Elm Avenue. To the crowd assembled, Colonel Brice Custer, grandnephew of the General, said: "The Custer family deeply appreciates the statue being brought out of the wilderness and up here in sight again." His brother, Colonel Charles Custer said: "The City of Monroe today keeps faith with the devoted wife and widow of General Custer."

Some Monroe residents will tell you that the equestrian monument, when at its original location in Loranger Square, had been placed so the rear end of the horse faced south because the homeowners south of it on Washington Street resented its presence.

Walter Gesell, whose barber shop was about fifty yards north of the monument at the time of its removal, when asked about the supposed weakness of the foundation said: "Hell, Doc, they dynamited for two days before they got it loose."

While a committee was planning to move the monument in 1955, former Congressman Lehr called to ask if any consideration had been given to facing it to the south. He was told that every consideration had been given to the thought he offered and that it had been decided to equally divide the corner with the statue so that it faced northeast. In that position it was in balance artistically and could be more easily seen and photographed.

The nearest corner to the statue was occupied by St. Marys Catholic Church, and the other two by a service station and by the Masonic Temple. Then he was reminded that should the statue be faced to the south the members of St. Marys Church would have to look at the rear end of the horse each time they went out the front door. Too, we felt that the Civil War should be considered in the past.

In the friendly discussion with Mr. Lehr, the matter of the

placement of the horse's feet was discussed. Sculptors of that period commonly had one foot of the horse raised if the rider had been wounded in battle, and two feet raised if the rider had been killed in battle. The question, naturally enough, was: "Why did this horse have all four feet on the ground since General Custer was killed in battle?" The answer was simple. This statue depicted Custer in a Civil War uniform as a Civil War general leading the Michigan Cavalry Brigade at Gettysburg. He was not wounded until some months later, and was not killed until thirteen years later.

During the fund raising stage—the committee agreed to raise half of the $12,000 needed to move it, the City matching and providing the other half—a friend who was an active member of the Knights of Columbus called to advise me that the K of C would be happy to give us the money we needed. "There was," he said, "one little string attached to the offer that he was certain our committee would accept."

"What is that?" I replied apprehensively.

"That you place the statue so that the rear end of the horse faces the Masonic Temple!"

The beautiful and arresting statue is known by every schoolchild. It is a common sight to see groups of them standing before it and discussing Custer's role as a military man. A newspaperman told me that he passed the monument each morning as he took his six-year-old to his first grade class. Whenever he had to stop for a red light at the intersection he would point at the horseman and say. "That's General Custer!" His little fellow would look up at the towering figure but say nothing. This was repeated many times. One rainy spring day the same stop was made. There was no such statement this gloomy morning. Suddenly the silence was broken by the little fellow who was pointing at the rain drenched horseman. "That's General Custer!" Nodding in agreement and happy in the thought that his heir was getting the idea, he said: "Yes, son." The little one with all the skepticism of a born newsman said: "But who's that on Custer's back?"

Chapter Two
An Uncivil War

In studying the Custer story no just conclusions can be reached unless attention is given to Custer's Civil War record. Many writers glibly condemn the man without any knowledge or consideration of his background or years of service prior to the 1876 campaign. And in most instances it is obvious they know little of the 1876 campaign or the events leading up to the battle of the Little Big Horn.

As a new graduate of the United States Military Academy young Custer was fortunate enough to be present at the first battle of Bull Run—July 21, 1861. Though assigned as a second lieutenant to the Second U.S. Cavalry he saw the first smoke of battle on that occasion but took no active role in it.

He participated in over one hundred engagements that followed, to earn the title of the Boy General. An appropriate title for a lad of twenty three; he was the youngest general in the Federal service.

When his service first began, a cavalryman was used for escort duty, scouting or message carrying. Indicative of their status was the infantryman's statement: "You'll never see a dead cavalryman." And the statement had merit.

Custer changed all that when, as the new commander of the Michigan Cavalry Brigade, he shouted: "Come on you Wolverines," as he led them in a charge against the seemingly invincible JEB Stuart at Gettysburg. Stuart was leading his

Old West Point Classmates Meet. Confederate Lieutenant James B. Washington, captured by General McClellan's men, had a reunion with his old friend Captain George A. Custer, who was serving as an aide on McClellan's staff. May 1862. James F. Gibson photo, courtesy Library of Congress.

superior force of veteran Confederate cavalry around the Union right on July 3 at the moment the Federal cannons were pounding Pickett's men as they crossed the wheat fields between Seminary and Cemetery ridges. Custer in his red necktie and braid-covered, velveteen uniform was in the front of that charge where he could easily be seen by his men and by his adversaries. An officer dressed like that was an easy target for the foe. He took that chance for he wanted his men to see him share their danger. Courage had to be incited by example. How else was he to instill it in his men than by being seen where danger is foremost?

This was no foolish act. By riding a fiery and fast-gaited horse he could move back and forth rapidly in front of his command thus presenting a moving target difficult to hit. Its effectiveness was evident. Though he had a dozen horses shot under him in the course of the war, he was wounded but once.

By taking a position in front of his command he had the opportunity to closely observe his adversary so that he could decide instantly when and where to lead a charge.

When Custer led the Michigan Brigade against JEB Stuart at Gettysburg he was facing overwhelming odds. In a series of charges and countercharges he drove the Confederate forces from the field saving the tender buttocks of the union line on Cemetery Ridge.

Some, like General Hugh S. Johnson,[1] feel that Custer's spectacular charge so shattered Stuart's cavalry it saved the battle for General Meade. Following that final day of July 3, it was Custer who ripped the rear of Lee's bedraggled forces as they made their weary way toward Virginia where they hoped to lick their wounds.

Custer was no armchair general. Though he was best known as a tactician—some considered him a genius on the field—he displayed some ability as a strategist. He and General Alfred Torbert planned a cavalry attack on Cold Harbor that was approved by Sheridan and supported by Meade and Grant. It was successful beyond all expectations, partially because Custer replaced his armchair with a saddle and led his men in the engagement.

If is not just a matter of "Custer's Luck" as some writers suggest—Custer himself referred to it as such—but a matter of being at the right place at the right time. His rapid rise in rank was the result of unusual courage, dash, flamboyance, an unusual sense of timing, and a charisma that charmed the men into following him against any odds he might decide to challenge.

Some writers have charged that he received high rank through political influence or by accident. Several months before being made a brigadier general he had applied for the appointment of colonel of the Seventh Michigan Volunteer Cavalry. He could not muster enough political influence to obtain it.

It was not mere chance or a matter of political influence that Generals Baldy Smith, Kearny, Hancock, McClellan, Hooker and Pleasonton appointed him to their staffs. All of them, including Barnard and Hancock, commended him for his ability and zeal. It was General Pleasonton, who put his own career on the line when he recommended that three of his cavalry captains be made brigadier generals—Custer, Elon J. Farnsworth of the 8th Illinois, and Wesley Merritt of the 2nd U.S. Cavalry.

Pleasonton and President Lincoln were looking for officers who could win battles. Each of the three named substantiated Pleasonton's judgment. Farnsworth died on the third day at Gettysburg, gallantly leading a charge ordered by Kilpatrick. Merritt and Custer were rivals until the latter's death in 1876.

Custer displayed his qualities of generalship in the battles of Cedar Creek, Five Forks, Cold Harbor, Yellow Tavern where one of his men killed JEB Stuart, Woodstock, Waynesboro, Falling Water and in the Shenandoah Valley Campaign of 1864.

In the final phase of the campaign in 1865 he drove his men hard. They understood for how else could the war be won? It was the cavalry's task to lead the relentless drive that would force Lee to surrender. Sheridan made every effort to head off Lee near Appomattox Court House. Near there on April 8 he reported: "Custer, who had the advance, made a dash at the

station, capturing four trains of supplies, with locomotives . . . .
Custer then pushed on toward Appomattox Court House,
driving the enemy ... charging them repeatedly."

Once the terms of surrender had been decided upon by
Grant and Lee, Sheridan purchased a pine table from the
owner of the house—Wilmer McLean—in which the
capitulation had taken place. Sheridan had given him a $20
goldpiece he had secreted on his person so that it might be used,
in the event he was captured, to purchase his release from a
rebel guard.

Once the small table was in his possession, Sheridan
addressed a short letter to Mrs. Custer, then presented the two
to Custer.[2] The letter read:

Appomattox Court House
April 10, 1865

My dear Madam:

I respectfully present to you the small writing table on which the
conditions for the surrender of the Confederate Army of Northern Virginia
were written by Lt. Gen. Grant—and permit me to say, Madam, that there is
scarcely an individual in our service who has contributed more to bring about
this desirable result than your very gallant husband.

Very Respectfully,
Phil Sheridan
Major General

With pardonable pride Custer passed through the throng
that surrounded the McLean house, carrying the small table on
his head. He knew the war was near its end and had evidenced
that feeling in a farewell order he had issued to the Third
Cavalry Division the day before.[3] In it he had said:

The record established by your indomitable courage is unparalleled in the
annals of war. Your prowess has won for you the respect and admiration of
your enemies. During the past six months, although in most instances
confronted by superior numbers, you have captured from the enemy in open
battle, 111 pieces of field artillery, 65 battleflags, and upwards of 10,000

Constant Companions. The General, his brother Tom and his wife Libbie were inseparable. 1865. Brady photo. Lawrence A. Frost collection.

Major General and Mrs. George Armstrong Custer. 1864. Lawrence A. Frost collection.

prisoners of war, including seven general officers. Within the past 10 days, and included in the above, you have captured 46 pieces of artillery and 37 battleflags. You have never lost a gun, never lost a color, and have never been defeated; and notwithstanding the numerous engagements in which you have borne a prominent part, including those memorable battles of the Shenandoah, you have captured every piece of artillery which the enemy dared open upon you....

And now, speaking for myself alone, when the war is ended and the task of the historian begins—when the deeds of daring have rendered the name and fame of the Third Cavalry Division imperishable, are inscribed upon the bright pages of our country's history, I only ask that my name may be written as that of the Commander of the Third Cavalry Division.

Custer's successful Indian campaigns are better known than his Civil War record. His last battle is the one of which we know the least and yet it is the one about which the most is written. Those hostile to him make the most of that day he died for neither he nor those who died with him can refute the loose statements of those who do not know what happened. As the noted Indian fighter who became General of the nation's army—General Nelson A. Miles—summed up the characters of those hostile to Custer, when he said: "His brothers and strongest friends died with him, while his enemies lived to criticize and cast odium on his name and fame; but it is easy to kick a dead lion." The lion has been dead a hundred years, yet the charges continue to prosper and grow. Some of the charges follow:

CHARGE

"His vanity, his desire to appear distinctive, led him to don whatever dress would make him most conspicuous and distinguish him from his companions."[4] The author of that statement goes on to say that during the Civil War "he took delight in outlandish costumes."

COUNTERCHARGE

Custer permitted his curly, blond hair to grow long, having it cut short only when he entered Richmond, when he married

Libbie Bacon, and when he started for the Little Big Horn and his doom. Instead of the regulation dress hat, he usually wore a broad-brimmed, flat topped, sombrero, either of straw or light colored felt.

Beginning with the hat it should be noted that Custer had a light complexion and a skin that burned readily on exposure to the sun. At West Point his skin was so fair and pink his friends called him Fanny. Out of necessity he was forced to adopt a broadbrimmed hat, the plantation type sombrero being his choice. The Southern cavalryman had learned that straw was cooler than felt, and that a light color reflected the warm rays of the sun. The Northern army seemed never to have learned this.

Barbers were not a common complement of the service. Shaves and haircuts were self-administered. Custer knew he had attractive hair and wasn't ashamed of it. He did have it cut short for his wedding in Monroe but later let it grow with the vow that it would never be cut again until he had entered Richmond. Before he left Fort Abraham Lincoln in the spring of 1876 it was cut short presumably because the coming campaign would be within a country known to be quite warm at that time of the year.

While campaigning on the plains Custer found both comfortable and durable a pair of buckskin trousers and a frontier fringed buckskin jacket waist length.[5] At times he wore moccasins but preferred Wellington cavalry boots because of the protection they afforded his legs while on the trail.

The officers and men were permitted to dress informally while campaigning. Many of the men would have canvas sewed onto their trousers at the points of wear on the seat and inner thighs. G. I. shirts were not mandatory. Checkered black and white shirts were popular, as were navy blue. Hats were every shape and size, for the regulation black felt hat was disliked by all. The hat was hot and unshapely after once in the rain.

For a time Custer wore red flannel shirts until Libbie begged that he not do so. In one he was an obvious target in combat.

Around the post Custer wore the standard and accepted uniforms lieutenant colonels customarily wore. While on garrison duty he dressed smartly and expected his officers to do likewise. They were soldiers in the public eye and he expected them to look like soldiers. He also believed that if they displayed little respect for themselves in the way the dressed they would have little respect for the outfit they served in. Little escaped him in developing *esprit de corps* in the Seventh Cavalry.

When Custer would visit New York during the winter he would wear civilian clothes.

When he was elevated to the rank of brigadier general he recognized the need for attracting attention to himself quickly. How much more quickly could this be done than by way of a bizarre uniform for, as a general officer, he had the prerogative of designing his own. General James H. Kidd, then a colonel in the Michigan Cavalry Brigade, described Custer as the Michigan Brigade viewed him when he first took command:[6]

> Looking at him closely, this is what I saw: An officer superbly mounted who sat his charger as if to the manner born. Tall, lithe, active, muscular, straight as an Indian and as quick in his movements, he had the fair complexion of a schoolgirl.
>
> He was clad in a suit of black velvet, elaborately trimmed with gold lace, which ran down the outer seams of his trousers, and almost covered the sleaves of his cavalry jacket. The wide collar of a blue navy shirt was turned down over the collar of his velvet jacket, and a necktie of brilliant crimson was tied in a graceful knot at the throat, the long ends falling carelessly in front. The double row of buttons on his breast were arranged in groups of two, indicating the rank of a brigadier general. A soft, black hat with wide brim adorned with a gilt cord, and a rosette encircling a silver star, was worn turned down on one side giving him a rakish air. His golden hair fell in graceful luxuriance nearly or quite to his shoulders, and his upper lip was garnished with a blond mustache. A sword and belt, gilt spurs and top boots completed his unique outfit....
>
> That garb, fantastic as at first sight it appeared to be, was to be the distinguishing mark which, during all the remaining years of that war, like the white plume of Henry of Navarre, was to show us where, in the thickest of the fight, we were to seek our leader—for, where danger was ... there was he, always.

General Kidd has indicated that this fantastic garb was a

distinguishing mark in the heat of battle. Like the company guidon, the personal designating flag or the regimental standard, he was the rallying point and none could fail to see where he was. He once said that by being in front where his men could see him in that uniform and red necktie sharing their dangers and inviting the enemies' bullets, he served to set an example. Few men failed to follow when he led.

General George Patton in our own time used a similar psychology. It was his practice to ride in a jeep at the head of a tank advance. When Patton was seen standing in the lead tank or jeep, a pair of ivory handled revolvers strapped to him, his men took on new courage. The faintest of hearts beat faster when they saw their commanding general up in front sharing their hardships and danger. Obviously the revolvers were symbolic of his horse cavalry days for they had no use in tank warfare. Who would doubt it was Patton when they were seen?

CHARGE

In the fall of 1864 the Confederate Ranger John S. Mosby stated, in a letter to General Lee, that during his own absence from his command, "the enemy captured six of my men near Front Royal; these were immediately hung by order and in the presence of General Custer. They also hung another lately in Rappahannock. It is my purpose to hang an equal number of Custer's men whenever I capture them."[7]

COUNTERCHARGE

Mosby was an attorney-turned-guerilla who led a band of parisan cutthroats that, during 1864, effectively harassed the Federal pickets, outposts and supply lines in the Shenandoah Valley of Virginia. He and his biographers have given the impression that Custer committed a war crime in 1864—the hanging of Mosby's guerilla command without the benefit of trial. Nothing could be further from the truth.

Mosby and his men have been glorified in recent years by being called Rangers. During the Civil War the U.S. Congress had passed a bill of pains and penalties against guerillas. Within its definition Mosby's men were considered to be guerillas.[8]

Nearly two weeks after his letter to General Lee, Mosby, in a communication to General Sheridan dated November 11, 1864, repeated the charge against Custer, then admitted to Sheridan that on November 6th "seven of your men were, by my order, executed on the Valley Pike.... Hereafter any prisoners falling into my hands will be treated with the kindness due to their condition, unless some new act of barbarity shall compel me reluctantly to adopt a course of police repulsive to humanity."[9]

This was indeed a strange letter coming from a man who trained as a lawyer admitted taking "an eye for an eye" in retaliation for alleged acts based on hearsay evidence. Mosby reported in his *Memoirs*[10] that his information had been obtained from Confederate newspaper accounts in which an "eyewitness" stated that Generals Merritt, Torbert and Custer were present. Mosby accused Custer of hanging the men in a spirit of revenge rather than on Sheridan's orders.[11]

Mosby commanded a body of several hundred picked men, usually using them in parties of a dozen to one hundred persons to harass the rear and flanks of the Federal troops. His skillful use of mounted troops made him a legendary figure both in the North and in the Confederacy. His guerilla warfare resembled the hit-and-run tactics of the Plains Indians and the North Vietnamese. Operating principally in the rolling countryside of Loudoun, Fairfax and Fauquier Counties in Northern Virginia, he forced his adversaries to spread out and attempt to protect literally a hundred points. His scouts and the sympathetic folks that inhabited the area kept him well-informed of all enemy movements. It was a simple matter for him to select a spot he wished to attack.

Though he and his men were considered unenlisted guerillas by the North he claimed all of his men had enlisted in the Confederate Army. The men took orders from no one but Mosby, and he received his orders from JEB Stuart.

Aside from the harassment and the loss of sleep his

command caused the Federal forces, the North's chief complaints against them were the looting, the frequent wearing of Union uniforms while scouting Union positions, or raiding outposts and pickets, and the assistance his men received from the residents of the area in which they operated.

This so enraged General Grant that on August 16, 1864 he issued a communication to General Sheridan stating that: "The families of most of Mosby's men are known, and can be collected. I think they should be taken and kept at Fort McHenry or some secure place as hostages for the good conduct of Mosby and his men. *Where any of Mosby's men are caught hang them without trial.*"[12] (my italics)

The very next day, Phil Sheridan advised Grant: "Mosby has annoyed me and captured a few wagons. We hung one and shot six of his men yesterday. I have burned all wheat and hay, and brought all stock, sheep, cattle, horses, etc., south of Winchester."[13] Sheridan's men, though acting under Grant's orders, found it necessary to deviate from them by shooting most of the seven guerillas captured rather than hanging them. So ended the first response to Grant's orders.

According to Monaghan,[14] who gives the most objective account of the next incident, Mosby's men attacked an ambulance train at Front Royal, Virginia on September 23. His men were captured in the act of destroying it. In the wreckage was mortally wounded Lieutenant Charles McMaster whose statement that he had surrendered, had been robbed then shot by his assailants caused Sheridan to retaliate.

One of Mosby's Rangers contended that: "Lieutenant McMaster was killed in the excitement of a fight, by men who were seeking to escape from a superior force and who were fighting for their lives."[15] He concluded that it was hardly possible at such a time to say whether McMaster had an opportunity of surrendering, for the affair was only of a few moments duration.

Six of Mosby's men were taken prisoner in the engagement. Three were shot and two were hanged near Front Royal. On one of the latter a paper was pinned which read: "Such is the fate of all of Mosby's gang."[16]

Thomas W. Carter, though listed as one of those hanged, wrote a letter to his home at Orange, Va., in 1908, that he was very much alive. He explained that he had been thrown from his horse on that occasion and had taken to a woods nearby and made his excape.[17] Ironically, there were "eyewitneses" who had seen him hanged.

One "eyewitness" recalled, over thirty years afterward, that while watching the hanging, "General Custer, at the head of his Division, rode by. He was dressed in a splendid suit of silk velvet, his saddle bow bound in silver or gold. ... He was distinguished looking with his yellow locks resting upon his shoulders."

How memory fails one in that period of time. During the 1864 Shenandoah Valley campaign Custer no longer wore a silk velvet suit nor did he wear his hair down to his shoulders. The worn out velvet suit had been replaced with sturdy woolens. Hair had been kept to a collar length, and the gold braid that another "eyewitness" thought he had seen had been discarded with the silk velvet suit of Custer's Gettysburg campaign days.

Mosby returned on crutches to his command on September 29. He had recovered from a bullet wound received near Centerville on September 14. A bullet had struck the grip of one of his revolvers, ricochetting into his groin.

Had Custer been present at the hanging, quite likely he would have been in charge, since both Merritt and Torbert ranked him and would have assigned the unsavory task to him.

Mosby, it must be remembered, was not present. He accepted the account in the Richmond paper as factual, even its incorrect date of September 22. All other accounts give September 23.[18]

It should be noted that the Battle of Fisher's Hill, Va., was in progress on September 22 and in which Custer's cavalry forces were actively engaged. On September 23, Early's battered forces were being pursued and fought at New Market, and Woodstock, Custer and his cavalry playing an active part.

It would be quite improbable that Custer would have been in the vicinity of the hangings. The all engrossing task of routing Early and attempting to emasculate his fleeing command would seemingly leave little time or interest in overseeing a hanging, had he been in the area of Front Royal.

Historian Jay Monaghan concluded that: "Custer might possibly have ridden through Front Royal September 23 but if so he took a 10-mile detour on a 40-mile march";[19] a very unlikely act when pursuing a rapidly retreating foe.

General Early's forces fell back through Woodstock on the morning of September 23rd, reaching Mt. Jackson in the afternoon.[20]

Sheridan was smarting from the knowledge that both General Alfred T.A. Torbert and General William A. Averell had failed to make any significant progress in the pursuit of Confederate General Jubal A. Early after the battle of Fisher's Hill. Sheridan knew that Early's retreating army was impotent and disorganized, an easy prey for his own victorious command.[21] Sheridan lost all hope of bottling up Early's rapidly retreating forces when Torbert was unable to reach the rear of the Confederate column.[22]

Shortly afterward—September 25, 1864—Sheridan removed Averell from his command because of his growing indifference. Sheridan had little use for officers with retiring dispositions. An event occurred soon afterward that sent Sheridan into another tail spin.

About dusk on the evening of October 3, Lieutenant John R. Meigs was murdered within the Federal lines. As an engineering officer he had gone out with two of his assistants to plot the countryside. While returning to camp he met three men dressed in Federal uniforms. Since they were less than two miles from camp, Meigs and his men assumed they were friends. After riding with them for some distance the three strangers revealed their identity by suddenly demanding that Meigs and his men surrender.

As Sheridan related the story in his *Memoirs*, it had been claimed that Meigs, in refusing to surrender, fired on them and was killed for it.[23] Sheridan goes on to say that one of Meigs' men escaped and reported at headquarters within a few minutes afterward, coolly relating the details. It was concluded that the three men dressed in Federal blues had been visiting their homes in the vicinity.

Custer, who had just been moved up to command the Third Cavalry Division—he had been commanding a brigade consisting of four Michigan cavalry regiments and the 25th New York Cavalry—was ordered by Sheridan to burn all houses within a five mile radius of the site of the "foul deed." Sheridan believed that a lesson had to be taught to those who were secretly aiding and harboring the enemy.

The area prescribed included the village of Dayton. After a few houses had been fired, Sheridan ordered Custer to discontinue the burnings but to sieze all able-bodied males.

Continually annoyed by the guerilla bands led by Mosby, White, Gilmore, McNeil and others who had forced Sheridan to weaken his forces on the line by using many of them to escort duty with the supply trains, Sheridan now directed General Wesley Merritt to desolate the Shenandoah Valley by clearing it of all forage and subsistence. By burning the grain and bringing in all cattle, hogs and sheep, partisans such as Mosby would find it difficult to continue their operations. Those who had supported him would tend to blame him for their forced impoverishment. Sheridan knew it was impossible to destroy Mosby's effectiveness in any other way.

On November 5, Mosby held a total of twenty-seven men belonging to Custer's Cavalry. Because of the execution of their men the feeling of the guerilla high command ran high. After a heated discussion it was decided that seven of the prisoners should be executed in retaliation for the six Mosby Rangers executed near Front Royal on September 23, and for the other Ranger hung at Gaines' Crossroad on the order of Colonel William H. Powell October 1.

In this last instance a Federal soldier had been sent ahead to locate cattle and horses that could be confiscated. According to Williamson[24] the soldier had passed himself off as a Confederate who had escaped from a Federal prison. When captured by Mosby's men he had been shot as a spy.

Colonel Powell retaliated for what he described as "the willful and cold-blooded murder of a U.S. soldier by two members of Mosby's gang of cut-throats and robbers," by ordering one of Mosby's men hanged. On the man's breast was placed a placard on which was inscribed: "A.C. Willis, member of Company C, Mosby's command, hanged by the neck in retaliation for the murder of a U.S. soldier by Messrs. Chancellor and Myers."[25]

Colonel Powell compounded this dramatic incident by ordering a detachment to burn the house, barn and outbuildings with all the forage on the Chancellor premises, then drive off the stock.

The twenty-seven prisoners held by Mosby included Custer's Commissary of Subsistence, Captain Charles Brewster. Of twenty-seven pieces of paper used for a drawing, seven were numbered. The bits of paper were placed in a hat, shaken up, and each prisoner was made to draw. Those receiving numbered pieces would be hanged; the remaining twenty would be sent to Libby Prison.

Before the lots were drawn, Brewster told Mosby he had not been at Front Royal, and knew nothing of the hangings there. Mosby brushed his explanations aside with "That will do; it will not help your case."[26] Brewster was fortunate in drawing a blank slip.

Five of the men were hanged on the Valley turnpike near Winchester. There being no rope left to hang the remainder, it was decided that the sixth man would be shot. While being permitted to pray this man managed to untie his hands. Suddenly he struck the lieutenant in charge, knocking him out, then escaped under the cover of darkness.

Mosby's biographer, Williamson, explains rather lamely that "Mosby was compelled to adopt this course, not only on account of these acts of Custer and Powell, but also *by the action of the higher powers.*"[27] (italics mine) Let's look at the record.

The escaped prisoner, according to a letter Williamson reproduced, was George L. Prouty, Company L, 5th Michigan Cavalry.[28] The letter, which in reality was an official report of the executions by Colonel O. Edwards on November 7, 1864, stated that "Of the 23 prisoners 7 were to be executed in retaliation for a like number of Mosby's command who were hung by General Custer. Of the 7 upon whom the lot fell, 3 were hung, 2 shot and 2 escaped. The wounded men, one of whom escaped alive by feigning death, are being cared for by Union families in the vicinity of the camp. The men who have escaped have reported at this post (Winchester, Va.)." With the report went the note Mosby had written and had pinned to the body of one of the victims of hanging, which read:

These men have been hung in retaliation for an equal number of Colonel Mosby's men hung by order of General Custer at Front Royal. Measure for measure.[29]

Williamson charges that Mosby was partly motivated "by the action of the higher powers." Mosby's report to General Lee of the six men allegedly hanged by Custer was dated October October 29. In the communication he indicated that it was his "purpose to hang an equal number of Custer's men." This letter was endorsed by General Lee and forwarded to the Secretary of War, J.A. Seddon, with Lee's endorsement and notation that he had "directed Colonel Mosby, through his adjutant, to hang an equal number of Custer's men in retaliation for those executed by him."[30]

Secretary Seddon had endorsed this communique on November 14, adding his approval to Lee's instructions to Mosby.

It was not until November 19 that final approval was obtained in the form of a communication from the Confederate Secretary of War sustaining Lee's instructions to Mosby.[31] On November 21, Lee referred the communicatoin containing Lee's approval to Colonel Mosby.

Though Mosby wrote afterward "No further 'acts of barbarity' were committed on my men,"[32] neither his nor Lee's orders and communications had the slightest effect on Grant or Sheridan. It seems that Federal officers regarded all Rangers and guerillas as brigands, highwaymen, freebooters, plunderers or partisans who, as irregulars, were not a part of the Confederate Army though led by some of its officers.

What appears to be an obvious disregard for Mosby's feelings in what Sheridan regarded as an all out war, Sheridan, on November 27, ordered General Darius Couch: "If you have arrested spies, hang them; if you are in doubt, hang them anyway. The sooner such characters are killed off the better it will be for the community."[33]

On that same day he directed General Wesley Merritt to move two brigades to the east side of the Blue Ridge mountains to a section that:

> has been the hotbed of lawless bands, who have, from time to time, depredated upon small parties on the line of army communications, on safe guards left at houses, and on small parties of our troops. Their object is plunder and highway robbery. To clear the country of these parties that are bringing destruction upon the innocent as well as their guilty supporters by their cowardly acts, you will consume and destroy all forage and subsistence, burn all barns and mills and their contents, and drive off all stock in the region the boundaries of which are described. This order must be literally executed, bearing in mind, however, that no dwellings are to be burned and that no personal violence will be offered to the citizens. The ultimate results of the guerilla system of warfare is the total destruction of all private property rights in the country occupied by such parties. This destruction may as well commence at home, and the responsibility of it must rest upon the authorities at Richmond, who have acknowledged the legitimacy of guerilla bands. The injury done this army by them is very slight. The injury they have inflicted upon the people and the rebel army may be counted by millions.[34]

One day earlier, Sheridan had informed Grant's chief of staff, General Halleck, that he would soon be working on Mosby. Sheridan indicated that there would be an intense hatred generated toward Mosby by the people in the Shenandoah Valley because they would see Mosby as the cause of the destruction of property they had worked a lifetime to acquire.[35]

It is extremely difficult to unravel atrocity stories years after their occurrence. Mosby's letters to Sheridan and Lee received wide publicity and acceptance. Few knew his charges against Custer were based on hearsay evidence and not on facts.

Mosby claimed that Custer was present at the hangings, and Mosby's biographers repeat the claim. No acceptable evidence has been offered to prove the charge. To the contrary, the evidence is quite clear that Custer had nothing to do with the hanging or shooting of Mosby's men.

Mosby had claimed that seven of his men were hanged— only two were, and not where he had said the hangings occurred. But then Mosby wasn't even present, nor was Custer. Mosby was recovering from a bullet wound and did not rejoin his command until September 29. On September 23, the day of the alleged hanging near Front Royal, Custer was forty miles away on the other side of the mountains.

Mosby even had the date wrong. Yet with all this misrepresentatiion and distortion of facts—and he surely was aware of these misrepresentations after the war concluded— there is no evidence that he ever attempted to correct them for the record.

The real victim is the person whose character is smeared unfairly with a charge of murder, the charge being perpetuated by writers who have neither the time, interest nor opportunity to search for the facts. The real victim was Custer.

Chapter Three
Let's Have a Fair Fight

GENERAL Winfield S. Hancock had tried to suppress the Indian plunderers in Kansas during the spring of 1867 but without success. In an attempt to obtain a winning momentum General Sherman ordered General Sheridan to take command of the Department of the Missouri and subdue the Indians Hancock had been unable to catch.

The Department of the Missouri included the states of Arkansas, Missouri and Kansas, Indian Territory, and the territories of Colorado and New Mexico.

By the spring of 1868 the Indians within the Department became adamant, defiant and warlike. Particularly irritating to them was the construction of the Union Pacific Railroad which, magnetlike, had drawn white settlers and frontiersmen.

Depredation was the only way the Indians could display their dissent. By autumn they had committed 154 murders of white settlers and freighters and had captured numerous women and children.[1]

Reprisals by settlers and soldiers followed with a varying degree of success. Hatred between the adversaries grew and the problem magnified to a point that General Sherman wrote to his brother: "The more we can kill this year, the less will have to be killed next year, for the more I see of these Indians the more convinced I am that they all have to be killed or be maintained as a species of paupers."[2]

57

Sherman was writing in a moment of frustration. He had been appointed to serve on the 1868 peace Commission and had thought the terms offered the Indians fair, but was now witnessing Indian outrages contrary to the terms both sides had agreed upon. "We have tried kindness," he said, "till it is construed as weakness."[3] He had declared war. Sherman proposed "to give them enough of it to satisfy them to their hearts' content."[4]

Sherman was a tough old warrior who recognized the formidable nature of his foe. The many do-gooders offering him advice were an anathema. Though he had, in a moment of anger, voiced his desire to rid the Department of all Indians he really did not want to exterminate them let alone fight them. He considered Indian fighing "inglorious" and a form of combat that offered no fame and little comfort for the soldiers involved. For them it was "all hell."

Both Sherman and Sheridan had been pressed from all sides to employ volunteer regiments of frontiersmen against the treaty-breaking hostiles. Sherman was willing to allow the people to protect themselves but would not accept the offer of volunteer regiments until they were requested by Sheridan.

When it became evident that the hostile Indians on each side of the Union Pacific Railroad had to be driven onto their reservations by force, Sheridan took measures to accomplish it. It was recognized that the hostile Indians were a minority composed of the young men of the tribes.

Sheridan's first response to the crisis was to organize a scouting party of fifty frontiersmen which Colonel George A. Forsyth was ordered to command.

On August 29, 1868, Forsyth left Fort Hays with his small command. Three weeks later it was attacked by nearly 1,000 warriors on the Arickaree Fork of the Republican River. There, from September 17 until the morning of the 25th, it was besieged by this larger force under Roman Nose until a detachment of the Tenth Cavalry from Fort Wallace came to its relief. Though Forsyth's small force had inflicted heavy casualties and lowered the prestige of the huge war party it in no way inhibited the Indian efforts to raid the frontier.

Though most of the officers had done well, Sheridan thought General Alfred Sully should be replaced with a younger officer.[5] Custer was the one who was always eager for a fight, so why not use him?

On September 24, 1868, Sheridan sent a telegram to Monroe, Michigan, advising Custer that Sherman, Sully and he were asking for him. Could he come at once?

Could he! He was on the next train! At Fort Hays, Sheridan outlined his plan to strike the Indians in their snowbound winter camps while the Indian ponies were weak from lack of forage. If the food supplies of the Indian encampment could be destroyed the Indians would be forced onto their reservations or starve.

Old and seasoned scouts said it couldn't be done. Custer didn't argue. He responded by asking Sheridan when he was expected to start.

On the morning of November 26th Custer, with a command comprising eleven troops of the Seventh Cavalry, struck the trail of a Cheyenne war party numbering about one hundred warriors, returning from the north. The ground was covered with twelve inches of snow. After pursuing it for almost twenty-four hours his Osage scouts discovered an Indian village a mile ahead on their front, bordering the Washita River. After reconnoitering, the Cavalry command was divided into four columns of almost equal strength. The surprise attack began at dawn of the 27th, with the band playing the Seventh's fighting music, "Garry Owen."

Since then many charges have been made, though most of them have been verbal.

CHARGE

That Custer struck and massacred a sleeping and defenseless village of peaceful Cheyenne women and children under Chief Black Kettle.[6]

COUNTERCHARGE

Taking a page from the Indian's method of warfare on the white settlements, Custer struck the sleeping village at dawn, catching it napping and totally unaware of his presence. As he said in his November 28 report to General Sheridan: "The Indians were caught napping for once."

Some critics of Custer called it a massacre, charging that the village was defenseless. It must be remembered that the war party the Seventh Cavalry followed had 100 warriors in it, and that they were housed in the village that night. The bodies of 103 warriors were counted on the ground after the two hour conflict. That they were armed is evidenced by Custer's loss of two officers and nineteen enlisted men killed, and three officers and eleven enlisted men wounded.

Women and children had taken up arms and were killed or wounded by soldiers in self-defense, several of the cavalrymen having been wounded by them. Captain Benteen was forced to kill a son of Black Kettle when the lad fired at him killing his horse. Boys were recognized as warriors at the age of fourteen. Then as now any civilian, male or female, firing a weapon at the military was considered a combatant.

The "peaceful" village was composed of forty-seven lodges of Cheyennes, two lodges of Arapahoes, and two lodges of Sioux, fifty-one lodges in all. The village housed four white prisoners. One was a white woman who was killed by her captors at the moment of the attack. A ten-year-old white boy was killed by a squaw who held him captive. Two white children were recovered alive.

The mail and scalp of an expressman killed by the Indian raiders Custer had followed were found in Black Kettle's camp. Circumstantial evidence, it is true, but evidence that hardly could be overlooked.

Sherman noted that Black Kettle claimed to be at peace but had not denied that some of his young braves had been on the war path. Sherman believed that Black Kettle did not wish any war but had lost control of his young warriors.

Sherman knew that the Committee of Indian Affairs of the

United States Senate would demand strong proof that Black Kettle's camp of November 27 was composed of hostile Indians. He was satisfied with Sheridan's positive report that the camp had contained four white captives, two of whom were children, and a woman and a ten-year old boy that had been murdered by squaws during the fight.

In response to charges by Indian agents that Black Kettle's band was on its reservation at the time of Custer's attack Sheridan asserted that the village was ninety miles off its reservation.

As to allegations that the band was friendly he stated: "Some of Black Kettle's young men were out depredating at (Fort) Dodge when the village was wiped out. Mules taken from trains, matter carried by our murdered couriers, photographs stolen from the scenes of outrages on the Solomon and Saline (Rivers), were found in the captured camp, and, in addition, I have their own illustrated history, found in their captured camp, showing the different fights and murders in which this tribe was engaged; the trains attacked; the hay parties attacked about Fort Wallace; the women, citizens and soldiers killed."[7]

CHARGE

Custer abandoned Major Joel H. Elliott and his men to their fate without even a shadow of an effort to save or find them.[8]

COUNTERCHARGE

The subject of Elliott's fate first appeared in an unsigned letter in the *New York Times*, February 14, 1869, as having been previously published in the *St. Louis Democrat*. Captain Frederick Benteen admitted to General Custer he had written it to a friend.

Major Elliott, a very promising young officer, led sixteen of his men in pursuit of some young warriors escaping to the south. Upon capturing them about two miles from the camp he began his return when he was attacked by over 1,000 Indians from the encampments below. They soon overcame his small party.

As Sheridan related it: "No one of those back with the regiment knew of Elliott's party having followed the Indian boys; no one heard the report of their guns and no one knew of their exact fate until they were discovered afterward, savagely mutilated almost beyond recognition."[9]

Custer, upon seeing the large number of Indians approaching from a series of Indian villages below him, realized that he was vastly outnumbered. His first concern was his own small force and the fact that it was without supplies. His men, just before the attack, had divested themselves of their overcoats and all unnecessary equipment. The wagon train containing the tents and all the supplies with a guard of eighty men had not arrived. Destruction of the wagon train could mean the loss of his entire command.

There was no time to search for Elliott and his men. There was little doubt at this point as to their fate. With the increasing and unexpected opposition from the Indians the safety of the command became Custer's paramount concern.

The destruction of the village, in compliance with Sheridan's orders, had been completed. Over 1,000 buffalo robes and skins, which included forty-seven lodges, were burned with huge stores of tobacco, dried meat, gunpowder, saddles, lariats, bows, arrows and guns. On Custer's orders over 700 ponies were shot so they could not fall into Indian hands. Without them the hostiles were reduced to immobility in the deep snow. An additional one hundred horses had been selected to carry the fifty-three captive squaws and three children with the troopers.

Custer lost Major Elliott, Captain Louis M. Hamilton and nineteen enlisted men. Colonel Alfred Barnitz, Captain Tom Custer, Lieutenant E.J. March and eleven enlisted men were wounded. At least one hundred and three warriors had been killed.[10]

When Custer discovered that Elliott and his men were missing he had sent out search parties, one of them under

Captain Myers. It was decided that if Elliott had not escaped to the wagon train he must have perished.[11]

In the so-called "abandonment of Elliott" it should be noted that Custer knew nothing of Elliott having left the battlefield until some time afterward. Elliott's move was not part of Custer's battle plan. No doubt Custer wanted him on the field as the second in command in case he, Custer, fell.[12]

Ben Clark, one of the reliable and trustworthy scouts with Custer, said that the charge of the abandonment of Elliott was made by Benteen because he was "anxious to weaken Custer's prestige." Unable to do so then, he continued his innuendoes and charges until the melodramatic account was printed in the St. Louis newspaper. Nearly eight years later on the Little Big Horn, Benteen abandoned Custer in the same fashion he always charged Custer had abandoned Elliott on the Washita.[13]

CHARGE

"Among the captive women and children was a young girl, Monahseetah, whom he (General Custer) kept with him all winter and spring and who bore him a son in the fall...."[14]

COUNTERCHARGE

A preliminary response might be "Very interesting!" Monahseetah was one of the Cheyenne Indian captives. Her father, Little Rock, ranked second among the chiefs in Black Kettle's village.

Those who like to read between the lines of Custer's account in his *Life on the Plains* and conjure an affair between the two charge that Custer "selected" her as a tent companion. They charge that it became a mutual understanding that resulted in her being delivered that summer—Sandoz' Indian informants informed her it was in the spring of 1869—of a yellow-haired, fair-skinned papoose named Yellow Swallow.

Interestingly enough Brill[15] and Sandoz obtained this information through squaw contemporaries of Monahseetah.

There is little doubt that it was a squaws' story. Dr. Thomas B. Marquis, in a booklet (*She Watched Custer's Last Battle*) he privately printed in 1933, reiterated the same story as told to him by Kate Bighead, a cousin of Monahseetah (Meotzi). Kate stated that her cousin claimed General Custer (the Northern Cheyennes called him Hiestze, meaning Long Hair) was her husband.

In June, 1954, I wrote to Miss Sandoz asking for the source of her evidence in alleging that her character Yellow Swallow in *Cheyenne Autumn*, was a son of General Custer. Graciously she replied that the Darlington school records showed that a Yellow Swallow attended school there, and that various Cheyenne squaws had told her of the existence of the boy and its mother. She also referred to the writings of Marquis and Brill as being sources for her "facts."

Since she had examined the Darlington records and found a Yellow Swallow listed as a student there, and had the testimony of a number of squaws as to his existence, one could accept that there was a Yellow Swallow, but that hardly could be considered the establishment of his paternity. If so, then paternity could be established on hearsay evidence or the wishful thinking of the mother and her female friends and relatives.

In replying to Miss Sandoz I told her that I could not "buy" her story of the paternity of Yellow Swallow. I wrote further: "To begin with it smacks of too much rumor. How can you accept as *fact* the paternity of a boy on the Darlington ration and school rolls just because he bore either the name of Yellow Swallow, Custer's Son, or Autie Jr., when you know it could have been placed there by a wishful thinking squaw or a malicious Indian agent?

"The old timers and the squaws were as given to rumor mongering and gossip as any other group of human beings. Certainly maintaining another Custer myth won't help or harm him now but when a man is alive it seems to be quite the custom to repeat such things.

"I've always had the impression that paternity was the sort of thing that a mother had to establish by law, and that usually means marriage, confession of guilt, blood typing, or even witnesses. Even then there are loopholes. So how can it be established in a case of this kind on the basis of the unreliability of old wives' tales?"

Several years later I made it a particular point to check the Darlington Agency files at the National Archives in Washington. The archivist in charge advised me that they had no records covering deaths, births, baptisms or medical care for the years 1867, 1868 and 1869, of the Cheyenne and Kiowa agencies of the Upper Arkansas. The correspondence files of the Central Agency were checked for the same years but nothing was found in reference to Yellow Swallow or Monahseetah.

I also examined the medical records of Forts Harker, Sill, Dodge and Camp Supply for 1867, 1868 and 1869, but found nothing relative or pertinent. The Fort Hays medical records for September through December, 1868, and January through October, 1868, showed no entries—just blank pages.

Since a rumor accompanied the rumor that Yellow Swallow died of a venereal taint I thought it best to check this out. In examining Custer's medical records, from his entry into the Military Academy through his service during the Civil War and the post war period up to his death, nothing could be found to indicate he had been anything but well. If Yellow Swallow died from a venereal taint it could be construed that Monahseetah was not as innocent as portrayed.

As to Yellow Swallow allegedly having fair skin and yellow hair, Mrs. Custer puts this to rest by describing Monahseetah's baby as "a cunning little bundle of brown velvet, with the same bright, bead-like eyes as the rest."[16] This observation she made when she first visited the prisoners placed in the stockade at Ft. Hays.

Historian Edgar I. Stewart, in the introduction to a reprint of Custer's *My Life on the Plains* (Norman, 1962, p. xx) evidenced his being taken in by the Yellow Swallow story. Since he stated that "while it cannot positively be asserted that Custer was the father of the half-blood son, neither can it be positively denied," it appears he had not read General Custer's letter to his wife written January 14, 1869, which stated: "One of the squaws among the prisoners had a little papoose a few nights since...." Mrs. Custer indicated that "the baby referred to was the child of an Indian princess described in a previous chapter."[17] The Indian princess was Monahseetah.

General Custer met Monahseetah for the first time on November 27, 1868. Monahseetah's son was born on or within a day or two of January 12, 1869. Hardly a premature baby or a Custer baby.

Benteen, Custer hater that he was, wrote to Theodore W. Goldin that the squaw "calved" at Fort Sill and that the baby was "a simon-pure Cheyenne baby, the seed having been sown before we came down on their fold at Washita."[18] The charge of paternity was absurd to Benteen; who else could posibly give the story credence?

CHARGE

General Custer used Monahseetah as an "interpreter" although she spoke no English from the time he left Camp Supply until he quit his command at Fort Hays four months later when he took leave of her...."[19]

COUNTERCHARGE

Here Brill attempts to discredit Custer and his relationship with Libbie by alleging that a romance existed on the basis that the Indian girl spoke no English. He makes no mention that Custer was extremely adept in the Indian sign language which Monahseetah, of course, could interpret. Brill makes little or nothing of the great service Monahseetah rendered in interpreting Custer's wishes to her tribe and her endeavors to encourage them to return to their reservation.

CHARGE

As a boy Custer had been mischievous, tenderhearted, kindly, but never bad. At West Point "he underwent a change of character, developing jealousies and engendering enmities which were continued throughout the remainder of his life."[20]

Lieutenant William B. Hazen, while serving as Officer of the Day at West Point, had occasion to arrest young Custer as Officer of the Guard, for permitting—even urging on—a fist fight between two cadets. Custer was tried by courtmartial and found guilty. "For this Custer never forgave Hazen, carrying the animosity in his heart toward this fellow officer to the day of his death."[21]

COUNTERCHARGE

Strangely enough one of the two cadets engaged in fisticuffs when Custer arrived on the scene was William Ludlow who was to be Custer's chief of engineers during his reconnaisance of the Black Hills in 1874. Both Custer and Ludlow were found guilty and both were given light punishment though Custer, in actuality, never received the reprimand that was to have been administered by the Superintendent.

Hazen, who had differing views with Custer on several subjects after the Civil War, testified at the courtmartial that Custer, while serving in his company "held a good character for conduct," and that he "only had occasion to report him for trivial offenses until the one for which he is now on trial."[22]

Hazen, because of his outspokenness, was given difficult assignments in the post-war West. He was honest and straight forward in his comments though they were tinged by a bitterness obviously the result of his placement. He and Custer, though friendly rivals, had occasion to assail each other because of opinions characteristic of each. Custer was an optimist while Hazen was a pessimist. Custer saw the Dakotas as a land of opportunity for the little man while Hazen saw it as an opportunity for the big man and the Northern Pacific Rail Road in particular.

CHARGE

Brill delighted in running Custer down. He admits Custer was "strictly devoid of vices and evil habits during his earlier days," then goes on to charge him with being "a heavy drinker and fast liver during the Civil War." To this he adds that "he was severe on any officer or enlisted man of his command who drank to excess."[23]

COUNTERCHARGE

So, let's settle this drinking thing. Custer was brought up under the rigid moral discipline of the period which his Methodist half-sister Anne embraced. Her influence on his life can easily be traced.

There is only one known instance in which young Custer drank to excess and that was on one of his visits home from the war while he was a youthful lieutenant. His adopted home at that time was Monroe, Michigan. The story has been told in an earlier chapter of this book. No instance has been noted, other than this one time, that he over indulged. If there be heavy drinking as charged, let the accuser produce the facts.

There were numerous instances where both he and Libbie went out of their way, and well beyond the call of duty, in attempts to direct young officers toward a path of restraint in the use of alcoholic beverages. Both knew the awful lonesomeness and boredom the young officers experienced in the western garrisons during the long winters. Away from family and female companionship and with too much idle time to while away they turned to cards and liquor.

Libbie managed to inveigle young women to accompany her back to the western posts for the winter season so there would be companionship for the officers. Her husband encouraged entertainments, horse racing and parties to occupy the men and officers. On a few occasions Custer acted with severity on officers who became drunk while on duty. Custer would ignore drinking off duty. It was an unpardonable offense to him for an officer to drink on duty when that officer had the lives of many men in his grasp in a country containing hostiles.

Custer was well aware of the drinking habits of his officers and would, though a teetotaler, serve wine to guests in his home, taking none for himself. On one occasion he ordered that a bottle of whiskey be given one of his men after a particularly dangerous swim in an icy cold river in the line of duty.

CHARGE

"Gen. George Armstrong Custer had a lady friend along at the disastrous battle of the Little Big Horn. The military men who revealed the secret described her as a camp follower," wrote Frederick C. Othman, a Washington columnist in the Toledo *Times* of November 20, 1957.

COUNTERCHARGE

Othman and his informant implied that "if Custer hadn't been paying so much attention to this pretty one, he might have escaped the Indians of Sitting Bull and Crazy Horse." The columnist went on to say that the powers-that-be didn't release the information out of respect for Mrs. Custer. He claimed that for many years the story was a "classified" secret, and that after Mrs. Custer died, no one seemed interested enough to bring up the subject. It was because of Representative John E. Moss of California, while heading a subcommittee investigating the pileup of ancient documents marked "top secret" that the stamp was taken off military secrets filling some 100,000 drawers.

In contrast, "a search of the records in the National Archives discloses no evidence of a romance with an Indian maiden," wrote Scripps-Howard reporter Lowell K. Bridwell in the Cleveland *Press*, December 2, 1957.

Though Mr. Bridwell's search may be accepted as conclusive there are no other facts that support him. It should be recalled that nearly three hundred men with Reno and Benteen survived the battle, all of whom would have been aware of any women who might have accompanied the expedition. Not all of these men would have kept the information confidential. Most certainly Captain Benteen would not have hesitated in so stating it in his letters to Theodore Goldin. Then too the Indians would have noted, and reported, the presence of a woman for they stripped every soldier they had killed in battle.

CHARGE

A capricious orphan by the name of Annie Jones made the statement that she had been the companion of various general officers during the Civil War having "joined General (Judson) Kilpatrick's command and went to the front as the friend and companion of General Custer."[24]

COUNTERCHARGE

According to this sworn statement from the Provost Marshal's file, Annie Jones left her home at Cambridge, Mass. in August, 1861, at the age of 17, to become a hospital nurse in Washington. Because of her youth she was unable to find such employment but did manage to obtain a pass from General John E. Wool to visit the army camps around Baltimore. Spending some months this way, "I was furnished by the commanding officers with a tent," she said, "and sometimes occupied quarters with the officers." Her object, so she stated, was merely curiosity.

"General Kilpatrick," she continued, "became very jealous of General Custer's attentions to me and went to General Meade's headquarters and charged me with being a spy. I was then arrested and sent to General Martindale, Military Governor of Washington, who committed me to the Old Capitol Prison."[25]

At the prison Annie made friends easily. She enjoyed special privileges because of her intimate relations with some of the men. One of the prison employees was discharged because of this.

She had been arrested three different times on the charge of being a spy. In each instance she was found innocent and released. The last arrest and investigation was based on a letter sent to the Provost Marshal. The Provost Marshal wrote in his report of February 2, 1863: "It is my opinion that the girl has been wrongfully accused by some one who dares not sign their own name to the statement for fear of getting into trouble themselves. There is something back of this.... The letter containing the charges was evidently written by a female who is jealous of her, as her former lover is paying some attention to this Miss Jones and I found that she was very anxious to have this Miss Jones out of her way."26

About six weeks after his marriage to Libbie Bacon, Custer replied to General Alfred Pleasonton's request for an answer to the charges Annie Jones had made. It was dated March 22, 1864. In this communication he referred to her as Annie E. Jones, though in the Provost Marshal's file she is sometimes referred to as Annie Jones and Annie Elinor Jones, both names applying to the same individual. However the file does contain a courtmartial summary of an Ann M. Jones (General Orders No. 93, October 7th, 1864) showing charges of being a spy and harboring and concealing enemies of the U.S. This Ann Jones was found to be "not guilty." It appears that this is not the same woman referred to as Annie E. Jones.27

Custer's statement to Pleasonton indicates that Annie came to his camp near Warrenton Junction, Va. in the fall of 1863, with passes issued to her by the War Department.

She expressed a desire to attach herself to one of the hospitals connected with the 3rd Divison," he said. "I gave her permission to remain at my headquarters until she could ascertain whether her services were required at any of the hospitals in the command. She remained at my headquarters about one week and desired to remain longer, but I denied her permission to do so.... Upon leaving I informed her that she must never visit my command again. A few weeks later she came in an ambulance and an escort furnished by Major General Warren.

At first glance I refused to see her and told my Adjutant General, Captain Greene, to order her return to General Warren, or at least to leave my command; it being nearly dark and she representing herself very much fatigued from having ridden nearly 30 miles, I gave her permission to delay her departure until morning when she left my headquarters after having been warned by me and my staff officers that in case she visited my command again she would be compelled to leave under charge of a guard. Since then I have never seen her....

Her whole object and purpose in being with the army seemed to be to distinguish herself by some deed of daring; in this respect alone she seemed insane. It was my disinclination to use force toward her that induced me to prevent her to stay the short time I have mentioned. So far as her statement in relation to General Kilpatrick and myself goes it is simply untrue. I do not believe she is or ever was a spy. This part of her reputation has been gained by her impudence."[28]

Before we draw any conclusions let's go back a bit. It has been noted in mid-January, 1863, Annie was unjustly accused, in a letter fictitiously signed, of being a Confederate sympathizer. The Provost Marshal cleared her of all charges on February 2, 1863.

She was arrested again on March 13, 1864, and charged with being a rebel spy. On the following day, according to a letter she had written to President Lincoln on March 23, 1864, the arresting officer, Colonel L.C. Baker, had forced her to sign a statement by threatening to commit her to the Old Capitol Prison if she didn't. It was the statement that had in it the defamatory remarks about Kilpatrick and Custer which Annie claimed in this letter to Lincoln "were utterly false and unfounded." This statement exonerates Kilpatrick and Custer.

Meanwhile Annie's defamatory letter had reached General Meade's hands, then was referred on to General Pleasonton, who was Meade's Chief of Cavalry, Army of the Potomac. Meade requested that the accused two make "such explanations, if any, as they may desire to present." Custer made his on March 22, 1864; Kilpatrick gave no reply, apparently thinking Custer did well enough for the both of them.

John C. Andrew, Governor of Massachusetts, became quite interested in the mistreatment of Annie Jones for on May 24 he forwarded her letter to the President, Lincoln referring it to Secretary of War Edwin M. Stanton, asking as to the evidence. Stanton in turn referred it to Colonel Baker, requesting an explanation. Baker denied the charge that he had forced or coerced Annie into signing the malicious charges. He claimed that he had read the charges to her three times and that she had signed them willingly enough. He did not explain why he was the one to draft them.

On July 9, 1864, the Secretary of War ordered Annie's release. The file indicates that Annie Jones was in Vicksburg, Miss., on May 14, 1866, in the capacity of a nurse.

The Annie Elinor Jones File was classified as top secret until some years ago—November, 1957—and now may be seen at the National Archives.

From the above one may conclude that an attractive and adventurous teen-age girl indiscreetly passed out her favors to men of position or influence in the military service. This is neither an unusual circumstance nor a first time that this sort of thing has happened during a war.

The girl, because of a certain freedom of movement permitted her in army camps and because of attentions showered on her by ranking officers, was the subject of repeated charges of being a spy. All charges, upon investigation, were dropped.

In the instance where she was pressured into signing a statement trumped up by Colonel L.C. Baker charging Custer and Kilpatrick with intimate relations with her, Annie denied the charges in her letter to President Lincoln. Custer had denied the charges. Kilpatrick, relying on Custer's statement of the circumstances in which he had met Annie, refused to view the matter important enough to add to Custer's explanation.

As Custer had stated, Annie Jones' "reputaton has been gained by her impudence." One can conclude that she was also imprudent.

Chapter Four
Custer was Court-Martialed Twice

CADET George Custer was completing his 66th Saturday[1] as the Officer of the Guard at the United States Military Academy. It was customary for West Point cadets to serve in this capacity at least once prior to graduation, but in young Custer's case he was serving extra tours of duty as punishment for his numerous violations of the Military Academy regulations.

Discipline had irked him during his four years there and to such an extent that he had accumulated 741 demerits[2] for 453 offenses. It is true that the marks against him were not of a serious nature since they consisted of such offenses as not properly standing at attention, improper saluting, an unbuttoned overcoat, food in his quarters, being late to dinner, and throwing stones. A cadet could be dismissed when he acquired 835 demerits. Young Custer had but ninety-four to go when he was graduated on June 24, 1861.

Six weeks earlier the regular five year class had been graduated. Custer's class had completed a course reduced to four years in response to an urgent call from the President for competent officers to train raw troops.

It was near evening of June 29th, just five days after graduation, when he heard a commotion near the guard tents. Hurrying toward the area he discovered two cadets squaring off for a fist fight. Several other cadets were trying to separate the two. Instead of arresting the two combatants as he was obliged to do, Custer instinctively called out, "Stand back boys: let's have a fair fight." It was a decision he was to regret.

Hardly had he uttered the words than the crowd seemed to melt away. The cause was soon apparent, for seen approaching were two regular army officers assigned to the Academy, Lieutenants William B. Hazen and William E. Merrill.

Lieutenant Hazen, acting as Officer of the Day, demanded, "Why did you not suppress the riot which occurred here a few minutes ago?" Overwhelmed by the thought that a fist fight could be interpreted as a riot, and realizing that he should have arrested the two belligerents and sent them to the guard tents, he was speechless. Hazen was obliged to report him.

Just a few hours later Custer's class was ordered to proceed to Washington for further assignments. His name was not on the list.[3]

The following morning he reported to his commandant, Lieutenant Colonel John F. Reynolds. He was unable to give him a satisfactory explanation. Reynolds reported the facts of the case to Washington, requesting a courtmartial.

Charged with "neglect of duty" and "conduct to the prejudice of good order and military discipline" with the specifications that he "did fail to take proper steps to suppress a quarrel between two cadets" and "did give countenance to a quarrel," young Custer pleaded "Guilty."

The trial took place on July 5th[4] before a court of nine officers of the regular army with Lieutenant Stephen B. Benet acting as Judge Advocate. Cadets Peter M. Tyerson and William Ludlow, the principals in the dispute Custer had observed, served as his first two witnesses. Both indicated their dispute was of no consequence.

Lieutenant William B. Hazen then took the stand in Custer's behalf, attesting to his good conduct and character. Custer requested and received permission to present his defense the following day.

In four pages of longhand he referred to the quarrel between the two cadets as a "trifling consideration" with no "serious results," since it was "merely a scuffle." In continuing, he expressed his grief and disappointment in not being permitted to accompany his graduating class into the military service. He believed his detention on the eve of war "surpassed in a hundred fold the punishment" that would have been meted out to him in time of peace. Added to this was his anxiety in awaiting the arrival of the members of the Court and the inconvenience of being in arrest with movement restricted until the court convened.

In conclusion, young Custer drew attention to "the peculiar merits and circumstances" of his case that had created an unusual situation. He ended by saying, "the detention and mortification which it has already occasioned me and the torturing suspension I must experience before I hear the findings of this Court will have their weight assigned to them by mature reflection and impartial justice."

The Judge Advocate, Stephen B. Benet, released the sentence on July 15th, stating the Court "finds the accused guilty and sentences him *to be reprimanded in orders*" and adding that "the Court are thus lenient in the sentence to the peculiar situation of Cadet Custer as presented in his defense, and in consideration of his general good conduct as testified to by Lieutenant Hazen his immediate commander."

In a few days the superintendent of the Academy received a telegraphic order releasing young Custer and ordering him to report to the Adjutant General in Washington for duty. Several classmates, through influential friends in Washigton, had managed to secure his release.

Custer never learned of the decision of the Court. It was unfortunate in one respect for he would have discovered that Lieutenant Hazen's testimony played an important part in the Court's final leniency in the disposition of the case.

In another six years, Custer, the Boy General, had another run in with his superiors. By 1867, he enjoyed an enviable Civil War reputation and record but had little experience fighting Indians. Major General Winfield S. Hancock too had a fine Civil War record but, like Custer, knew nothing about fighting Indians. When the Plains Indians began to murder, rob and rape the Kansas settlers, then disrupt and halt the construction of the Kansas Pacific Railroad, bringing travel and communication to a standstill, Kansas Governor Samuel J. Crawford demanded that the Government provide protection.

General Sherman assigned the problem to General Hancock, conveying to him his wish that the campaign should begin in the spring of 1867, and that the Indians be offered "no quarter."[5] Custer and his newly formed Seventh Cavalry were ordered to join Hancock since it was the only cavalry regiment immediately available.

Early in April Hancock and his command of some 1,500 men set out for Fort Larned where a council was arranged with some Cheyenne chiefs. It became apparent that the Indians had no intention of approaching the troops or allowing the troops to approach toward their village.

Another council was finally arranged which several Cheyenne chiefs and a dozen warriors attended. Hancock explained to them that the purpose of his expedition was to promote peace. To this their resplies were vague. They did remark that they thought the visit would not be peaceful because Hancock had brought so many soldiers with him.

The following morning Hancock marched his entire command twenty-one miles to the Indian village on the Pawnee Fork. During the following evening the inhabitants of the village disappeared. Fearful of another Sand Creek massacre, their solution was flight. Hancock had been unable to convince the Indians that the movement of his troops next to their village was made with honorable intentions. The Sioux and Cheyenne mistrusted him. They could not forget the time when Col. J.M. Chivington and his 800 men attacked a peaceful Cheyenne camp of 100 lodges. Three-fourths of the 100 Indian dead were women and children.[6]

Custer was ordered in pursuit of the escaping Indians. When he gained on them they broke up into numerous small bands and separated. The trails were difficult and, finally, impossible to follow on the hard, dry ground. By this time Custer had concluded that: "The hasty flight of the Indians and the abandonment of, to them, valuable property, convinces me that they are influenced by fear alone, and it is my opinion that no council can be held with them in the presence of a large military force."[7]

Custer moved on toward the Smoky Hill trail where he discovered that the stage stations along the route had been attacked and were in a state of siege. A number of civilian occupants had been tortured and killed. Custer moved on to Fort Hays where he learned that a party of 800 Sioux, Pawnees and Cheyennes had been seen heading north, painted and ready for war.

With the knowledge of all this, Hancock could hold back no longer. On the morning of June 19, he ordered the Cheyenne village of 251 lodges completely destroyed. This included 942 buffalo robes, 436 saddles and vast amounts of housekeeping articles. Indian Commissioner N.G. Taylor was of the opinion that this act brought on another Indian war which could have been averted.[8]

Taylor was right. Hancock's order to fire the village was the opening gun of a summer of Indian plundering. These intensified to the degree that they were uncontrollable. Custer reported seven years later: "Of the many important expeditions organized to operate in the Indian country, none, perhaps, of late years has excited more general and unfriendly comment, considering the slight loss of life inflicted upon the Indians, than the expedition organized and led by Maj. General Hancock in the Spring of 1867."[9]

Sherman wanted the area between the Arkansas and Platte rivers cleared of all hostile Indians. Custer and his cavalry were assigned the task. On June 1, Custer left Old Fort Hays with six companies of the Seventh Cavalry riding north in the direction of Fort McPherson on the Platte River. In this scout they were to describe a semicircle to the south, touch the Republican River, then move up north to Fort Sedgwick on the Platte River. Once the supplies were replenished at that point they would move south to Fort Wallace on the Smoky Hill River, and then back to their starting point at Fort Hays. The distance to be traveled would be about 1,000 miles.

On the 200 mile trek to Fort McPherson, Maj. Wickcliffe Cooper shot himself to death while intoxicated. When

McPherson was reached, supplies, rations and forage were replenished, then the column moved on in a westerly direction. At the camp of that first evening a Sioux Chief, Pawnee Killer, along with several other Sioux chiefs, appeared for a talk with Custer. Their obvious purpose was to obtain information, food and ammunition. Custer's response was limited to food.

When Pawnee Killer found his efforts to discover where Custer was going were unsuccessful he made promises to bring his band to Fort McPherson to camp. He never kept his promise.

Before Custer left the vicinity of Fort McPherson, Sherman received word from Fort Wallace that every garrisoned stage station seventy-five miles east and west of the fort had received an average of four Indian attacks. There was no question that the Smoky Hill stage route was under siege.[10]

Sherman did not send the cavalry south to Fort Wallace immediately. Instead Custer was sent over toward Fort Sedgwick with orders to search the area thoroughly for Indians. When about seventy five miles southeast of Fort Sedgwick and about the same distance from Fort Wallace, Custer decided to send a small detachment up to Fort Sedgwick for any message meant for him, and send a larger detachment with the wagon train south to Fort Wallace for provisions.

Major Joel A. Elliott led the dangerous 100-mile mission to Fort Sedgwick. Five days later—June 28—they returned, their mission accomplished. There was no message for Custer. Capt. Robert M. West and Lt. W.W. Cooke had left for Fort Wallace with a train of twelve wagons and a company of cavalrymen. On their return they were attacked by an overwhelming number of Indians but managed to extricate themselves from the situation by putting up a vigorous defense.

At this time, Custer was acting without specific orders. Elliott had found none for him at Fort Sedgwick, and Cooke had found none for him at Fort Wallace. Meanwhile, Gen. Sherman, who was at St. Louis, learned that Custer had sent to Fort Wallace for supplies. His orders, relayed on to Fort Sedgwick, stated:

I don't understand about Gen. Custer being on the Republican (River) awaiting provision from Fort Wallace. If this is so, and all the Indians be gone south, convey to him my orders that he proceed with all his command in search of the Indians towards Fort Wallace, and report to Gen. Hancock, who will leave Denver for the same place today.[11]

With his command completely united Custer led it west then north to Riverside Station on the Platte River to determine if any orders were available. Great was his surprise to learn there that a detachment of ten troopers and an Indian guide under command of Lieut. Lyman Kidder had left Fort Sedgwick with Sherman's orders. Kidder had left the day after Elliot had left, but no more had been heard of him.

Custer was greatly concerned. Kidder was on a suicidal mission, for he was totally inexperienced in Indian warfare. Then, too, there were the Sherman orders Custer had been so anxious to receive. But copies of it were available and he was soon made aware that Sherman wanted him to march his command "across the country from the Platte (River) to the Smoky Hill River, striking the latter at Fort Wallace."[12]

Custer started his command at daybreak. There was no time to lose. His supplies were low, for none of the promised provisions had been available at either Fort Sedgwick or Riverside Station. He and all of the officers were becoming anxious about the Kidder party.

Then a real tragedy struck the cavalry column. "Inferior and insufficient rations, nearness to the overland route of travel to some newly-discovered mining claims in Colorado Territory, and the supposed opportunity to amass great wealth as prospector or miners proved too great a temptation to many of the enlisted men. Forgetting that they had sworn allegiance to the flag, that they were in enemy country and in a state of war, and that the penalty for desertion under those circumstances was death, a number of them made plans to desert."[13]

As they were about to leave the Platte it was discovered that of his command of less than 300 men, thirty-five had deserted. This was a serious misfortune but there was no time for pursuit. The column moved southward. By noon they have marched fifteen miles. Believing that they were encamped for the rest of the day about one-third of the remaining members of the command conspired to desert that evening. Learning of this, Custer gave orders to repack and move out so that he could put a greater distance between the men and temptation.

When the order to repack was given, thirteen troopers, seven on horseback, left camp in a northerly direction. They seemed unable to hear the shouts or the officers or the trumpeter sounding "Recall." Maj. Elliott, Lieut. Tom Custer, Lieut. Cooke and seven of the men mounted and pursued the deserters. The mounted deserters easily pulled away for they had taken the fleetest horses in the command. Those on foot presented no problem, for, after a chase of several miles, they were ordered to halt. This order they ignored. When they were approached, the ringleader raised his carbine to fire at his pursuers. He and two of his companions were shot down. The other three promptly surrendered.

That evening every officer was placed on guard duty. There was no attempt at desertion nor was there for the balance of the campaign. The column moved south then east the next day until they struck Captain West's old trail toward Fort Wallace. Continuing along it they kept a close watch for Kidder's trail. The heat was blistering, for there was not a cloud visible as they pressed on. Time and distance was forgotten as the tension grew. Suddenly an object was seen on the trail a mile or so away. The scout, Medicine Bill Comstock, and his Delawares galloped toward it and discovered it was the carcass of a white horse displaying a U.S. brand. The horse had been killed by a bullet within the past few days. It was decided that this horse had been in Kidder's command.

An examination of the surrounding area resulted in the conclusion that the horse had been killed in an Indian skirmish. Several miles further another dead horse was found and nearby were pony tracks registering the obvious presence of Indians. Obvious too were signs indicating that both horses and ponies were running at a gallop. As the trail gradually descended into a valley a small stream was seen several miles in the distance. Noticeable also were buzzards flying to the left of the trail within a mile of the creek. The rank stench of decaying corpses was quite discernible.

Comstock and the Delawares, with several of the officers, conducted a hurried search to either side of the trail. Suddenly one of the Delaware scouts some distance away let out a whoop. Jumping off his horse he was seen examining something on the ground. Custer said: "Lying in irregular order, and within a very limited circle, were the mangled bodies of poor Kidder and his party, yet so brutally hacked and disfigured as to be beyond recognition save as human beings."[14]

In reconstructing Kidder's movements it was decided that he and his detachment had discovered the trial of the wagon train to Fort Wallace and had followed it thinking Custer had gone that way instead of up to Riverside Station. That was Kidder's undoing. Several days later the cavalry column arrived at Fort Wallace to make camp there late in the afternoon of July 13. The main column had traveled 705 miles since June 1.

When they arrived, Custer rode over to Fort Wallace to determine if Hancock's orders had arrived. They had not. Fort Wallace literally was in a state of siege. Mail and supplies had been interrupted by the Indians for several weeks. Cholera had made its presence known just outside the post. The first to die from it was a civilian employed at Fort Wallace by the Quartermaster Department. He died on July 15. Within ten days five soldiers and three citizens succumbed to the disease.[15]

In appraising the situation at Fort Wallace, Custer suffered considerable mental discomfort. The available food was unfit to eat and the reserve food supplies were extremely low, medical supplies were almost depleted, and neither mail nor dispatches had been received for some time. The entire situation had to be improved immediately if the cholera epidemic was to be checked.

Orders were imperative if he was to continue the campaign against the Indians. Hancock was not at Fort Wallace to issue orders as Sherman had said he would be. The latest information available indicated that Hancock was at Fort Leavenworth and would remain there for an undetermined period of time. The situation was critical.

Custer had two choices. He could send a detail for the badly needed medications and supplies, or he could go himself. He had reason to believe the detail might not reach its objective. A week earlier there was the real possibility that one-third of his command intended to desert.[16] That would have meant the loss of near to 100 of his men. If he sent 100 men east to Fort Hays on this mission, what would have prevented them from doing the same thing? The obvious solution was to go in charge himself. He never had been one to shirk responsibility.

The situation was peculiar in one respect. *He had to leave Fort Wallace without permission*, to go to Fort Harker where his commanding officer, Col. Andrew J. Smith, was stationed, *to obtain permission to leave Fort Wallace.* To Custer that was a mere detail.

Adding the best of his worn horses to those available at Fort Wallace, and selecting one hundred men from his command, he started out on the 150-mile trek to Fort Hays, leaving at sunset on July 15. There were twelve stage stations between Fort Wallace and Fort Hays, varying from five to thirteen miles apart. The column arrived at Fort Hays at 3:A.M. on July 18, a ride of fifty-five hours, including all halts.

Custer pressed on to Fort Harker, some fifty-two miles east, with Lieutenants Cooke and Tom Custer and two troopers, arriving there at 2:A.M. on July 19. It had taken twelve hours. Col. Smith was immediately informed of all details of the expedition, of the fate of the Kidder party, of conditions at Fort Wallace, then he arranged for a train of supplies to be taken back on his return trip to Fort Wallace. Once this business was concluded he requested permission of Smith to go on to Fort Riley to see Libbie. The permission was granted.

Custer critics are strong in their condemnation of Custer's march to Fort Harker without orders. They ignore the conditions Custer faced when he arrived at Fort Wallace and that there was no one there to give him further orders. These critics not only imply but state that he led the detachment east to see his wife and that his other reasons for the trip and for personally leading it were merely window dressing. They would be the first to have loudly complained had there been members of their family at Fort Wallace during an epidemic of cholera while Custer rested his horses and men without making an effort to remedy the situation.

Quite properly, Custer was concerned about his wife for he had heard nothing from her during the latter half of the expedition, for he was aware of the spread of cholera from eastern posts. And hadn't he known of the cases at Fort Wallace, one civilian employee having died of it on the very day he rode east for medical supplies and provisions?

On arriving at Fort Hays, where Custer believed his wife to be, he was alarmed to learn that she had been sent east to Fort Harker where cholera was raging. Ordering his train to rest overnight, then moving on to Fort Harker where medical supplies and provisions were abundant since it was the terminus of the railroad he, with his brother Tom and Lieut. Cooke, pushed on to Fort Harker, arriving there about 2 A.M.

Quite likely he became extremely concerned about Libbie when he had reached Fort Harker for there he learned she had been moved to Fort Riley. Just two days before he had arrived there the post surgeon's wife, Mrs. George Sternberg, had died from cholera after a few hours of illness. Coincidentally, the first cholera death at Fort Wallace—on July 15—occurred on the date of the first cholera death at Fort Harker, that of Mrs. Sternberg.

With permission from Col. Smith to visit Fort Riley, Custer traveled the ninety miles by way of the Kansas Pacific Railroad. No sooner had he reached his destination than he was handed a telegram from Smith placing him under arrest and ordering him to remain at Fort Riley pending a courtmartial on the charge of leaving Fort Wallace without authority.

Capt. Louis Hamilton, whom Custer had placed in command of his detachment when he arrived at Fort Hays, arrived at Fort Harker on the twentieth. Smith immediately readied him for the return trip with a train of supplies, and on the twenty-second, Hamilton, with Lieutenants Cooke and Custer, returned with the supply train to Fort Wallace. Maj. Joel Elliott was ordered to assume command of the 7th Cavalry at Fort Wallace while Custer was under arrest.

General Grant set Custer's general courtmartial for September 17 at Fort Leavenworth. Though the original charges were preferred by Col. A.J. Smith, it was his superior, Gen. Hancock, who had instigated them. Smith had intended to treat the charges against Custer lightly. Hancock, perhaps, would have wanted to follow the same course but circumstances forced him to do otherwise. Congress had been quite disturbed over the fruitless results of his summer campaign. Senator Henderson of Missouri had charged that it would "cost us $100,000,000 without having accomplished anything."[18] Hancock was forced to find a "goat" to take the heat off himself. Custer did the wrong thing at the right time.

Up to this point the charges against Custer were of a minor nature. Courtsmartial were a common occurrence, few officers escaping them in a lifetime of duty. The semi-official *Army and Navy Journal* published a list in every issue. But this one took a different turn.

Brevet Col. Robert M. West was a captain in the 7th Cavalry. He was a competent officer and an experienced Indian fighter but was having trouble with his battle with the bottle.[19] West had suffered the indignity of seeing Lieut. Cooke placed in charge of the wagon train to Fort Wallace while he, with higher rank, was placed in charge of its guard detail. Then, on arriving at Fort Wallace, while officer of the day, he became quite drunk while on duty. This occurred in the presence of the regiment at a time the post was having considerable difficulty with hostile Indians. Custer was placed in a position where he was forced to prefer charges. West saw an opportunity for revenge when he learned of Custer's arrest and of the charges placed against him. Vindictively he tacked on some additional charges not directly relating to those placed by Smith. Even the Leavenworth *Daily Conservative* (August 31, 1867) presumed Custer would be not be dealt with very severely on the original charges. West's additional charges changed the picture entirely.

The courtmartial opened at Fort Leavenworth, Kansas, on September 15, 1867, at 11:00 A.M., the Court consisting of ten officers, one of whom requested and received permission not to serve. The first charge against Custer was that of absenting himself from his command without authority. To this, other charges were added that he had marched a portion of his command upon private business without proper authority, that he used Government vehicles (ambulances and mules) for private business, and that he had failed to take proper measures to repulse an Indian attack upon his escort or recover the bodies of several of his command killed by those Indians. Under ordinary circumstances, Custer probably would have suffered a reprimand had the charges ended there.

Capt. West thought it should end otherwise. He was convinced that Custer had misused him. To even the score he had additional charges to those of Col. Smith. Out on the trail he was one of the officers who had wholly approved of Custer's handling of the wholesale desertions. Now at the post, under the influence of alcohol and angered because Custer had been forced to prefer charges against him for his dereliction of duty, he had a reversal of his former convictions.

He began by charging that Custer "when ordering a party of three commissioned officers and others of his command in pursuit of supposed deserters who were then in view leaving camp, *also order* the said party to shoot the supposed deserters down dead, and to bring none in alive," causing three to be severely wounded. He also charged that the wounded, on Custer's orders, were hauled eighteen miles in a Government wagon without the benefit of any medical attention. The result, according to the charge, was the death of Private Charles Johnson, caused by Custer's orders that no medical attention be rendered any of the wounded deserters.

As the trial proceeded, the Judge Advocate admitted that Gen. Sherman's order to Custer to report to Gen. Hancock did not reach him in time.[20] Both Lieutenants Cooke and Custer testified that on or about June 16 they had heard Gen. Sherman tell Gen. Custer "he would receive orders from Gen. Augur, but not to confine himself to those orders, if his judgment led him elsewhere. That if he wished, he could go to Denver City, or he could go to hell if he wanted to. That he could go to any post he wanted to."[21] Custer never received any orders following that conversation until he received the one from Sherman directing him to go to Fort Wallace for orders from Hancock. On arriving there and finding Hancock's whereabout unknown, it became a question of whether Custer had the right to make a decision at that time for the welfare of the garrison.

The courtmartial was the chief subject of conversation at Fort Leavenworth and nearby Leavenworth City. Courtsmartial were common enough but it wasn't every day the likes of Custer were talking subjects to them. Though the testimony was not to be discussed with others by the members of the Court it leaked to those on the outside. Sides were taken and opinions offered. Even bets were made.

Was the establishment trying to use Gen. Custer as a scapegoat in order to whitewash Hancock's disastrous summer campaign? Could it be possible Gen. Grant was placing the blame on Custer in order to take the heat off himself thereby furthering his own ambition to become President? Would Custer be slapped on the wrist or would they throw the entire book at him? Was Custer really at fault?

The townspeople would have been surprised had they known that Gen. Sheridan had told Custer the authorities in Washington regarded the trial as "an attempt by Hancock to cover up the failures of the Indian expedition." They would have been even more surprised had they known that Hancock had telegraphed Sheridan to shoot down deserters in the spring of 1867 to deter its increase, and that Sheridan, in turn, had ordered Custer to shoot down deserters without trial for the same offense. Perhaps they were not very surprised to learn that Capt. West would not be placed on the witness stand by the prosecution. He had been drinking so heavily he had delirium tremens.[22]

Custer admitted in his testimony that he had ordered, in the pursuit of the deserters, "to bring in none alive," but his command was given only to the officer of the day, Lieut. Henry Jackson. He explained that this was said for its effect upon the members of the regiment who were in hearing distance. The attention of nearly the whole command had been directed toward him to see what he was going to do. Lieut. Jackson understood the intent of the order. Had he obeyed literally he would not have brought back the remaining three prisoners unhurt. Had Custer expected him literally to obey the order, he would have arrested Jackson for not fully obeying it.

Dr. I.T. Coates, the 7th Cavalry surgeon who accompanied the expedition, testified that Custer had given him orders, so all could hear, that he was not to give the wounded deserters medical attention, this for the effect it would have upon the rest of the command. He gave them medical attention a short time later with the knowledge that the orders given by Custer were not intended to restrict him.[23]

The testimony was concluded on October 11 and a verdict of "Guilty" was rendered. Several of the charges, namely the one of using ambulances for private business and the other of refusing to allow the wounded deserters to receive medical attention, drew an added statement with the Court's verdict that they would "attach no criminality thereto." Custer was sentenced "to be suspended from rank and command for one year, and forfeit pay proper for the same time."[24]

It is obvious now, and probably was then, that had Gen. Sheridan appeared or had given a deposition to enter into the Court records, his remarks would have proved that Custer had the sanction of higher authority to shoot deserters without benefit of trial. This show of interest and statement of fact by the commander of the department could have provided enough weight to have had Custer acquitted.

Of interest too is the fact that the Court consisted of four members inferior in rank to Gen. Custer, two being majors and two being captains. Military law required trial by one's peers who were superior in rank, if they could be assembled without inconvenience. There would have been no inconvenience in obtaining members of equal or superior rank at Fort Leavenworth. Another interesting observation about the composition of that Court is the fact that three of its members, including the Judge Advocate, were members of Gen. Hancock's staff.

There was little doubt in the minds of Custer and his friends that he had been used. He didn't expect favors and he had told Sheridan he didn't want any favors. His West Point class ring had engraved on it "Thro Trials to Triumph." Time would tell.

Chapter Five
The Day is Yours

ANECDOTES are foundations to many of our best legends.
The story may be told to illustrate a trait of character, a human
failing, a highlight in history or a highly colored incident that
stirs the imagination. Then again it may be told only because it
brings a laugh.

Back in 1906, so the story is told, the General's brother
Nevin gave William F. Haight—Monroe's fire chief at the
time—a Green River type hunting knife, informing him it had
belonged to the General. The sturdy 13-inch knife had been
skilfully made from a tool file for General Custer by Elija F.
Frazier.

When Chief Haight's son presented it to the Monroe
museum he told me that his father once had a farm just out of
town on which he raised turkeys. From time to time friends
were invited to turkey dinners in his home. As was the custom
he would carve and serve the bird from the head of the table.
When it came time for second portions to be served he would
hold up this knife and remark that they were being honored by
eating a turkey carved with a knife that had belonged to
General Custer. Then he would add that it had been used by
Custer to scalp many an Indian. Mr. Haight concluded, "and it
was surprising how much turkey was left over each time."

Monroe has circulated its share of unfounded tales. Many
townspeople believe Custer was born there. Most of those who

91

know he was born in New Rumley, Ohio, are of the opinion that he came to Monroe at the age of ten to live with his half-sister, Mrs. David Reed.

As mentioned earlier, the Custer family broke up housekeeping in New Rumley in May, 1842—George Armstrong Custer was two and one-half years of age at the time—and moved to a small farm just south of Monroe. His father Emanuel's horses were stolen shortly after they arrived. They remained but six months, just long enough to make good the loss, then returned to New Rumley.[1]

At the age of ten, young George traveled to Monroe to live with his half-sister, Anne, for two years. Then back to New Rumley he went, remaining there for two years, before returning to reside in Monroe again for another two years. It was during this last stay in Monroe that he attended the Stebbins Academy.

Now sixteen years of age, he returned to New Rumley to attend the McNeely Normal School at Hopedale nearby. After securing his teacher's certificate from the Harrison County Board of School Examiners he obtained a job teaching at the Beech Point School. While there he was nominated to the U.S. Military Academy by Ohio Congressman John Bingham. Young Custer reported to West Point in the summer of 1857.

The Custer plot in Monroe's Woodland Cemetery is one of the points on the Custer trail most frequently visited by Custer students. Though the General and his wife Libbie are not buried there, the rest of the Custer family are. There one may see the simple headstone marked "Boston." And next to it is the Reed plot where one may see the final resting place of Harry Armstrong (Autie) Reed and that of of his mother—the General's half sister. The next plot is that of the Heath family. A large stone there indicates the grave of Dr. George F. Heath, the Custer family physician who so carefully guarded the health of the General's aging parents. On his stone is a medallion indicating that he was the founder of the American Numismatic Society.

In the Custer plot is a headstone with a single name—
Margaret. It is that of Maggie Calhoun, the widow of Lt. James
Calhoun. A Monroe story commonly told is that Maggie
Custer's second marriage, which was to a New York contractor
by the name of John Maugham, was frowned upon by the
Custer family. It is said they evidenced their dislike by leaving
his last name off her stone.

This charge is without foundation. A simple search
through the cemetery will reveal many stones displaying given
names and no more. The Custer plot evidences another in a
similar pattern—that of Boston. It was the custom of the time.

There was a time when it was my lot to settle barroom
arguments over the telephone on various debatable aspects of
the Custer story, sometimes at 2:A.M. Highest in number of
queries was the question as to the placement of the Custer
equestrian statue at the time of its unveiling. "Wasn't the
Custer monument placed with the rear end of the horse facing
South Washington Street just to spite those living there who
opposed it?" I had to answer that it was placed facing his Civil
War enemy and peace time friends—the South.

I have close to 2,000 books relating to General Custer in my
library, and over 1,000 magazine articles. Over 1,000 paintings
and sketches have been made relating to General Custer. Each
year many, many more are produced, and additional facts are
added to the fascinating story. Those who have something to
say usually write books. Those who don't, critically review
them, though this does not always hold true. Fortunately some
reviewers have a background permitting them to present their
thoughts incontestably. The one that follows is one of the best.
Its author, Gen. Hugh S. Johnson, a West Point graduate and
the former Director of the National Recovery Act under
President Franklin D. Roosevelt, presented in *Today
Magazine*, Dec. 29, 1934, a review of *Glory Hunter*, a biography
of Gen. Custer by Frederic F. Van de Water.

Gen. Johnson Rides to the Defense

"Heralded by some reviewers as the 'Custer book to end Custer books,' comes a volume from the pen of a hunter who himself seeks to attain glory by trying to tear the shining mantle from the shoulders of one of the country's most romantic figures—by debunking Gen. George Armstrong Custer.

"Your reviewer is not a Custer fan, but he was once a mounted soldier. He knew the American Horse Service and the Seventh Cavalry. As a boy he knew and talked to Cheyenne braves who remembered that furious fight. He used to sit fascinated, listening to old Mrs. Benteen tell about the glorious days preceding, and the tragic weeks following, the day Custer led his troops out of Fort Lincoln, threw his hat in the air and yelled: 'Custer's Luck!'—luck that led directly to death for many at the Little Bighorn. And her impression of that great mystery was not in the least like the one that is given in this book.

"Just as in France, where the mark of Napoleon Bonaparte still is everywhere—as of a man but lately gone—so not only in the Seventh Horse, to an extent at least, in the whole American cavalry, something of Custer remains. One can even go a step further and say that our air corps, organized largely by cavalrymen, is not without its debt to this incarnation of the spirit of headlong assault—without which neither cavalry nor air corps would be worth keeping.

"The book pillories Custer because he was flamboyant, swaggering, boastful, untamed and remorseless in attack. Such incidents as his shooting of a fleeing horseman after calling for surrender, attacking unknown forces mounted and on the spur, wearing loud uniforms, letting his horse run away at parade before a grandstand, fighting mounted and not on foot when somebody's hindsight would have dictated dismounted action—all are overemphasized in an effort to expose the clay feet of this idol. Other far more important happenings, such as the little-known charge at Hanover, are reduced to insignificance. His quarrels with Sec. of War Belknap are turned to Custer's disadvantage. Old army obscurities, such as the fate of Elliott at Black Kettle's camp on the Washita, are dragged from their oblivion to invoke suspicion where fact will not sufficiently serve.

"The circumstance that Custer had enemies and detractors among his comrades is continuously thrown into the highlight. Any youth appointed Brigadier General over his seniors is sure to reap this reward.

"Such hero-sniping is a profitless, shameless business. A cavalryman who does not like his brilliant trappings ought to shift to the infantry. The zest for colorful, even bizarre, uniforms has characterized horsemen not only since Murat and LaSalle, but from the beginning. Swagger, boastfulness, elan, and boisterousness among cavalrymen are part of the oldest of military traditions. The attack on an opponent's left rear and the maneuver to get there are the first things taught a mounted recruit. Custer's charge at Five Forks into soft ground was a misfortune, but there is only one moment for the charge in mass, and if it comes it cannot be delayed for scouts, unless the leader is just a mounted infantryman.

"But Custer's little-known headlong cavalry charge at Hanover broke up the Confederate ground strategy at Gettysburg and prevented Stuart from harassing the Union rear line, at the very moment that Pickett reached the highwater mark of the Confederacy. Stuart was in a position to interpose between Meade and Washington, and this may have been the turning point in the Civil War. It was as fateful a moment as ticked the Lost Cause to its doom. The prejudiced spirit of the whole book is revealed by the derogatory treatment of this deathless instant.

"As events quickly proved, Custer's attack on the old post trader racket uncovered one of the meanest grafts of the most graft-ridden administration in our history, and exposed Belknap as the least-worthy Cabinet officer of whom we know. To rake in review the conduct of a small Indian campaign, to make a mountain out of the Black Kettle incident, but reduce Gettysburg to a molehill, leaves the reader with no just appraisal of the intense and varied career of the most striking figure in the annals of the United States Cavalry.

"As history, this is just adversary advocacy. As biography, it is merely muckraking. As military criticism, it sounds like the musings of a daisy-crunching doughboy.

"Custer was a poor student, a 'sloppy' cadet, a boastful and pugnacious subaltern. But he first became prominent in the Union cavalry when it was little better than a bunch of grooms, horseholders and orderlies, while the Confederate cavalry was near perfection. With Sheridan, Kilpatrick and Gregg, he helped to reverse these relative standings completely. To hard work and discipline, he, more than any other general, added the indispensable ingredients of a good mounted service—zest, brilliant tradition and above all (as Napoleon often insisted) first, audacity; second, audacity; and third, audacity. Even this detractor does not deny him that. He states it, but only to decry it.

"Well, if the author does not respect Custer as a cavalryman, his general—Sheridan—did, and, even more, his enemies did. Crazy Horse, Rain-in-the-Face, and the bloodthirsty Gall—Sioux, Cheyenne and Arapaho—they rode around that devoted band firing into it until all the whites were dead, and left Gen. Custer—not a hair of his scalp having been ruffled—stretched out on top of that gory peak.

"The wild plains horsemen who have felt again and again the thrust of his headlong assault, as a signal mark of savage respect left his body and his fame untouched. But not so this writer, who rises nearly sixty years after Custer's death to do that which even an acorn-eating Digger Indian would scorn to consider—scalp an heroic warrior found dead on the field of honor."

Various stories have been told how Custer became a General. The one most frequently told is that portrayed in the motion picture *They Died With Their Boots On*. In it General Scott accidentally commissioned Custer a Brigadier General instead of a Second Lieutenant immediately after his graduation from the U.S. Military Academy. To put that and

other related stories to rest one should read the following list of
Custer's U.S. Army Commissions that are in the possession of
the Custer Battlefield National Monument:

June 24, 1861	Second Lieutenant in the Second Regiment of Cavalry. Signed by Abraham Lincoln, Sept. 9, 1861.
June 5, 1862	Additional Aide-de-Camp with the rank of Captain. Signed by Abraham Lincoln, July 30, 1862.
July 17, 1862	First Lieutenant in Fifth Regiment of Cavalry. Signed by Abraham Lincoln, June, 6, 1863.
June 29, 1863	Brigadier General of Volunteers. Signed for Abraham Lincoln, March 11, 1864.
July 3, 1863	Brevet Major for gallant and meritorious services at the Battle of Gettysburg, Pa. Signed by Andrew Johnson, August 3, 1866.
May 8, 1864	Captain in Fifth Regiment of Cavalry. Signed by Andrew Johnson, June 1, 1865.
May 11, 1864	Brevet Lieutenant Colonel for gallant and meritorious services at the Battle of Yellow Tavern, Va. Signed by Andrew Johnson, August 2, 1866.
Sept. 19, 1864	Brevet Colonel for gallant and meritorious services at the Battle of Winchester, Va. Signed by Andrew Johnson, August 1, 1866.
October 19, 1864	Brevet Major General of Volunteers for gallant and meritorious service at the Battles of Winchester and Fisher's Hill. Va.
March 13, 1865	Brevet Major General for gallant and meritorious services during the campaign ending with the surrender of the insurgent army of Northern Virginia. Signed by Andrew Johnson, July 28, 1866.
April 15, 1865	Major General of Volunteers. Signed by

Andrew Johnson, March 10, 1866.

July 28, 1866   Lieutenant Colonel of the Seventh
Regiment of Cavalry. Signed by Andrew
Johnson, March 5, 1867.[2]

From the above one may determine that Custer was made
a general on five separate occasions, three of which were by
brevet. After the war, when regular army officers who held
high rank in the Volunteer army had been dropped in grade to
their regular army grades in keeping with the need for fewer
officers in a much smaller post war army,[3] there was a wild
scramble for the available openings in the service.
Appointments were made often on the basis of the influence of
friends in high places as well as the professional background
and abilities of the applicants.[4]

A brevet usually was a commission giving an officer
higher nominal rank than that for which he received pay. It
was an honor conferred by the Senate for meritorious service or
heroism. Many were conferred upon staff officers who saw no
active combat, creating much resentment among those officers
who were serving on the line of action.

For a time an officer with a brevet frequently was assigned
a command commensurate with his brevet rank and was paid
accordingly. For that reason the honor was not an empty one.
In addition, the recipient bore the title of his highest rank for
all of his career. General Custer is a case in point. Socially and
oftentimes officially, he was addressed as General though his
rank in the Seventh Cavalry was that of Lieutenant Colonel.[5]
In this last instance he received the pay and the emolument of a
lieutenant colonel.

All of this may be a bit confusing. To add to the confusion,
turn back a few pages and refer to the list of commissions. As of
July 17, 1862, Custer was commissioned a First Lieutenant in
the regular army. While on the staff of Gen. Alfred Pleasonton
and holding the rank of Captain—apparently a temporary
field promotion, for he was still a regular army lieutenant—he,
along with Capt. Wesley Merritt and Capt. Elon Farnsworth,
both of whom held the rank of captain, was commissioned a

Brigadier General of Volunteers.

Libbie Custer received many letters in her lengthy life. Much of her time was spent answering them, and always in longhand. For brief periods she resorted to using her left hand, her right temporarily incapacitated with a recurrent painful neuritis. In most instances the letters were from men who had served with her husband. There were recollections, requests for photographs, requests for financial aid or assistance in obtaining an appointment or employment. She answered all. Following the 50th anniversary of the battle, when her right arm bothered her considerably, she doggedly continued her letter writing against her doctor's wishes. There were hundreds of letters awaiting her attention and she meant to, and did, answer every one.

Some of the letters contained bits of information useful to her in the quest to present the truthful story of her gallant husband. One such letter arrived in the summer of 1897 from an officer she had never met. He was a man in the position to reveal information about the conduct of the Reno Court of Inquiry in an objective manner for he had been the Recorder of that inquiry. This is what he told Mrs. Custer:

I want to say to you in all frankness, that at one time I was in some degree influenced by the prejudicial opinions of those whose motives I did not understand, and whose sources of information I then had no means of testing. But soon after I was brought into close contact with thousands of Indians, the Sioux, Cheyennes and others; and in January 1879, I was Recorder of the Reno Court of Inquiry; a year later I visited the field of battle.

Now, I tried to be honest and fair minded and allow nothing but *facts* to make an impression on my mind. So it came about in the light of long and confidential talks with Indians under my charge, in the light of what was said to me by witnesses *before* they went on the stand, and in the light of much testimony *on the stand,* and finally in the light of my visit to the field, my judgment could no more escape the conclusion of *facts* than to deny that I am penning these lines. That conclusion I referred to in my letter to General Miles and I am glad you consider it 'generous and fair.' *It is true!* I do not believe an unprejudiced mind—any one whose heart is free from the contact of jealousy could with a knowledge of all the facts come to any other conclusion. When I got all the facts it was easy to understand how *self interest* influenced opinions; how Jealousy being unopposed could unmask its horrid power and loosen its tongue of calumny—with none to answer; how the living could extol themselves for *prudence* and *delay*—and condemn the dead as *rash* and *impetuous,* how Authority through inexperience, sought to evade the responsibility through a loophole of escape. Had some one blundered? Then how easy to censure those who could not answer. It was both cruel and unjust for *anyone* to send that dispatch: 'Orders were disobeyed but the penalty paid.'

This dispatch reveals both weakness and incompetency. The sender, as I believe, knew but little if anything about Indians, but he did know General Custer, and it verges on imbecility to suppose that any one would expect Indians to be held in position several days by one column waiting and making it convenient for another column to attack them.

I was glad to see that General Miles had gotten at all the material facts, and of course there could be but one conclusion. I think Capt. Philo Clark in his life time—got the fact, and the conclusion was the same. Major Godfrey when Captain of the 7th Cavy—wrote a very fair article on this subject. There has been so much misrepresentation—so much from personal and interested motives, that it would seem that the truth is hard to separate from the chaff, but I believe that the *impartial historian* will do justice to your distinguished husband.

"My opinion, as such, is of but little account one way or the other, but I believe as an unprejudiced person I have had better opportunities to get at the *facts* than almost any other person. These facts show beyond successful contradiction:

1st: That General Custer was *not* disobeying General Terry's orders in attacking the Indians. Any other course under the circumstances would have been ridiculous and absurd.

2nd: Major Reno, according to General Gibbon's testimony—left, *abandoned,* a splendid position where he threatened the entire village and thus enabled the entire force of Indians to concentrate on General Custer, who was thus compelled to meet them with *less* than 2/5 of the effective force of his regiment.

3rd: Major Reno's disastrous retreat in *keeping out of the battle at a critical period fully 3/5 of the effective force,* and in doing this all chance for victory over the Indians was lost.

I had not the honor of a personal acquaintance with General Custer. I saw him but once in my life; but I feel that I would be remiss to Truth were I to fail to say and write on appropriate occasions that which I know is in accord with his great reputation.[6]

The Custers inherently displayed a common trait. They loved to play practical jokes on each other though they did not limit them to members of their own family. Libbie relates a number of them in her books, some of which were on her. The reader begins to feel sorry for Father Custer, for he was the frequent subject of some rather rough play, until one realizes that he developed this trait in each of his offspring. He was a realist. He knew that life had its rough spots. If one learned to laugh when the going got tough, it made things much easier.

During the course of writing one of her popular books Libbie wrote to her husband's brother Nevin to see if he could recall some of the incidents in her husband's youth. Nevin told her the story of the drilling of the New Rumley militia—muster, it was called. Every able bodied man was subject to it. "Autie," he said, "always walked along with his father carrying his little wooden sword. At one of these drills he got a toothe ache. In the evening his father took him to Dr. Black's office and had it pulled or twisted out as they used to do. Autie never flinched or said a word, and going home he says, 'Pa, we can whip all Michigan.' Now we don't know how he came to speak of that. There was some trouble between Ohio and Michigan about the boundary line so he might have heard something that way."[7]

After Autie had grown enough to do some of the chores, he was walking down the lane one day with his father. Father Custer, noticing that Autie had some good dress shoes said: "Armstrong, you can't afford to wear such good shoes as them on a farm" Autie replied: "I never intend to make my living by working on a farm." Nevin noted that his brother always had a book along to read when he and Tom had something to do. While living in New Rumley there was not too much work for the Custer boys. This gave more time to think of pranks to play.

Mother Custer, as was her custom just before Christmas, made quite a large number of mince pies which she stored in a large box upstairs. All the boys happened to sleep upstairs, and all of the pies happened to disappear. Nevin added: "I don't say the boys took them."

Father Custer had reached a point where he decided that his income as a blacksmith in the small community was not adequte for his growing brood. He was well on the way to raising a third family. His first marriage (to Matilda Viers) had provided him with three children. By his second marriage (to the widow Maria Ward Kirkpatrick) he had inherited her four children. He now had Autie, Tom and Nevin by this second union, and probably suspected that a fourth son was on the way. The few dollars obtained as a justice of the peace in a crimeless community added little to his diminutive income. He had tried a new life in Monroe, Michigan, but that had ended with the theft of his horses. A farm two miles out of New Rumley had a practical allure. He had some brawny boys to run it while he turned his attention to blacksmithing, church work and politics.

Father Custer was a strict Methodist and never missed a Sabbath going to church. As Nevin told Libbie: "His boys was just as punctual as he was, but not of their own free will."[8]

Father Custer saw to it that the boys had chores to do. There was a market for eggs in town so Autie, who was a good horseman, was directed to deliver a basket to New Market. Platt, a French pony they had brought with them from Monroe, was his mount. When Mother Custer handed the basket of eggs to Autie the pony became frightened and started off on a dead run. Mother Custer, fearing that her son would be injured by the pony, yelled to Autie to drop the basket. He did drop it and, as Nev reported: "He did not take any eggs to market—not out of that lot."

One fall, Autie came home on furlough from West Point unannounced. Nevin was dragging ground for wheat at the time. Autie told his mother he intended scaring Nev, so he put on hoops, one of his mother's dresses and a shake bonnet. Going out to the field Nev was working in, he leaned on the fence, his head resting on his arms as if in distress. As Nev drove his team to the end of the field he viewed, with a feeling of alarm, the figure of his mother. Nev said that if Autie had made a move to get over the fence he would have known who it was. As it turned out he was completely fooled and startled.

During the Civil War Nevin had a farm in Tontogony, not far from Toledo. Father Custer was living in Monroe at the time so this would have been in 1863. General Custer and Libbie, with Father Custer and sister Maggie, visited Nev at his Tontogony farm. As Nevin told Libbie the story:

"To make things pass off pleasantly we had to have something going, so Autie says to Father: 'I can give you so many rods in the start and run forty rods and beat you.' Well, Father took the banter and I was to hold the money and first one out got the money. I went up about ten rods to see that everything was all right, and when they came I was to grab Father and hold him until Autie caught up. You may guess who got the money. That was the Custer of it. They can't help it; it is born in them. It is in the young generation too. They want to have somebody in hot water."[9]

Attorney John Bulkley, Autie's boyhood friend, had been his seatmate at the Stebbins Academy for Boys. Libbie had encouraged him to write a biography of his old friend other than the short sketch in his two-volume "History of Monroe County" published in 1913. This never came about. The nearest to a biography was an article he prepared for a New York newspaper. Recalling their Academy days, Bulkley wrote:

"Professor Stebbins would steal from the aisle of the study hall in his felt slippers, and suddenly detect Custer, his head buried under the raised lid (of his desk), poring over the pages of 'Ivanhoe,' 'Harry Lorreque,' or 'Charles O'Malley, the Irish Dragoon.'

" 'Armstrong,' he would mildly say, 'as you seem to prefer romance to grammar, you may stay an hour after the morning session and we will have an interview on the subject—or some other!'

"Custer loved adventure and excitement; he craved it, and withal had the keenest sense of humor....He loved his fellowmen, and he loved animals; of these he was always surrounded by magnificent specimens of both horses and dogs.

"Custer had not the flight of oratory of a public speaker at all, neither was he a great conversationalist, but he was a clear, agreeable writer....While in Detroit together entertained by K.C. Barker, then Mayor, who was a friend and admirer of the General, he opened a letter from his publishers, requesting an installment of copy for the story then running. Custer laughed and said, 'This is pretty short notice, when my authorship is done by my wife, who is far away; however, I will write a chapter or two, if you will excuse me.' He wrote for half an hour, enclosed the MS to the magazine, and exclaimed with a laugh, 'Well, you fellows know I wrote this, anyhow.' When this particular chapter was printed, all agreed, with all deference to

Mrs. Custer, it was one of the best things he had written."[10] The story frequently told was that Libbie had been the author of a series of articles appearing in the *Galaxy Magazine.*

Bulkley was, perhaps, the last to have an in depth conversation with Custer prior to the tragedy on the Little Big Horn. On his return from Washington to join his troops at Fort Lincoln, Custer stopped off in Monroe to bid his aging parents goodbye. He spent the evening at the Bulkley residence with a number of friends who had called to wish him farewell. After all had left, he sat down with Bulkley to review events of past years. There were no regrets, Bulkley recalled. Custer's only sore spot was the unjust manner in which he had been treated by President Grant while in Washington during the past weeks. Grant had believed that Custer was instrumental in the expose of Belknap's post tradership frauds. Though Custer had made no criticisms of the President, he had made a statement that was considered by Grant to be harmful to his friend Belknap. Grant never forgave anyone who was supposed to have done Belknap an injury.

Custer believed that if Grant would have understood his position more fully he would not have humiliated him. He was yet to receive a more humiliating experience from Grant—his arrest and detention in Chicago the following day.

Before leaving the Bulkley home, Custer made a statement about Grant that appears prophetic: "It is a long lane that has no turning. I don't believe that a man ever perpetrated a rank injustice, knowingly, upon his fellow man but that he suffered from it before he died."[11]

Once the date was set—June 4, 1910, to dedicate the equestrian monument in Monroe, Libbie mentally prepared for the culmination of her greatest dream. She arrived in Monroe on June 2nd to be greeted by a pouring rain which did not deter any of her schoolmates who turned out to greet her. Several of them were very frail but they had braved the cold, wind and rain, and that touched Libbie.

She hadn't seen them in some years for, as she said: "Instead of going to Monroe when I was tired with work and my nerves exhausted from constant endeavor to perpetuate my husband's memory, I have gone to the other side where I would meet people and see sights that had nothing to do with my past. Dear, yes, precious as my life work is, I have to drop it all occasionally."[12]

It had rained most of the time for weeks but on June 4th the day was perfect. It was a day of thanksgiving for which she had hoped for many years. What a day it was! Monroe, a village in size, had suddenly exploded into a city. Electric lines and four railroads poured 25,000 people into the small community.

The streets were a mass of color. As Libbie observed: "The festoons and garlands of flags and bunting made the town look at a distance like the gardens of a giant." Even farmhouses up the River Raisin were draped with flags and cotton streamers.

Libbie had two fears: newspaper people and the gaze of the public. On this occasion she was willing, very willing, to brave both. As one friend reminded her: "The day is yours!"

Because of an oversight another fear arose. Just as the audience was asked to arise while she was to unveil the bronze statue the thought struck Libbie that she had not asked anyone how statues were unveiled. Her heart sank as she recalled what John Bulkley had said: "Libbie! I hope the ribbon won't break as it did at West Point when the first statue of Armstrong was unveiled. The old sculptor wouldn't let anyone help him but sent for a ladder and unveiled the statue himself, and there was a long, awkward wait."[13]

Her heart sank even more with the knowledge that an accident had happened just before she had arrived. Someone had brushed against the ribbon and down had come two huge flags that were being used as drapes. The ladders used to redrape the statue had been taken away just as Libbie had arrived.

As she stood beside President Taft, she pulled the ribbon very gently. The great flags swung apart easily, "floating off on either side on the wires across into the foliage of the great branches of the trees that were old when I was a child," she recalled. "I turned in an instant, and it seemed to me there never was anything more lifelike and beautiful than that golden image of the hero of the day."[14]

Chapter Six
Come on You Wolverines

THE BATTLE of Gettysburg was no picnic. Yet, compared to many of the battles of World War I and II, it was just a skirmish. One American division in 1918 was composed of 50,000 men. Lee's entire army had only 75,000 men. Any average day of battle in France could chalk up more casualties than the three days at Gettysburg. And one hour of gunfire from a single artillery battalion on the Somme shot up more ammunition than both the Confederates and the Federals did in the artillery duel preceeding Pickett's charge across the wheat fields.

There have been many decisive battles in world history. Perhaps none was more decisive than that last day at Gettysburg. Emphasis has been placed upon the "high water mark" where Pickett's charge faltered and broke. Little is said of the spectacular cavalry action that took place several miles behind the Federal lines at the very moment they were confronted by Pickett's forces.

The three days of action had been a blunder from the start. The site for the battle hadn't been selected by any general on either side. The North was being driven back by the Confederates and stumbled on it. In the bungling, neither side recognized the impregnability of Gettysburg when it was first reached.

The North had superiority of numbers, supplies and position. Under ordinary circumstances it would have taken another licking for it had lost every Eastern battle up to that point except Antietam, and that had been disputed.

On this occasion Lee was at a disadvantage. Lee had lost Jackson. JEB Stuart was absent the first two days of the battle. Stuart, acting on what have since become highly controversial orders from Lee, found himself north of Gettysburg at Carlisle.[1] There, on July 1st, he found the town in the possession of the Federals under command of General William F. (Baldy) Smith, who in answer to Stuart's demand, declined to surrender. "Shell away," he said, and Stuart did, after which he burned the U.S. Cavalry barracks there. He had hoped to find news of the Confederate army, for he had lost it.

While shelling Carlisle, Stuart received a dispatch from General Lee advising him that the Confederate forces were at Gettysburg and had had a successful engagement against Meade's infantry that day. Immediately Stuart began the 30 miles trek toward Gettysburg, arriving there on July 2nd.

It was noon when Stuart met Lee. Burke Davis, Stuart's biographer, describes the scene as an emotional one. Lee began sharply: "General Stuart, where have you been? I have not had word from you for days and you are the eyes and ears of my army."

"I have brought you 125 wagons and their teams, General." Stuart replied.

Lee's brusque manner changed to one of gentleness: "Yes General, but they are an impediment to me now. Let me ask your help now. We will not discuss this matter longer. Help me fight these people." Stuart nodded his head in assent.

From the 25th of June, Stuart had been on a raid that had Washington officials in an uproar. He had detoured to Carlisle, forced in that direction after striking the rear of a cavalry column under Brigadier General Judson Kilpatrick. Stuart's column was so spread out in its endeavor to shield the slow moving wagon train he had captured that it was all he could do to hold his force together under the impact of Kilpatrick's counter attack.

Stuart's command was worn out when it joined Lee, the result of six days and nights of hard work. The mile-long, well-loaded supply train he had captured had no effect upon the Federal Army. He had exhausted his men and animals in a

long and useless march for he had gained no useful
information. He had been absent from the main command
when he was needed most.

Meanwhile Kilpatrick had received orders to move down to
Two Taverns, about five miles southwest of Gettysburg. He
bivouaced there at daylight of July 3rd. It had been a weary
night march, the men being in the saddle continuously. Most of
them were members of the Michigan Cavalry Brigade
commanded by the newly commissioned Brigadier General
George A. Custer.

"At an early hour on the morning of the 3rd," Custer wrote
in his report, "I received an order, through a staff officer of the
Brigadier General commanding the division (Kilpatrick), to
move at once my command, and follow the First Brigade
(Farnsworth's) on the road leading from Two Taverns to
Gettysburg.

"Agreeable to the above instructions, my column was
formed and moved out on the road designated, when a staff
officer of Brigadier General Gregg, commanding the Second
Division, ordered me to take my command and place it in
position on the pike leading from Hanover to Gettysburg,
which position formed the extreme right of our line of battle on
that day."[2]

Federal scouts on Cemetery Ridge had observed Stuart
moving out on the York Pike just beyond the Federal right. The
intelligence had been hurried rearward to General Gregg. It
was obvious that Stuart was attempting to slip behind the
Federal lines. If successful, the damage he could do would be
irreparable.

Then an incident occurred that some point to as an
example of Custer disobeying the orders of a superior.
Kilpatrick, in his report, stated that he had been ordered to
move his entire command to the left of the Federal line and
attack the enemy's right and rear. "By some mistake," he
wrote, "General Custer's Brigade was ordered to report to
General Gregg, and he (Custer) did not rejoin me during the
day."[3]

Custer's move was no mistake. It was due to Gregg's

premonition of a serious diaster. With only two small brigades under Colonels John B. McIntosh and John Irvin Gregg, in addition to Captain Alanson Randol's single battery, he realized he had no chance against Stuart's four brigades and three batteries. Like a good general should, he took the responsiblity of intercepting Kilpatrick's largest brigade (Custer's) and turning it off to the right. Had he not done so....But this was not the only time General Gregg, modest man that he was, took it upon himself to make a bold and decisive move..

Continuing his report, Custer wrote:

"Upon arriving at the point designated, I immediately placed my command in position, facing Gettysburg. At the same time I caused reconnaissances to be made on my front, right, and rear, but failed to discover any considerable force of the enemy. Everything remained quiet till 10 a.m., when the enemy appeared on my right flank, and opened upon me with a battery of six guns. Leaving two guns and a regiment to hold my first position and cover the road leading to Gettysburg, I shifted the remaining portion of my command, forming a new line of battle at right angles to my former line. The enemy had obtained correct range of my new position, and were pouring shot and shell into my command with great accuracy."[4]

Custer ordered one of his batteries to silence the enemy's, an order they promptly complied with. Then placing his command in the form of the letter L, the shorter branch consisting of the 6th Michigan Cavalry facing east toward Gettysburg, and the long branch composed of the remainder of his command—the 1st, 5th and 7th Michigan Cavalry—extending northerly along the Low Dutch Road, he prepared to repel any attack.

At noon he received another order from Kilpatrick directing him, upon being relieved by a brigade from Gregg's Second Division, to move his command and form a junction with the 1st Brigade on the extreme left. When Col. McIntosh arrived with this brigade, Custer prepared to comply with Kilpatrick's orders. Before he could leave, Gen. Gregg arrived. He, on learning the condition and circumstances confronting him, and rightly concluding that Stuart was on his front for no good purpose, ordered Custer to remain in the position he then occupied. Thus, for a second time, Gregg countermanded Kilpatrick's orders to Custer.[5]

Some claim that Custer had already withdrawn from his position. Custer had not. He had been fired upon by Confederate artillery beyond the Rummel buildings to the northwest, and had received reports as to Stuart's movements toward the Rummel woods just north and west of the Rummel farmhouse.

Earlier Stuart had his men replenish their ammunition while he discussed plans with Gen. Lee then moved east on the York Pike for two and a half miles without sighting the enemy. He turned off the pike riding southeasterly toward several ridges just west of the Rummel farm and there he positioned two brigades in the Rummel woods. From the ridge he had a commanding view of most of the roads in the Federal rear.

From this vantage point he had an excellent view of the rolling farmland around him and of the Federal line on Cemetery Ridge to the West. His first object was to observe the enemy's rear. He had an excellent observation point from which to do that. His second object was to strike the enemy flank if an opportunity arose.[6] He intended striking the rear of the Federal Army "in cooperation with Pickett's grand attack upon the center."[7]

Then Stuart had a gun from Griffin's battery placed at the edge of the woods. He personally directed it to fire at several points on his front. No explanation was given to his officers but his adjutant, Major Henry B. McClellan, assumed it was a prearranged signal to Lee that he was in a favorable position, or that he, finding no enemy in sight, wished to determine whether any Federal cavalry were in the vicinity before leaving this strong position. Receiving no response to this fire he sent to Gettysburg for his two brigade commanders, General Wade Hampton and Fitz Lee. He proposed to arrange with them for an attack upon the enemy's rear. In the interim he ordered a battalion to dismount and occupy an area near the Rummel barn.

The moment they were in position a Federal skirmish line advanced to meet them. Then a Federal battery of 3-inch rifles opened up. The first shot struck the muzzle of a Confederate gun killing the entire crew. The second shot struck the carriage of the next gun, destroying it. The Federal gun crew had displayed uncanny marksmanship.

A period of calm followed during which General Gregg arrived and took command. Hampton and Fitz Lee arrived at this point and took positions in the woods on Stuart's left.

Suddenly the sound of the terrific cannonading that preceeded Pickett's charge rolled down on them. The earth shook while the heavens echoed and re-echoed continuously. In a short time Custer directed Col. Russell Alger to advance his 5th Michigan Cavalry and engage the enemy. The 5th moved toward the Rummel woods its right flank protected by McIntosh's brigade, and its left by part of the 6th Michigan. As they advanced from fence to fence their adversaries moved out from behind the Rummel buildings to engage them, only to be met by the rapid fire of the 5th Michigan's newly issued eight-shotted Spencer carbines. Though outnumbering their enemy the gray line was unable to stand up to the superior firepower. They were forced to yield, making a final stand behind a heavy fence immediately in front of the Rummel buildings.

The new rapid firing carbines had given the 5th a decided advantage but it used up ammunition faster than had been anticipated. After advancing to within a few hundred yards of the foot of Cress Ridge they found themselves out of ammunition. When this became apparent, the Confederates sprang forward with renewed zeal. The blue line fell back stubbornly, pursued by the men in gray.

As the retreating blue line neared one of its batteries a regiment of Federal cavalry advanced from the rear, sabers drawn and colors flying. It was the 7th Michigan. Gregg had ordered it to charge. Once it was clear of the battery, Custer, with drawn saber waving, took a place at its head and shouted: "Come on you Wolverines!" The dismounted Confederate line, unable to face a mounted charge, broke and fled.

Dashing six or seven hundred yards in good order, the 7th Michigan ran into an oblique post-and-rail fence. This caused indescribable confusion. Many of the men dismounted and began lifting the deeply set posts while others kept the Confederates at bay. A passage was soon effected and the charge resumed, the Confederates falling before it. Another fence was encountered within 300 yards of the Confederate battery. There the 9th and 13th Virginia Cavalry flanked and stopped the 7th Michigan, then a series of blows and counter blows were struck by each side.

After a brief pause "a body of mounted men began to emerge from the woods on the left of the Confederate line, northeast of the Rummel buildings, and form column to the right as they debouched into the open field," General Kidd recalled. "Squadron after squadron, regiment after regiment, orderly as if on parade, came into view and successively took their places."[8]

Lieut. Alex Pennington could not let the opportunity pass. Firing his six field pieces as rapidly as they could be loaded, he tore huge gaps in the Confederate ranks. And just as quickly, the Confederate cavalry closed them.

Kidd, who witnessed all of it, continued: "With sabers glistening, they advanced. The men on foot gave way to let them pass. It was an inspiring and imposing spectacle, that brought a thrill to the hearts of the spectators on the opposite slope. Pennington double-shotted his guns with cannister, and the head of the column staggered under each murderous discharge. But still it advanced, led on by an imperturbable spirit that no storm of war could cow."

While the 5th Michigan retired slowly and stubbornly before the Confederate advance, the 7th Michigan waited patiently a little to the left. McIntosh too was waiting at the edge of a woods on the opposite side.

The oncoming Confederate horsemen charged straight for Randol's battery, the charges of cannister seeming to goad rather than deter them. Gen. Gregg had ridden over to the 1st Michigan prepared to give an order to Col. Town to charge. Custer arrived at the same moment with similar instructions.

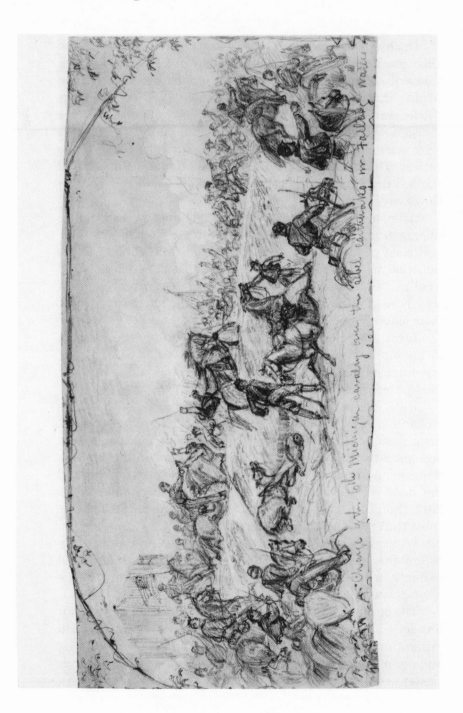

Charge of the 6th Michigan at Falling Waters on July 14, 1863. Custer's men constantly harassed Lee and Stuart's ... ... Pencil ... ... by A.R. Wood. Library of Congress.

When the sabers were drawn at Town's order, Custer rode by his side at the front of the lead company. The force they were about to encounter outnumbered them three to one.

For a ways they moved at a trot, then the trumpet sang out the charge. With a shout they were off. When the two columns met head on, so violent was the impact many horses turned end over end, crushing riders beneath them. The Confederate force staggered from the blow, for it had been struck simultaneously on the left flank by the 3rd Pennsylvania and on the right flank by the 1st New Jersey and the 5th Michigan. While the grey column was being swept back to its starting point, Wade Hampton was seriously injured.

This was a hand-to-hand encounter, the sabre and pistol being the favored weapons. For once the cannons were silent though they had played an effective role in the earlier stages of the engagement. Once the lines were reformed and the wounded cared for there was no evidence that the Confederate cavalry was readying for another bout. That evening they withdrew to the York Pike and camped.[9]

The Confederate cavalry force was about 6,000 men, whereas the Federal force was about 5,000 men of which only 3,000 were actually engaged. Capt. Rawle claimed there were between 7,000 and 8,000 Confederate cavalrymen.[10]

The casualties on both sides were high. Gen. Gregg's Division lost one man killed, seven officers and nineteen men wounded, eight men missing. Total loss: thirty-five.

Custer's Brigade lost one officer and twenty-eight men killed, eleven officers and 112 men wounded, and sixty-seven missing. Total loss: 218.

Stuart reported a loss of 181 but this did not include a return from the artillery or from Col. M.J. Ferguson's command. It had been generally agreed that the losses on both sides were about equal. Both sides laid claim to a victory for both maintained they were in possession of the battlefield after the engagement.

In his report of the engagement, Custer (who had learned that modesty reaped no rewards) wrote: "I challenge the annals of warfare to produce a more brilliant or successful

General Jeb Stuart's Cannon on Cress Ridge. The barn in the center housed many of the wounded of the Michigan Cavalry Brigade and of Stuart's cavalry force four miles east of Gettysburg on July 3, 1863. Author's photo.

charge of cavalry than the one just recounted." Yet he took no personal credit in his report. There is little question it was one of the fiercest and most spectacular cavalry charges in history.

Gen. Gregg, previously, had ordered all newspaper correspondents out of his cavalry camps because of the mischief he had seen result from their activities. They repaid him by withholding all coverage and comment about his outstanding achievement at Gettysburg. Custer was part of Gregg's command for the moment. Though he was to be the correspondents' delight for the remainder of the year, on that occasion they didn't know how to spell his name.

Pickett's charge was the dramatic climax of the Gettysburg campaign because there were so many witnesses to it. The cavalry engagement out on the right was hardly heard of, and was soon forgotten. Gettysburg was the turning point of the Civil War. The repulse of Stuart on the Rummel farm was the turning point of Gettysburg. Had Stuart charged through the Wolverines, had the Michigan Brigade been routed, Stuart would have been left free to strike the Federal rear as it faced Pickett's brave Virginians. Had Stuart been successful, perhaps we in the North would now be talking with a Southern accent.

Palm Sunday, April 9, 1865, was the end of a great tragedy. Two great generals, Robert E. Lee and Ulysses S. Grant, met in the Wilmer McLean house at Appomattox to take a first step in the settlement of the differences within a divided nation. They met there at 1:30 P.M. By 4 P.M. the final terms of the surrender of Lee's army had been drafted by Grant and signed by Lee.

Gen. Lee was wholly satisfied with the terms Grant offered. They were generous to his way of thinking. "This will have the best possible effect upon the men," Lee stated. "It will be very gratifying and will do much toward reconciling our people."

Grant had said that Confederate officers could keep their sidearms and their horses. The men who owned horses or mules could retain them "to work their little farms."

The Federal victory at Five Forks, on April 1, had set the

stage for this scene at Appomattox. Lee had turned his army west to obtain more men and supplies. Grant's column relentlessly pursued them. Lee's army, weakened by losses, captures and desertions, was hungry and exhausted, while the arrival of troops from other theaters was strengthening Grant. Disaster seemed to be following Lee.

At Sayler's Creek, 6,000 of his men were cut off and captured. At Farmville he was so closely followed by Grant he had no time to destroy the main bridge across the Appomattox. It was Saturday night, April 8, immediately east of Appomattox Court House that he realized he was trapped. There were Federals on every side. They were moving too fast for him. His men lacked shoes and clothing. His horses needed forage. There was no food though word had been received there would be three railroad train loads[12] of rations awaiting him at Appomattox Station. There just might be a chance if he could obtain the rations and move toward Lynchburg.

Just after daybreak of April 8th, one of Sheridan's scouts informed him of three railway train loads of supplies arriving at Appomattox Station, sent from Lynchburg for Lee's Army. Major General G.A. Custer's Third Cavalry Division and Brigadier General T.C. Devin's First Cavalry Division were within striking distance and so were promptly ordered by Sheridan to advance. Custer, who was in the lead, marched twenty-eight miles before sundown, to reach a point one mile from the Station. There he waited for Major General Wesley Merritt who was to join him with Devin's Division. But there was no sign of Merritt. Custer had made an effort to communicate with him but had been unable to make contact. Communications had been extremely difficult to maintain since the cavalry units were spread out over a wide area.

By this time Custer had received additional word from other scouts that the supply trains had reached Appomattox Station. Growing impatient because Merritt had not appeared, and realizing that an opportunity to strike a decisive blow could disappear, he resolved to disregard his orders to await contact with Merritt before attacking the enemy.[13] If Merritt didn't appear in a half-hour he would move to capture the trains "and if possible reach and hold the road to Lynchburg."[14]

An hour before sunset Custer jumped to his feet and exclaimed: "By George! There's a train; let's go for it." Vaulting into his saddle he rode over to Colonel A.M. Randol and said: "Go in, old fellow. Don't let anything stop you. Now is the chance for your star. Whoop 'em up and I'll be after you."[15]

Randol moved out in a gallop, arriving at the station just as the engines were getting under way. Their engineers had taken alarm and had decided to make a run to the west for Lynchburg. The Federal cavalrymen spurred their horses alongside the engines, covered the engineers with their revolvers and ordered them to stop. They stopped. Custer now had all of Lee's commissary supplies in his hands and controlled the railroad upon which they had been carried.

A call for firemen and engineers to man the captured engines brought forth a dozen competent volunteers. Those selected were in a playful mood, all of them recognizing that the end of the Confederacy was near. Playfully they ran the woodburning engines back and forth, ringing bells, belching smoke, and blowing whistles. After venting their feelings they moved eastward toward Farmville, passing Devin's and Crook's columns on the way.

Near the point the engines and supplies were captured was " a camp of hospital train, a large pack of wagons and a park of surplus artillery."[16] The artillery was being guarded by a small division of Confederate infantry and full division of cavalry. About the same time Custer's cavalry reached the depot a detachment from Lee's army arrived. Custer struck it the moment he had secured the engines. The contest was sharp and hot, and continued until after dark and the enemy were driven off. It was apparent that the Confederate forces were defenseless, the attack being wholly unexpected.

Custer had no advance information of the presence of the artillery train, the scouts having failed to inform Sheridan of its presence. He had expected a detail of cavalry at the depot, and this he had routed. "Then," as Newhall said, "he turned his attention to the guns, and dashed into the woods to see who was firing so wildly, and to see if it couldn't be stopped."[17]

"Custer might not well conduct a siege of regular approaches," Newhall continued, "but for a sudden dash, Custer was against the world. Many another might have pricked his fingers badly with meddling gently with this nettle, but he took it in his hand boldly and crushed it; for it was a nettle, and a very keen one, as appeared in a moment when there opened on his slap-dash party a banting of batteries going off like a bunch of firecrackers."[18]

The Confederate artillery had opened fire with grapeshot and cannister, the havoc among Custer's troopers being fearful. Most of Custer's attacks were repulsed until 9 P.M. As the Confederates had withdrawn their main batteries, leaving a few to defend the rear of its retreating column, it appeared to Custer's officers the enemy line could be broken. When Randol told of this, Custer exclaimed: "Go tell the men that those guns must be taken in five minutes."[19] When Custer's words got to the cavalrymen, they shouted and charged. In a matter of minutes the batteries were taken. It wa now after nine o'clock and the day was done. Twenty-five pieces of artillery, over 200 wagons, three (some reports say four) railroad trains of supplies, and uncounted numbers of prisoners were captured.

Custer's cavalry then advanced on the road to Appomattox Court House, meeting resistance on the way. Encountering an infantry barricade, he halted his command and established a line in front of it.[20] But for the mercurial Custer the day was not over. It was after midnight before he rode to the hospital to visit the wounded men.[21]

That evening, in a last council of war, Lee and his generals had decided that an attempt at a break-through would be made if they were opposed by nothing other than cavalry. An enemy infantry force blocking the Lynchburg Road would be their undoing. The road was their only avenue of escape.

At dawn on April 9th, Major General John B. Gordon made an attempt to determine the Federal strength on his front. The Federal use of repeating Spencer carbines gave him an impression he was confronted by a large enemy force. Then began a series of Confederate attacks that brushed aside the

Federal cavalry. Advancing they met Gen. E.O.C. Ord's infantry, were stopped, then pushed back to the western edge of Appomattox Court House.

By 10 A.M. it was all over. And at 1:30 P.M. Gen. Grant was walking his horse to the red brick McLean house to meet Gen. Lee.

In a general sense the war was over. It was fitting that Custer recognize those who had valiantly followed him through the final stages of the campaign to reunite a divided nation, so he wrote:

Headquarters Third Cavalry Division
Appomattox Court House, Va.
April 9, 1865

SOLDIERS OF THE THIRD CAVALRY DIVISION:

With profound gratitude toward the God of battles, by whose blessings our enemies have been humbled and our arms rendered triumphant, your commanding general avails himself of this his first opportunity to express to you his admiration of the heroic manner in which you have passed through the series of battles which today resulted in the surrender of the enemy's entire army.

The record established by your indomitable courage is unparalleled in the annals of war. Your prowess has won for you even the respect and admiration of your enemies. During the past six months, although in most instances confronted by superior numbers, you have captured from the enemy, in open battle, one hundred and eleven pieces of field artillery, sixty-five battle flags, and upwards of ten thousand prisoners of war, including seven general officers. With the past ten days, and included in the above, you have captured forty-six pieces of field artillery and thirty-seven battleflags. You have never lost a gun, never lost a color, and have never been defeated; and notwithstanding the numerous engagements in which you have borne a prominent part, including those memorable battles of the Shenandoah, you have captured every piece of artillery which the enemy has dared to open upon you. The near approach of peace renders it improbable that you will again be called upon to undergo the fatigues of the toilsome march or the exposure of the battlefield; but should the assistance of keen blades, wielded by your sturdy arms, be required to hasten the coming of that glorious peace for which we have been so long contending, the general commanding is proudly confident that, in the future as in the past, every demand will meet with a hearty and willing response.

Let us hope that our work is done, and that, blessed with the comforts of peace, we may be permitted to enjoy the pleasures of home and friends. For our comrades who have fallen, let us ever cherish a grateful remembrance. To the wounded, and to those who languish in Southern prisons, let our heartfelt sympathy be tendered.

And now, speaking for myself alone, when the war is ended and the task of the historian begins—when those deeds of daring which have rendered the name and fame of the Third Cavalry Division imperishable are inscribed upon the bright pages of our country's history, I only ask that my name be written as that of the Commander of the Third Cavalry Division.

G.A. Custer
Brevet Major General Commanding

Chapter Seven
Detractors Try Slander

A LITTLE-known chapter in Gen. Custer's life is that
dealing with his presence in Texas immediately following the
Civil War. He was there but a few months, the time and events
having been scarcely reported. Had it not been for his wife's
account of it in her book *Tenting On The Plains*, very little of it
would have been made known to the general public. A recently
published study of the Custers in Texas has brought new light
and an acceptable interpretation.[1]

Libbie Custer, by nature, is a symbol of absolute loyalty.
Some thought she carried it too far. To carry a loyalty to the
memory of a good husband for fifty-seven years has been
unthinkable to his detractors. Libbie, who knew him best, had
many opportunities to remarry in the years that followed his
tragic death. Twelve years of marriage with her Autie
outweighted fifty years of married life with another, no matter
how exalted his position. She had given up a life of ease to join
her husband in a rugged camp life not patterned for a
gentlewoman. It was by her choice, and she never complained
for fear he would send her back to civilization. There was no
question in her mind where she would rather be, for life with
Autie, no matter what danger or hardship faced them was her
prime interest in life.

Though Libbie lived to within a few days of being ninety-
two, she did not live long enough to see the penned efforts of the
"Great Detractor" Frederic Van De Water. His book, *Glory-*

123

Hunter, boldly faced the dead lion. It was published a year after Libbie's death as if sensing the timing was right. What defense could he expect from an aged warrior even if she was a female? Had she been alive, he would have—and justly—learned what every male should learn, that women are equal, and many times superior, to the male.

Van De Water was a belittler, who made much ado of nothing. His kind, and there are many, flyspeck and criticize, fog and besmog, either to make a buck or to raise an ego. Character assassins find it a way to build a bank account or a career. As an example:

Point:

On May 23, 1865, a Grand Review of the victorious Federal combat troops was held in Washington. Past the Presidential reviewing stand they marched, Sheridan's cavalry in the lead. As they approached the grandstand Custer's horse, *Don Juan* ran away with him. Custer's hat blew off—some say it was knocked off by his saber as he attempted to salute the President while passing by the stand—and he dropped his saber in an attempt to gather in his reins and bring the frightened animal under control. Van De Water goes on to say: "The whole man with his flaws and his flairs is epitomized in that dash. He has been, he will ever be, prone to spectacular outbursts against ordered regularity; insurgent in his hunt for Glory. That runaway is at once his biography and his epitaph."[2]

Counterpoint:

An eyewitness to the incident in describing it for the *Detroit Evening News* said, that a group of 300 girls dressed in white sang "Hail to the Chief" each throwing a bouquet or wreath at him as they did so. "Instead of dodging the floral missiles he began trying to catch thelm. The sudden rush, the pelting of bouquet and the peal of 300 voices frightened his stead, and before he could gather up the reins the excited animal had made the rush we saw from the other end of the avenue."[3]

Down the avenue they raced, Custer's yellow hair and red

flannel necktie floating in the air. In rocketing past the reviewing stand Custer thought to draw and present his saber in full salute to President Johnson and General Grant. In doing so his saber caught his wide hat, causing it and the saber to fall to the ground. Once both hands were free he easily brought the terror-stricken animal under control.[4]

The Federal government following the surrender of Appomattox had sensed that there would be a lot of trouble in Texas if more troups were not moved down there soon. Kirby Smith and his Confederate army were defying the Government, refusing to consider surrender. Gen Grant had ordered Gen. Sheridan down to Texas for the purpose of subduing Kirby's forces so that the Southern states could proceed in an orderly manner to be restored to the Union. Grant want on to explain that there was another motive in sending troops to Texas that could not be mentioned openly.

Emperor Maximilian and his French army had invaded Mexico and set up an empire there while the Federal Government was involved in a civil war. Maximilian had received encouragement from the Confederacy which led Grant to believe that the French invasion of Mexico was linked with the rebellion. Many of the Confederates were escaping across the border and joining with them. Grant foresaw the trouble that would result but was opposed by Secretary William Seward from committing any act that might involve the Union in a war. Seward preferred negotiating with Napoleon. In consequence, Grant asked Sheridan to be prudent in any move he might make and to maintain a strict neutrality. Seward's policy was a show of weakness that Maximilian quickly took advantage of. By the fall of 1865 he had occupied northern Mexico all along the Rio Grande.

Sheridan had little use for the State Department's "slow and poky methods." His was a temperament that demanded action. His practical military mind saw the French occupation as a threat to peace in the South. Disregarding Seward's wish, Sheridan decided upon a hostile demonstration. Gen. Merritt and his Fourth Corps had been stationed at San Antonio.

Using these troops as a feint as if to cross the Rio Grande into Mexico he caused the French and Austrians, who were alarmed at this strategem, to withdraw from Metamoras and abandon most of northern Mexico. This permitted the Liberals under the Mexican general Escobeda, by using the arms and ammunition supplied him by Sheridan, to control the area relinquished by the Imperialists.[5]

Meanwhile, Custer, who was in command of another cavalry column near Houston, was made aware of what was transpiring south of the border. His was the difficult task of readying his troops for a possible invasion of Mexico; troops who had enlisted for the duration and were now anxious to go home. There was grumbling, discontent, and insubordination in the ranks of the volunteer force before Custer took over. The men were aware that most of the Eastern regiments had been mustered out. They too had served their time and wanted to go home. They had enlisted for a war now over, but had no interest in a reconstruction of the South. They were aware that they were stationed there to control civil affairs until Congress took action restoring the Southern states into the Union. They were not aware of the threat south of the border, for Custer was not at liberty to tell them should he be so inclined.

The men were not aware of a role they might have to play nor were they aware that the Mexican government had offered Custer handsome inducements to take over a Mexican cavalry command. Custer would be given the rank of a major general and serve as adjutant general with a salary of $10,000 in gold. Both Grant and Sheridan had given him their blessing. Libbie was not in favor of the proposition but would go with him if he decided to move into Mexico and command its cavalry forces. He applied to the Government for a leave. It was denied. The Government had need of his services in Kansas where hostile Indians were making life miserable for the white settlers.

But while in Louisiana, just prior to moving into Texas, he had inherited a command of grumblers, undisciplined, slovenly, insubordinate and mutinous. They did not, or refused to, understand the need for their presence now that the war was over. Their Government had offered no word of explanation for having delayed mustering them out of the army, and their officers had done no better. Some of these officers had lost control of their commands. One of the colonels complained to Custer that his men were shooting at his tent each night after Taps.

As Libbie Custer had written: "Texas was in a state of ferment from one end to the other.... Jayhawkers, bandits, and bushwackers had everything their own way for a time." The soldiers in Custer's command were no better to loyal Texans. In one instance "without even the excuse of want, a party of soldiers, belonging to this (Custer's) division butchered a number of cattle belonging to Dr. Peebles, who is probably the most thorough Union man in the State, having been incarcerated in prison for nearly a year by the rebel authorities owing to his strong Union sentiments, and afterwards forced to leave the State to save his life from rebel mobs."[6]

Custer took stringent measures to see that this violation of human rights did not recur. The men had been raiding, robbing and pillaging to such a point and degree that Custer had reported it to General Sheridan. Sheridan responded with "Use such summary measures as you deem proper to overcome the mutinous disposition of the individuals in your command." From this came Custer's General Orders No. 2, June 24th, 1865, while in Alexandria, Louisiana, well before the incidents in Texas, giving ample warning that depredations upon the persons or property of citizens would result in punishment to those so charged by having "his head shaved and in addition will receive twenty-five lashes upon his back, well laid on."[7]

From the application of this order came the charge of both Surgeon Charles Lothrop and Lieutenant Colonel A.G. McQueen of the First Iowa Cavalry that Custer had flogged their men unjustly, issued inedible rations and inadequate clothing, claiming it caused extreme destitution and intense suffering to their men. The floggings, they claimed, were administered without trial or any opportunity at self-defense. Nothing was said about one of the regiments that had sent a petition to Custer requesting the dismissal of its colonel, or of another colonel who said that his men wanted the general to explain the reasons for an order he had issued.

It is a matter of record that Quartermaster C.G. Sawtelle was incompetent, and because of his incompetency there were insufficient supplies, low quality rations and too few horses for the command. That men had their heads shaved and received lashes on their bare backs is also a fact. Custer had inherited all of these problems and had to make the best of them. Lothrop and McQueen were partially responsible for the conditions that existed, for they had encouraged the men to rebel and to force the issue with the commanding general. They persisted in making an issue of it by viciously sending false stories about Custer to officials in their home state.

When Custer ordered the execution of two men, one for desertion and the other for mutiny, both of whom had been tried and sentenced by courtsmartial, there was considerable resentment in the ranks. A petition was circulated and presented to Custer asking a pardon for one of the two men, the one who had participated in a mutiny. Custer advised that he would consider the matter, and there it rested.

The men swore vengeance, saying that their commanding officer did not dare carry out the sentence. Custer did dare. Of the many things he had been charged with by his detractors, cowardice was not one of them.

Many threats came to his attention and his officers asked him to go about armed. This he refused to do. He did place a pistol under his pillow each night, unknown to his wife. On the day of the executions he ordered his command of 5,000 soldiers to form a hollow square in a field near town. Slowly he rode around the entire square within reaching distance of the nearest men. Unarmed, he was followed by his alarmed staff. As his wife recalled the incident:

The wagon, drawn by four horses, bearing the criminals sitting on their coffins, was driven at a slow pace around the square, escorted by the guard and the firing party, with reversed arms. The coffins were placed in the center of the square, and the men seated upon them at the foot of their open graves. Eight men, with livid countenances and vehemently beating hearts, took their places in front of their comrades, and looked upon the blanched, despairing faces of those whom they were ordered to kill. The provost marshall carried their carbines off to a distance, loaded seven, and placed a blank cartridge in the eighth, thus giving the merciful boon of permanent uncertainty as to whose was the fatal shot. The eyes of the poor victims were then bandaged, while thousands of the men held their breath as the tragedy went on. The still, Southern air of that garden on earth was unmoved by any sound, save the unceasing notes of the mocking birds that sang night and day in the hedges. Preparations had been so accurately made that there was but one word to be spoken after the reading of the warrant for execution, and that the last that those most miserable and hopeless of God's creatures should hear on earth.

There was still one more duty for the provost marshal before the fatal word "Fire!" was sounded. But one person understood his movements as he steathily drew near the sergeant (the one charged with mutiny), took his arm, and led him aside. In an instant his voice rang out the fatal word, and the deserter fell back dead, in blessed ignorance that he went to eternity alone; while the sergeant swooned in the arms of the provost marshal. When he was revived, it was explained to him that the General believed him to have been the victim of undue influence, and had long determined upon pardon; but some punishment he thought necesesary, and he was also determined that the soldiers should not feel that he had been intimidated from performing his duty because his own life was in peril.[9]

The march from Louisiana to Texas was an orderly one. There was no lawlessness, no disobedience, no mutiny. The men still resented Custer and continued to lay their detention and compulsory service on Custer but they respected him and his wishes. Gradually he was bringing order out of chaos. In consequence, the Texans were amazed at the fine deportment of an army from which they expected nothing but trouble. There was no unwanted foraging by the men, no outrages against private citizens and their property as had been perpetrated in Louisiana. What had been a lawless and mutinous command had become one of resentful orderliness. As Mrs. Custer remembered: "They hated us, I suppose. That is the penalty the commanding officer generally pays for what still seems to me the questionable privilege of rank and power. Whatever they thought, it did not deter us from commending, among ourselves, the good material in those Western men, which so soon made them orderly and obedient soldiers."[10]

Captain Frederick W. Benteen, Custer's senior captain, had taken an instant dislike to Custer the moment they first met. The dislike ripened into an intense hatred made very evident in a reading of the Benteen-Golden letters.[11] Benteen was a likeable person, but he was a personage with a problem which in his later years became apparently a psychosis.

Benteen was not long in encouraging factionalism in the regiment nor did he reject the opportunity of acting as a leader for the dissidents. His true colors were first made evident immediately following the Battle of the Washita. He was six years older than Custer, a circumstance that did much to aggravate his huge ego. It became obvious, soon after he was assigned to the Seventh Cavalry in 1866, that he resented Custer's prestige, rank and youth. As time passed Benteen's hostility grew.

Custer too had his share of egotism, for what successful general officer does not. His exploits during the Civil War had earned him much acclaim both in the newspapers and in the homes of the veterans who had followed his guidon. This and Custer's outstanding military ability was too much for the jealous nature of Benteen. There could be neither admiration nor respect for Custer, only resentment which grew into a hatred following Custer's success on the Washita.

A few days after the battle Benteen went to Ben Clark, one of the scouts in the compaign, and asked him if he would "be willing to make the statement that Custer knowingly let Elliott go to his doom without trying to save him." Clark, who had seen Major Elliott, without permission or direction, ride off after a call of volunteers, refused to have any part of Benteen's proposal.

Clark was of the opinion that Benteen was charging Custer with abandoning Elliott so that he could "weaken Custer's prestige."[13] Whatever Benteen wished to do to Custer, he received no support for it from Ben Clark. Clark had been a witness to all of Elliott's actions prior to the unauthorized pursuit of some of the Indians. It was a foolhardy act at best, for Elliott was second in command and, had Custer fallen, he would have had to assume command immediately. Riding off as he did he could not have been, under ideal conditions, in any position to assume command had Custer been severely wounded or killed.

Clark was well-known to high ranking officers as a competent and trustworthy scout and was considered to be both honest and frank.

The charge Benteen made, appeared two months after the battle in the form of a letter to the *St. Louis Daily Democrat,* February 9, 1869. The unsigned letter obviously had been written by a participant in the battle and had been sent to a friend in the St. Louis area who had seen to it that the newspaper received a copy. The letter was dated two weeks after the finding of the bodies of Elliott and his detachment. The paper containing this letter reached Custer's hands while the Seventh Cavalry was encamped in Indian Territory.

Custer read the fanciful melodramatic account that unmercifully censured him. In part it read:

"Round and round rush the red fiends, smaller and smaller shrinks the circle, but the aim at the devoted, gallant knot of heroes is steadier than ever, and the death howl of the murderous redskins is more frequent. But on they come in masses grim, with glittering lance and one long, loud, exulting whoop, as if the gates of hell had opened and loosened the whole infernal host.". . .

"And now return with me to the village. Officers and soldiers are watching, resting, eating and sleeping. In an hour or so they will be refreshed, and then scour the hills and plains for their missing comrades. The comander occupies himself in taking an inventory of the captured property which he has promised the officers shall be distributed among the enlisted men of the command if they falter or halt not in the charge. . . .

"Our chief exhibits his close sharpshooting and terrifies the crowd of frighted, captured squaws and papooses by dropping the struggling ponies in death near them. Ah! he is a clever marksman. Not even do the poor dogs of the Indians escape his eye or him as they drop dead or limp howling away.

"Take care! do not trample on the dead bodies of that woman and child lying there! In a short time we will be far from the scene of our daring dash, and night will have thrown her dark mantel over the scene. But surely some search will be made for our missing comrades. No, they are forgotten."

A strange letter, to charge Custer and his fellow officers with having left Elliott without a search. That would mean that the officers were as guilty as Custer, for none had protested the leave-taking, yet all knew that Elliott had either been killed or had escaped and returned to the wagon train. And there was evident contempt for the officers and the men who had won this outstanding victory at a point the Indians had been making the Army a laughing stock.

When Custer read the letter he undoubtedly thought it was from the pen of some malcontent in the lower ranks of his command. All of his officers had read the letter and were waiting to see what he would do about it.

They did not have long to wait. Officers Call was sounded and all responded. As he stood before them he tapped his boots with his riding whip then, referring to the letter, he remarked that he intended horsewhipping its author once he learned his identity.

Colonel Bates got the story from General John F. Weston who was present at the scene as a lieutenant. Benteen amazed all of them by shifting "his revolver to a handy position on his belt," then said, "'All right, General, start your horsewhipping now. I wrote it.'" Weston added that "Custer seemed to be dumfounded, hesitated a moment, dismissed the assemblage and hurriedly left the tent."[14]

It is obvious Custer never suspected that Benteen was the culprit. Though astounded by Benteen's admission, he had observed Benteen's shifting of his pistol in readiness for a confrontation. Custer feared no man. He had faced braver men than Benteen. Even Custer's foes granted him the highest of commendation for his courage.

As he had on many battlefields, Custer instantly decided upon a plan of action—in this instance it was one of inaction—for he had been faced with surprises before. Dismissing the assembled officers, he left. A quarrel at that point, while in the midst of an Indian campaign, would do immense harm to the morale of the Seventh Cavalry. To Custer the Seventh was always first. His threat was an impulsive act. All knew he would not have carried it out; there was too much at stake. He displayed his true character by regaining his control and recognizing that there was no need to punish Benteen for "There was enough in Benteen's having branded himself as disloyal before his fellow officers."[15]

"Custer's Luck" is a phrase commonly tossed about by those on both sides of the fence. None of those who used it, either disparagingly or complimentally, originated it for it was Custer himself who first recognized he had fared well in the dispensation of opportunities. He gave himself no credit for recognizing each opportunity when it knocked nor did he pat himself on the back for having successfully accepting each of these challenges and bringing each of them to a successful conclusion.

General of the Army Nelson A. Miles had some very definite views about luck and "Custer's Luck." While in the midst of a rugged winter campaign against the Sioux, he wrote to Mrs. Custer:

"Custer's career has few parallels in the history of any war in any country. His success was no more the result of luck than are the rewards of any human effort, for if there is any calling in life where the fruits are gathered in accordance with real merit it is in the profession of arms, where patient study, sleepless vigilance, laborious toil and iron nerve are requisite in order to reap the harvest of glory. "Custer's Luck" was the result of judgment to do the right things at the right time, and to his devotion to his profession and to his great energy and persistency."[16]

But General Grant had recognized Custer's capabilities ten years earlier when he wrote a letter of introduction saying:

"This will introduce to your acquaintance Gen. Custer, who rendered such distinguished service as a cavalry officer during the war. There was no officer in that branch of service who had the confidence of Gen. Sheriden to a greater degree than Gen. Custer, and there is no officer in whose judgment I have greater faith than in Sheridan's. Please understand than that I mean by this to endorse Gen. Custer in a high degree."[17]

Custer knew many thought highly of him, yet he was not reluctant to admit he had not always been thought so well of. In one of the last articles he had written for publication he observed that : "My career as a cadet had but little to commend it to the study of those who came after me, unless as an example to be carefully avoided. . . . My offenses against law and order were not great in enormity, but what they lacked in magnitude they made up in number. . . . The resignation and departure of the Southern cadets took away from the Academy a few individuals who, had they remained, would probably have contested with me the debatable honor of bringing up the rear of the class."[18]

This brings us to another Custer legend—that at his graduation in 1861, he was number 34 of the 34 graduating member of that class. Therefore he was the "Goat" of his class. That class had started in 1857 with 79 names on the roster. The shrinkage began immediately. Some 22 cadets didn't show for admission, or dropped out; one died on sick leave; and 22 resigned because of the Civil War. Many of the latter, and some had less than a semester to graduate, joined and fought on the side of the Confederacy. John Carroll, one of the country's leading Custer authorities, is of the belief that 23 members of the class that started with Custer in 1857 conceivably could have finished behind Custer. As he said in a comprehensive study of the subject: "It is not only completely wrong, but faulty to claim Custer as the "Goat." True, he finished last, but this was because of a decimated class and not necessarily because of an earned academic standing."[19]

The term "Goat" as applied to Custer is a traditional one that was applied to the graduate who was at the very bottom of his class. Actually it didn't apply to Custer for the term was not yet in use. Classes up to 1861 were scheduled for five years. Because of the impending war, his class was reduced to four years, the year 1861 graduating two classes, the other being the regular five-year class.

In the final analysis Custer has been victimized; made to appear, through inaccurate research, as the "Goat" of his class. Carroll has now laid that myth to rest.

When Custer arrived at the West Point wharf in the summer of 1857 to begin the five years of training then required to graduate from the United States Military Academy, he became one of the nearly 300 boys granted this privilege. With so few attending the Academy they became intimately acquainted with each other. During the war years, when forced to face each other on opposing sides, this knowledge became quite useful. Like a poker club of many years standing, those likely to bluff were well-known.

Except for a few, there was no hard feeling displayed when Southern boys began leaving at the early state of the Rebellion, to return home to join the armed forces of their homes states. Most of the cadets were broad-minded professionals-to-be who respected their future adversaries capabilities and loyalties. Young Custer expressed this feeling for his fellow classmen when he declared to an obstinate Northern cadet that "any Southern cadet who wants to leave the academy and go home and fight fo his home State has a clear right to. I'm going to stick to the Union, but I refuse to hold the slightest bitterness against any Southern cadet or Southern army officer who resigns and follows the fortunes of his own State."[20]

He had taken his share of hazing while a plebe as good naturedly as he had the practical jokes in the Custer home in New Rumley. In his second year his turn came. Attracted by a new arrival sporting a great beard, Custer asked him his name.

"Myers, sir," the plebe replied.

"Well, Mr. Myers, I am sorry but there seems to have been a serious mistake," said Custer. "I think you had better go right home and send your son, Mr. Myers."[21]

Brig. Gen. Evans Andruss wrote to Mrs. Libbie Custer: "His boyish—but harmless frolics kept him in constant hot water. . . . He was beyond doubt the most popular man in his class and even the plebes (and Andruss was one while Custer was a cadet) deemed it an honor and a pleasure to be 'deviled' by him."[22]

Another schoolmate who became a brigadier general was Peter Michie. He recalled that: "He (Custer) never saw an adjutant in full uniform that he did not suspect that he was the object of his search for the purpose of being placed under arrest, and to have five minutes more freedom he would cut and run for it, to delay if possible the well-known formula: 'Sir, you are hereby placed in arrest and confined to quarters, by direction of the superintendent.' He had more fun, gave his friends more anxiety, walked more tours of extra guard, and came nearer being dismissed more often than any other cadet I have ever known."[23]

Apparently Custer believed there were two positions of distinction in his class. Since he could not be at the head of the class he made every effort to establish himself at the foot of it. He was distinguished in several other respects. He was the strongest man in his class and, while lying down, could spring to a standing position. In horsemanship he excelled, having made the highest jump on record with the exception of a higher jump made by Cadet U.S. Grant.

If one examines the Academy records of Custer the conclusion is soon reached that his was a phenomenal scholastic performance. To hang on to the tail end without being sent home at the head of those who were too deficient to remain, was no mean achievement. As the dare devil of his class he became one of its "immortals." As one classmate wrote: "Custer, ever at the head of his regiment, and Custer (without disparagement) ever at the foot of his class."[24]

Another schoolmate, Major General James Wilson, referred to him as an indifferent scholar but having tremendous vitality and vigor. He described him as being "six feet tall, with broad shoulders, deep chest, thin waist, and splendid legs; he had a perfect figure and was one of the best horsemen of his day." At the Academy and afterwards his close friends called him "Cinnamon" because he had brought a bottle of cinnamon hair oil to West Point and showed a preference for it.[25]

His yellow hair and fair complexion soon earned him the name of "Fanny" among other cadets. The recipient of many nicknames in later years, the two most commonly applied to Custer by the Indians were "Yellow Hair," and "Long Hair."

And during the Civil War the correspondents commonly referred to him as the "Boy General." The troopers who followed him while he chased after Indians raiding the Western frontier soon took to calling him (but not in his hearing) "Old Hard Ass."

It was while at the Academy that Custer endeavored to let his hair grow long. Two cavalry instructors, Charlie May and Charlie Field, wore their hair a la Cody. Custer was intrigued, After having been reported several times for his long hair he instructed the barber to give his head a clean shave. It was a laughing matter for his classmates but not for him. He was relentlessly pursued and, at all military inspections and on sight, was reported for having "Hair out of uniform." So numerous were the demerits acquired that he wore a tan-colored wig to prevent his dismissal.[26]

On another occasion in Spanish class he asked the instructor to translate into Spanish "Class dismissed." When the request was complied with, the class arose and left in a body.[27]

Of Custer's many delinquencies, there was one for which he received no demerits, though every cadet knew of it. From the window of Custer's 8th Division tower room one could look down on the garden of Lieutenant Douglas. In this garden could be seen Douglas' rooster proudly leading his small flock among the vegetables. From time to time the rooster would crow defiantly and boastfully from the top of the fence. He crowed once too often for one night Custer slipped down and quieted him. The rooster was next seen in a kettle boiling over a gas burner, the feathers carefully piled on a newspaper. Once the rooster was disposed of it became the obligation of one of the guests to get rid of the feathers. This was done rather carelessly for the next morning a trail of yellow feathers could be seen leading from the 8th Division tower, across the grounds.[28]

In spite of his disregard for regulations there was no question that Custer had a great love for the Academy. This was apparent in a letter he wrote to a girl friend in August, 1857:

I like West Point as well if not better than I did at first. I think it is the most romantic spot I ever saw. I am becoming accustomed to the strict discipline and have escaped with but few demerits though. Some find it difficult to avoid getting their number as one hundred and fifty marks would dismiss a person next January, and after January it requires but one hundred in a year to dismiss a person, and as some offenses give five demerits, a person has to be very careful in his conduct.

We have permission to go on public lands but there are limits which must not be crossed, but occasionally some of the cadets have the boldness to cross the sentinental's post at night and go to a small village two or three miles down the river for the purpose of getting things which are not allowed, such as ice cream, candies, fruit, and (I am sorry to say) some even go for wine and liquors. They always change clothes for citizens to prevent detection for the punishment of this offense is very severe and occasionally persons are dismissed and if not dismissed are confined in a light prison for three or four months.

Night before last one of my classmates in company with two elder classmen left camp about 11 o'clock at night, went to town and were seen by an officers who caught two of them, one of whom is my classmate, and both are now confined in their tents...They will be court-martialed and it is very probable that the "old cadet" will be discharged, and my class mate will be confined in prison for a few months...This seems hard but military law is very severe and those who overstep its boundaries must abide the consequences.[29]

Chapter Eight
No Place for Cowards

THE GREATEST myth maker of all was the Battle of the Little Big Horn. Some refer to it as Custer's Last Battle while many others call it the Custer Massacre. In a literal interpetation it was a massacre for it was a merciless or wholesale slaughter of Custer and his men. And it was an overwhelming defeat of the cavalry whatever one may wish to call it.

Though intended to be a campaign to drive the Indians onto their reservation by the use of force, General Custer and General Alfred Terry in particular, did not anticipate any great resistance on the part of the Indians they were to encounter. Little did they know that the resistance Custer was to encounter would result in the greatest of Plains Indian victories. The Indians won the battle but it was this battle that lost the war for them. Because of it the American people rose up in wrath and demanded that Congress provide the West with troops sufficient to conquer those who interfered with its settlement.

Many historians rate the Battle of the Little Big Horn as unimportant. It was not unimportant. It was as important as the Japanese strike at Pearl Harbor. Each served to stir an indifferent nation.

In 1875, there were 746 men on frontier duty in Montana where the Custer battle took place. In 1876—the year of the Custer Battle—Montana contained 2,056 soldiers. In 1877, there were 3,298 men engaged in Indian campaigns. This escalation in 1877 would not have have been possible had

Custer merely been checked, as General Crook's forces had been at the Battle of the Rosebud one week before the Custer engagement.

The well-known Custer battle authority Captain Mike Koury believes that: "The war would have gone on and on unless the nation would have been shocked by what became a great disaster to a national hero, and to what supposedly was the best regiment in the U.S. Cavalry, probably the entire army."

"Had the Sioux and Cheyennes merely defeated Custer, killing 30 or 40 men," he said, "the war would have gone on and on. By killing Custer, by wiping him out, the Sioux and Cheyennes sealed their own fate."[1]

You may be certain that the nation would have appropriated the money for additional troops, and it would not have built Forts Keogh and Custer in the heart of the Sioux reservation, had not this showcase regiment of cavalry been decimated.

Indeed, the Battle of the Little Big Horn was most important for it brought to an end any further recognition of the Sioux and Cheyenne treaties. The days of the Indians were numbered after that. With an increase in its numerical strength, the army, led by officers seeking revenge and glory, pursued the stubbornly defiant Indians until they were able to capture or destroy them. The leader of these defiant Indians was Sitting Bull.

For some years the Plains Indians had evidenced their displeasure at the migration of whites through their hunting grounds. To add to their discomfiture many of the whites began occupying some of the choice land. The Indian hostility was first directed toward the trappers,[2] then against the immigrants, prospectors and settlers.

The terms of a treaty had been decided upon in 1868 by both the Indians and the whites. Both seemed to believe that treaties were made to be broken for violations were immediate. The whites began to trespass upon Indian land; the Indians— the younger element—continued their raids upon the settlements. Though Colonel John Gibbon contended later that there had not been a single treaty made with the Indians that the whites did not violate[3] there were many who held the same view of the Indians.

For the five years following the Treaty of 1868, ungovernable Indians continued to murder, rape, and loot any white within reach. Neither side respected the treaty boundaries "even when clearly defined and understood."[4] The young warriors crossed the boundary lines to carry out their depredations. On other occasions they would attack parties of whites who had ignored the boundaries of Indian owned land by settling, hunting, or seeking gold on it. Soon the Sioux and Cheyenne warriors were raiding well beyond the limits of their reservations or hunting grounds.

General Sherman, acting in behalf of the Government, had placed soldiers in the field during the summer of 1873 to act as an escort for the party surveying the route of the Northern Pacific Railroad. The rail had been laid across the prairies of Minnesota and Dakota up to the Missouri River as far as Bismarck. The government regarded its completion to the West coast as an absolute necessity. It was the nation's umbilical cord to the West coast settlement.

The Sioux had differing views. The railroad—or any road—was obnoxious. It would bring in more whites and would drive away the buffalo. Without the buffalo the Indians would be forced to retire to their reservations and become welfare recipients.

Sherman anticipated trouble during the construction across Dakota. He had indicated to Sheridan that he expected it and that he would back him in his efforts to subdue any Indian hostilities. He concluded that the Indians now recognized they must oppose this road construction. In doing so, this might be their last opportunity to stem the white tide.[5] Looking at it from the standpoint of a military interest Sherman saw the railroad as a means of permanently controlling the Indians.[6]

The Commissioner of Indian Affairs, Francis Walker, was wholly in accord with Sherman's solution to the Indian problem. "Columns moving north from the Union Pacific, and south from the Northern Pacific," he said, "would crush the Sioux and their confederates as between the upper and nether millstone."[7]

Since Sherman anticipated a vigorous resistance from the Sioux he placed Col. David S. Stanley in command of almost 1,500 soldiers and 400 civilians to protect the surveyors during the summer of 1873. This escort included Lt. Col. George Armstrong Custer and ten companies of the Seventh Cavalry. During its three months in the field that summer the Seventh Cavalry had two sharp engagements with the Sioux, defeating them on both occasions. This had the effect of infuriating the Indians all the more.

The experiences the Stanley expedition had encountered caused Sheridan to take stock. It was his view that the Indian did not know what he was doing when he murdered or depredated since it was the only way of life with which he was acquainted. "If some wise system of punishment could be arranged and carried out," he said, "it would much sooner terminate the Indian trouble on our frontier."[8]

To his way of thinking the completion of the Northern Pacific Railroad would greatly assist and hasten the settlement of the West. The panic of 1873 was delaying its completion but that would be only temporary. With its completion would come a tide of whites which would augment the Indian problem.

In his annual report of 1873 Sheridan had recommended the establishment of a military post at the base of the Black Hills "to secure a strong foothold in the heart of the Sioux country, and thereby exercise a controlling influence over these warlike people." He wanted to locate a post there so he would be in a position to "threaten the villages and stocks of the Indians if the latter raided the settlements."[9]

This last post would complete the ring around the Hills. Fort Fetterman was to the west, Fort Ellis to the northwest, Fort Union to the north, Fort Abraham Lincoln to the northeast, and Fort Laramie to the southwest.

President Grant and General Sherman accepted Sheridan's recommendation and ordered him to plan a reconnaissance for the following spring. On April 24th, 1874, General Sheridan in company with General Terry, visited Fort Lincoln to discuss details of the coming expedition with General Custer. Sheridan had Custer in mind to head the reconnaissance before he ever broached the subject to Grant and Sherman. Three days after the meeting, Custer supplied Sheridan with figures to prove "that the proposed reconnaissance can be made and result in an actual saving to the Government."[10] No appropriation from Congress appeared necessary.

Just two weeks earlier, Bishop William H. Hare, on learning of the proposed expedition, wrote to the President to remind him that the Government had planned special efforts during the summer of 1874 to pacify the northern Sioux. Western newspapers were encouraging the public to enter the Hills in search of gold. It was his opinion that this and the Custer expedition would cause an influx of adventurers, and war with the Sioux would result.[11]

Little did Hare know that the President, the Congress, the public and the army were fed up with the Government's Peace Policy. Quite likely the public was tired of paying for a peace they never seemed to get. The humanitarians and the do-gooders had had their day and had no lasting result to show for their efforts. The army was even more dissatisfied. They had observed an Indian Bureau appeasement policy that had provided the Indians with the latest multiple fire weapons while supplying the army with single shot weapons, apparently for the purpose of evening the contest.

On July 2, the Black Hills expedition left Fort Abraham Lincoln. With more than 1000 men in its ten companies of Seventh Cavalry and two companies of infantry it composed one of the largest of exploratory assignments in the country's history up to that time.

For sixty days it combed the Black Hills in search of a satisfactory site for a military post and an easy access to it. It was an area near Bear Butte on the northeastern border of the Hills that Custer decided upon as the most feasible location.

Fort Lincoln Staff Outing in 1875. General Custer in center, standing with arms folded, and wearing light hat. Author's collection.

Fort Abraham Lincoln, North Dakota Territory in the winter of 1875. Missouri River to the left. D.F. Barry photo in author's collection.

Sight of the lush grazing land and the heavy timber aroused Custer's agrarian instincts. Though gold had been discovered by men attached to his command, Custer played this down but described the opportunities for farming and cattle raising in glowing and rapturous terms. The accompanying correspondents and their editors paid small heed to Custer's remarks about the rich soil but instead gave an over-emphasis to the discovery of gold.

Custer was overzealous in his effort to avoid friction with Indians. He realized he was operating within the understanding of the 1868 Treaty but that some Indians might not interpret his actions in the Hills as General Sherman did. Sherman, who was a party to the drafting of the Treaty, was of the opinion "that it was not intended to exclude the United States from exploring the reservation for roads or for any other national purpose."[12]

By August 30th the Custer expedition was back at Fort Lincoln. There had been no confrontation with the Indians though the Sioux were well aware that the military had entered the Indian sanctuary.

Following the Custer battle charges were made that the 1874 expedition was the direct cause of the Sioux resistance that led to the annihilation of Custer's command. Nothing was further from the truth. It has been shown that there had been a mounting resentment against encroachment upon the Indians' hunting grounds. The construction of railroads across these hunting grounds had added irritation to the presence of settlers and military posts. The existence of gold in the Black Hills was well known to the whites who were awaiting an opportunity to get it with safety. Parties of prospectors had invaded the Hills prior to the expedition but the fanfare and publicity given the gold discovery on this expedition was enough to start a boom. Excitement ran high as parties organized and equipped in Bismarck, Fargo, Sioux Falls, Omaha and Chicago. Sheridan and Terry had to step in and order all such parties out of the Hills.[13]

General George Crook felt rather strongly about the settling of the Black Hills. It was his feeling that "the

Custer's Wagon Train on the 1874 Black Hills Expedition. The column of 110 wagons accompanied by over 1,000 men, three Gatling guns and a three-inch rifle prepare to move out. The dark room wagon of photographer William H. Illingsworth is in the foreground presumably to give his stereo view an additional third dimension. Courtesy of the South Dakota Historical Society.

occupation by the settlers of the Black Hills country had nothing to do with the hostilities which have been in progress."[14] It may be argued thusly or it may be argued that "the Black Hills gold rush had nothing to do with the causes of the Sioux War in 1876."[15]

Any transgressor irritated the Sioux. The Crows and the Pawnees, traditional enemy of the Sioux, could vouch for that. They hunted on Sioux land at the risk of their lives, and it was land that the Sioux had once taken from the Crows. When emigrants, railroads or the military—each in its turn—made use of the plains, more fuel was added to a fire that had burned for many years.

The inevitable would have happened after Custer's reconnaissance. Prospectors were ready to go in prior to Custer but were prevented from doing so by the military. As soon as the press ballyhooed the expedition the real invasion of the Hills took place and it was all the military could do to hold it down. Arrests upon arrests were made. Once the prospectors were turned over to the civil courts they were immediately released. The trespassing was repeated until the small force of soldiers was unable to cope with the situation. It became apparent that the only solution was for the Government to purchase the Black Hills.

During 1875 while the Government was attempting to purchase the Hills, Chief Red Cloud, through the intervention of Professor O.C. Marsh, had managed to obtain an investigation of alleged graft and corruption on the part of various Indian agents. There were charges that the annuity goods had been in the form of undersized cattle, poor quality blankets and a short measure of foodstuffs. This caused additional disatisfaction amongst the Indians.

Then began the negotiations to purchase the Black Hills. Legally and morally they belonged to the Sioux, yet they were now in the possession of the whites. All attempts to keep the white man out had been unsuccessful. This circumstance resulted in a public demand for an opening of the territory. Once the white man discovered that this portion of the Indian reservation was valuable he, as in many previous instances,

Permanent Camp on French Creek. Though General Custer played down the discovery of gold on his expedition to the Black Hills the newspaper correspondents with him thought it should be front page news. 1874. Illingworth photo from South Dakota Historical Society.

Golden Valley Camp on French Creek near present day Custer, South Dakota. This was the 7th Cavalry's "permanent camp" in 1874. The Pioneer Mountains are on the left. French Creek lies beyond the tents on the right. It was here that gold was discovered. Illingworth photo courtesy of the South Dakota Historical Society.

made every effort to deprive the Indian of his established rights and ownership.

As usual the whites wanted to purchase the Hills at bargain prices—literally, for nothing. The offers made were unacceptable. At no time did the Government offer to buy the land with an agreement to share the mining rights or royalties with the Sioux. Fairness was not an element permitted to enter into the Government's bargaining process.[18]

Near the end of 1875 the prospectors had entered the Hills by the hundreds. It was a foregone conclusion that the tide could not be stemmed by the army. The army had almost given up in disgust. The Indians attacked the wagon trains, destroying them when they did so, killing and wounding many of the trespassers. Though these hostilities continued they never reached a dangerous state. It was becoming apparent, however, that in the spring with the coming of the grass, the Indians would begin their opposition in earnest. This was the word passed along the frontier.

During the first week in November, 1875, the trend of events was discussed at the White House. President Grant, Secretary of War Belknap, Secretary of the Interior Chandler, Commissioner of Indian Affairs Smith, and Generals Sheridan and Crook came to the decision that all Indians off their reservations must return to them or suffer the consequences.[19]

On December 6, Indian Commissioner E.P. Smith, on Chandler's directive, ordered all Sioux who were off their reservations to return to them by January 31, 1876. By not returning as ordered, they would be considered hostile and the army would deal with them accordingly.[20]

Some writers contend that the Indians could not return to their reservations because of the bitter cold weather and deep snow. This is not entirely true. Most of the treaty or peaceful Indians did return. Agent James S. Hastings of the Red Cloud Agency, in a telegram dated February 24, 1876, reported that "over 1,000 Indians from the north have arrived in obedience to your request communicated to them by couriers sent from here. More are expected daily."[21] Crazy Horse and Sitting Bull and

Custer Family and Friends at Fort Lincoln in 1874. Bottom row, left to right: Tom Custer, Emma Wadsworth of Monroe, Mich., and General Custer. Center seated: Mrs. Maggie Calhoun (Gen. Custer's sister) with her husband, Lieut. James Calhoun standing on the right, and Mrs. G.A. Custer standing on the left. Courtesy of the J.C. Custer family.

their followers refused to comply, but many other Sioux did.

On February 1, the matter of non-compliant or hostile Indians was turned over to the army to force those Indians who were off the reservations to return. The army's operation was not intended to be toward the Sioux nation but only against hostile parts of it, namely the followers of Crazy Horse and Sitting Bull.

It is interesting that General Crook led 1,300 men into the field from Fort Fetterman in the latter part of February in search of Crazy Horse. Crazy Horse was at Bear Butte at the time, on his way to the Red Cloud Agency. He and his village had elected to remain there for a time because of the extremely cold weather.

Col. J.J. Reynolds and his force under Crook's orders struck the village on March 17. The results were unsatisfactory. Crook was forced to retire to Fort Fetterman on March 26 because his troops were not properly clothed or equipped for the inclement weather. Yet Crazy Horse and his followers were criticized and condemned for not returning to the Red Cloud Agency in spite of the severely cold weather.[22]

Since Crook's expedition was neither satisfactory nor conclusive, General Sheridan decided upon concentric movements by ordering three large columns toward a common center. Under General Terry's command one column of about 450 men would move from Fort Ellis in Montana under Colonel John Gibbon, and another column of about 1,000 men directly under General Terry with Lieutenant Colonel Custer in command of 600 cavalrymen starting out from Fort Abraham Lincoln. General Crook led the third column of over 1,000 men from Fort Fetterman.[23]

The movements of all three were concurrent "so that the Indians avoiding one column might be encountered by another." Military authorities assumed that all the peaceful Indians had returned to their agencies and that at no time would any of the three columns meet with more than 800 warriors. The Indian Bureau estimated the hostiles at 500 warriors.[24]

General Custer's last letter home to his mother indicated

that they expected to meet no more than 500 Indians during the campaign.[25] Had any greater danger or likelihood of disaster been anticipated, it is unlikely he would have taken along his youngest brother Boston or his young nephew Autie Reed.

One wonders if Custer took into account the Indian Agent's method of taking a census at the agency. Custer was quite familiar with the technique used in taking such a census—some agents would indicate there were many more Indians present during the distribution of annuity goods than actually were. That portion not distributed could be disposed of through a friendly Indian trader. The number of Indians said to be present usually was exaggerated. When this information was relayed to the army the impression given was that there were only a few hostiles out in the field.[26] It was common knowledge that thousands of Indians known to be hostile would come into the agencies each winter just to obtain the annuity goods. In the spring they would leave the reservations to do as they wished.[27]

Crook's column was the first to make a contact with the Indians. On June 17 his scouts ran into a war party of Sioux on the Rosebud River. It was a surprise for everyone. The Sioux, accompanied by some Northern Cheyennes, had been returning from a sun dance on the Rosebud to join a large number of Indian tribes moving slowly toward the valley of the Little Big Horn. Crazy Horse and Sitting Bull were with those they were joining though Sitting Bull was recovering from the painful and weakening effects of the sun dance in which he had a part.

An engagement between the two forces immediately ensued. For six hours the two sides fought tenaciously. The Indians displayed surprising spirit. Undoubtedly they had gained considerable confidence following their previous success against Crook in March. They battled the rest of the day in a series of charges and counter charges which ended when Crook drove the Indians from the field. The hostiles returned the following morning and harassed his retreat to Goose Creek, remaining there with him until June 20, then left abruptly.

Crook claimed a victory, a rather strange victory. His mission was to drive the Indians before him. They had halted him in his tracks. He had lost but nine killed, twenty-one wounded. The number of Indians opposing his 1,300 men have been estimated to have been from 1,000 to 1,500. The Indian loss was eleven killed and five wounded.[28]

Crook now did a curious thing. For nearly six weeks he dallied around his Goose Creek camp, spending most of his time hunting and fishing. No serious effort was made to inform Terry of his whereabouts or of his engagement with the Indians.

On July 10 he received a dispatch from Sheridan informing him of the diaster to Custer and the Seventh Cavalry. In referring to Crook's Rosebud fight Sheridan said to him: "Hit them again, and hit them harder." After reading the telegram, Crook sarcastically remarked: "I wish Sheridan would come out here himself and show us how to do it."[29] Crook was waiting for reinforcements. Crook, obviously, had no intention of fighting Indians until he had a big edge on odds.

Terry never learned of Crook's defeat until after Custer's column was destroyed on June 25. The two unsuccessful encounters with Crook served to fire the Sioux with a feeling of invincibility which served them well when they faced Custer and the Seventh Cavalry. This same force that faced Crook was joined by others who had left their reservations that spring. Crook made no effort to follow the Indians he reported he had defeated. He left that to Terry.

Crook's campaign was a complete flop. Fighting Indians when he had them outnumbered was one thing; he found that in fighting them with equal numbers, they were more than a match.

Crook's two campaigns against the Indians that year served only to inflame the Indian ego by providing them with two victories. He would have served Custer better by staying home.

Agnes Bates and General Custer in Costume for an amateur theatrical performance at Fort Abraham Lincoln in 1874. They assume the role of a Sioux chief and his bride. E.B.C. collection, Custer Battlefield National Monument.

Chapter Nine
Hero or Fool?

THE WESTERN column had left Fort Abraham Lincoln on May 17 and by June 10 had reached a point on the Yellowstone River about twenty five miles above the mouth of the Powder River. General Alfred Terry, who commanded this column, had gone ahead to meet both the supply steamer *Far West* and Colonel John Gibbon, who commanded the Montana column. No Indians had been seen up to this time and all signs indicated that the buffalo had moved farther west.

The Indians Terry sought apparently were west of the Powder River. Gibbon, who had come in from the northwest, was certain they were south of the Yellowstone River. Both were positive that the Indians would follow the buffalo herds.

On June 10, six troops of the Seventh Cavalry under Major Reno left on a scout that led them to the forks of the Powder River, down Mizpah Creek to its confluence with the Powder River, then down Pumkin Creek to the Tongue River. After scouting up the Tongue they were to return to its mouth and rejoin the regiment.

In the meantime General Terry and his staff had boarded the *Far West* which took them to the mouth of the Tongue. Custer marched the command to meet Terry there. A supply depot had been established at the mouth of the Powder River. There the wagon train and the supplies were left under guard of the infantry.[1]

On June 18, Reno returned with his command from the

scouting expedition, arriving at the mouth of Rosebud Creek, thirty-five miles west of where Terry was waiting with Custer and the balance of the Seventh. He had given Reno specific orders to return to the confluence of the Tongue and the Yellowstone rivers. Terry learned of Reno's arrival late the following afternoon.

Terry, mild mannered man at all times, was thoroughly angered by Reno's gross disregard of orders. He had commanded Reno to scout the Powder River Valley for traces of Indians, and more explicitly to scout the Tongue River, but not to go as far west as the Rosebud. For three and a half days he had waited for Reno and, as he described it to his sisters:

> Here we lay in idleness until Monday evening when to my surprise I received a note from Colonel Reno which informed me that he had flagrantly disobeyed my orders, and that instead of coming down the Tongue he had been on the Rosebud.
> It appears that he had done this in defiance of my positive orders not to go to the Rosebud, in the belief that there were Indians on that stream and that he could make a successful attack on them which would cover up his disobedience.[2]

Reno had discovered a wide Indian trail at the Rosebud and had followed it some distance before turning back over it. Near the mouth of the Rosebud he was ordered by Terry to halt and await the arrival of Custer.[3] He had not followed the Indian trail far enough "to determine in which direction it finally turned."[4] The net result was more confusing than helpful to Terry. Though Terry believed the Indians were heading for the Little Big Horn River, he could not be certain they had not turned to the east instead. As a result he was ambiguous in his final instructions to Custer.

Terry had indicated in the letter to his sisters that Reno did not have "the supplies to enable him to go far and he returned without justification for his conduct, unless wearied horses and broken-down mules would be a justification. Of course, this performance made a change in my plans necessary."[5]

Terry believed that the Indians were on the Little Big Horn. To be certain they were not on the Tongue or the Powder he had sent Reno on his scout. Once assured there were no Indians on the Tongue he planned to send Custer up the Tongue then over to the Rosebud so he could move north from there toward Gibbon's column, which would be moving southerly up the Rosebud. If done concurrently, without first having been discovered, there was every chance the Indians would be caught between the two columns.

Terry may have been mild mannered but this was too much even for him. Reno was told off in no uncertain terms, and Custer added his bit when he discovered that Reno had not determined the number of Indians moving over the trail and the exact direction they were traveling.[6]

There was some concern that the Indians might have learned of Reno's presence and, alarmed, had moved further west. Custer wrote to his wife on June 21, from the mouth of the Rosebud, that Reno and his scouting party had returned and that "they saw the trail and deserted camp of a village of 380 lodges. The trail was about one week old. The scouts reported that they could have overtaken the village in one day and a half. I am now going to take up the trail where the scouting party turned back. I fear their failure to follow up the Indians has imperiled our plans by giving the village an intimation of our presence. Think of the valuable time lost!"[7]

It was the consensus among the officers that the Indians were fearful of the troops and were making every effort to get away from them.

The question in many minds then and since is, why didn't Terry prefer charges against Reno and have him courtmartialed for exceeding his orders? The importance of his disregard for Terry's wishes seems to have been played down and ignored.

On the evening of June 21 Terry, Gibbon and Custer met in the cabin of the *Far West* to discuss the details of Terry's strategy.[8] Gibbon was to march along the north side of the Yellowstone River to the mouth of the Little Big Horn, then up the Little Big Horn by June 26. Custer with the whole of the Seventh Cavalry would move up the Rosebud until he could determine the direction of the Indian trail Reno had followed. If it led to the Little Big Horn, it was not to be followed. Instead he would move further to the south then turn in toward the river. In this way he would be certain to prevent the Indians from escaping around his left and, by taking this longer march, he would permit Gibbon's slower moving infantry column to move up.

Throughout, Terry's plan was more concerned with preventing the Indians from escaping. Terry admits in his report he did not know the exact spot on the Little Big Horn the hostile Sioux would be found and for that reason did not expect that his columns would move "in perfect concert."[9]

He did expect that they would be in supporting distance should either become engaged independent of the other. There had been no reason to fear the Indians. As mentioned earlier, the prevailing fear was that the Indians might escape.[10] And there was no reason to believe, when Custer and the Seventh left the mouth of the Rosebud on June 22, there would be no more than 1,000 to 1,500 warriors opposing them. Most of the officers expected they would meet fewer.[11]

Indians had rarely offered a stand up fight. As experts in guerilla warfare they found it wiser to hit and run. Custer had learned as an Indian fighter that a surprise attack on an Indian encampment was the only means of overwhelming it. Given any warning at all they would scurry like quail to all points of the compass.

Because there was a prevailing opinion that either of the columns could handle the hostiles they expected to come upon, there was no great concern. Lieutenant James H. Bradley, who served with Colonel Gibbon, stated in a journal he kept that "It is understood that if Custer arrives first he is at liberty to attack at once if he deems it prudent. We have little hope of being in at the death, as Custer will undoubtedly exert himself to the utmost to get there first and win all the laurels for himself and his regiment."[12]

Prior to that, Sheridan had advised Sherman that each column could take care of itself if Indians were found. He had expressed the hope "that one of the two columns will find the Indians."[13]

Following the conference on the *Far West* Custer offered "Officers' call." At the assembly Custer gave orders that the pack mules were to carry "15 days' rations of hard bread, coffee and sugar; 12 days' rations of bacon, and 50 rounds of carbine ammunition per man. Each man was to be supplied with 100 rounds of carbine and 24 rounds of pistol ammunition to be carried on his person and in his saddle bags."[14]

He indicated that they would follow the Indian trail Reno had discovered for fifteen days unless they could catch up with them sooner. He closed his remarks with the suggestion that they should take along an extra supply of salt in the event that they have to live on horse meat. One can gather from this last comment that he expected the Indians to flee before him and he intended to give chase no matter how long it took to catch them.

It had been suggested that Custer take along Colonel James Brisbin's battalion of Second Cavalry consisting of one hundred sixty men. He refused the offer. There was insufficient forage for the Seventh's horses as it was. Another detachment of cavalry "could not affect the result of the battle and might cause friction."[15]

The three Gatling guns were available but Custer decided not to take them. They were drawn by condemned horses that had difficulty keeping up with the command. Reno had had trouble with them on his scout and Gibbon was to have trouble with them on June 25.[16] They would have been an impediment over the rough terrain approaching the valley of the Little Big Horn.

Custer's command of twelve companies—the entire regiment of the Seventh Cavalry—consisted of about 625 officers and men. With them were about forty Crow and Arikara (Ree) Indian scouts. They were to travel as quietly as possible—no trumpets would be employed—and as nearly invisibly as possible by raising little dust on the march.

Terry sent Custer his instructions in writing the next morning. In essence they reiterated the discussion on the *Far West* of the previous evening. They began:

The Brigadier General commanding directs that as soon as your regiment can be made ready for the march, you proceed up the Rosebud in pursuit of the Indians whose trail was discovered by Major Reno a few days ago. It is, of course, impossible to give you any definite instructions in regard to this movement, and were it not impossible to do so, *the Department Commander places too much confidence in your zeal, energy and ability to impose upon you precise orders which might hamper your action when nearly in contact with the enemy.*

He will, however, indicate to you his own views of what your action should be, and he desires that you conform to them *unless you see sufficient reason for departing from them.*"[17] (Italics are mine.)

The balance of the letter provided additional instructions. All in all, the letter was one of instruction. It contained no positive order.[18] Custer's objective was the Indians he was pursuing. Terry stated that in his very first sentence. It was not necessary to tell him that he was not to let them escape. Custer had a fifteen day food supply—and salt—so that pursuit could have been lengthy. When he saw that the large Indian trail he followed was the only trail, and that it led in only one direction, he did exactly what Terry had suggested he do—he departed from Terry's suggestions. He saw "sufficient reason for departing from them."

For the past ninety-nine years there has been considerable discussion and controversy over the interpretation of these orders, and in particular how Custer interpreted them. The ultimate charge and counter charge centers around the question, Did Custer disobey his "orders"? This will be covered in greater detail in the next chapter.

Following receipt of the letter of instructions, Terry visited Custer at his tent and said to him in the presence of Mary, General Custer's servant: "Use your own judgment and do what you think best if you strike the trail."[19]

The Seventh Cavalry moved out from the mouth of the Rosebud at noon for a distance of twelve miles, then camped for the night. The next morning the column left at five o'clock. The terrain was rough and the rate of travel necessarily slow so that the distance traveled by the evening of June 24 was another sixty-five miles, less than thirty-five miles each day. The rate of travel was minimal.

It was Custer's plan to rest his command the day of the

25th. He was hot on the trail of the Sioux and it obviously led to the Little Big Horn valley. His horses and men were tired so why not bed down east of the divide between Rosebud and the Little Big Horn? He was twenty-four hours ahead of the suggested schedule. That would provide ample time to scout the area. His men and horses could stand a rest.

Terry had suggested in his letter to Custer that he should pursue the Sioux up the Rosebud, and if the trail turned toward the Little Big Horn, he should turn off it to the south, "then toward the Little Big Horn, feeling constantly however to your left." This latter move was to prevent the Sioux from escaping around Custer's left flank.

At this point two things happened that placed everything in a different perspective. On the night of the 24th, Captain George Yates' troop had lost a pack of hard bread. A detail sent back to recover it found an Indian opening it with a tomahawk. It was Captain Tom Custer who reported the incident to his brother. "Officers' call" was sounded. The incident was reported and it was also stated that the scouts had observed Indians watching their movements from the ridges nearby. That the cavalry column had been discovered was obvious. In four days the column had moved 108 miles, the last ten so that his command would be concealed. Though he had expected to attack the Sioux on the 26th, this plan no longer was feasible.[21]

After crossing the divide just before noon of June 25, Custer began dividing his regiment into four battalions. Captain Benteen was to command three companies of 125 men with orders to scout the country to the left and drive any Indians he might find toward the village.

Earlier that morning—near 10 A.M.—Custer had ascended a high hill called the Crows' Nest to view the Indian village his scouts had discovered from that vantage point. Custer remained skeptical of the discovery since he could see nothing of the huge hostile camp in the valley fifteen miles distant, even though he used his field glasses. Custer's observations were made several hours after those of the scouts and at a time when the heat of the sun had developed an aerial haze that tended to obscure any distant view. It was after his visit to the Crows' Nest that he was informed of the Indian discovery of his regiment.

Just after noon, Benteen led his battalion off to the left at an angle of 45 degrees from the regiment's line of march.

From that point, Custer and Reno moved westerly along what has since been named Reno Creek. Reno led his three companies of about 112 men along the left bank and Custer led his three companies of about 225 men along the right bank, both columns proceeding parallel to each other for about ten miles until Custer motioned Reno to cross his men over and ride side by side.[22] The remaining company of 130 men commanded by Captain Tom McDougall convoyed the pack train in the rear.

About 2 o'clock a single tepee was sighted. In it was found the body of a warrior who had been killed in the fight with Crook on the Rosebud June 17. The tepee was fired by the scouts—though the Crow scouts blamed it on the soldiers—and left smoldering as the column moved forward. A few Indians were seen from this point on, well in front as if inviting pursuit.[23]

From here a heavy cloud of dust could be seen four or five miles down the Little Big Horn River. This tended to give Custer and his staff the opinion that the Indians in the village were in flight. An interpreter, Fred Girard, rode onto a nearby knoll. From here he claimed he could see the Indian village and its pony herd. Turning to Custer, he shouted: "Here are your Indians, running like devils!"[24] It appeared as though the Indian village was being vacated.

Lieutenant W.W. Cooke, Custer's adjutant, was told to order Reno's battlion to cross the river and begin the attack and that Reno would be supported by the whole outfit. Reno moved toward the river at a trot. While he was crossing, Custer moved along the right bank of the river down stream.

Once Reno was across and had reformed his column on the left side of the river within a narrow belt of timber he moved forward in columns of four. By this time a few warriors appeared on his front firing as they came. The time was about 2:30 P.M.

The column moved forward about half a mile then formed in a line of battle that stretched across the valley. The scouts were on his left. The Indians on his front were increasing in numbers but offering no resistance. After advancing another mile Reno ordered his men to form a skirmish line. By this time the battalion was moving along at a gallop. The Indians opened a brisk fire and in some force charged toward Reno's left flank. Most of the scouts, on seeing this charge, fled.

Reno, not seeing Custer within supporting distance, disobeyed his orders. He did not charge the village. He ordered his command to dismount and fight on foot.[25] This placed his men on the defensive.

On his right was a stand of timber bordering the Little Big Horn and to this he ordered his men. Up to this point but one man had been wounded, though two men had been carried into the village on the backs of their unmanageable horses. Once in the timber a second skirmish line was set up by Reno. The timber, on their side, and the steep banks of the river on their front, provided the cavalrymen with a strong defense position. Nearly surrounded by Indians, though not heavily so, Reno was comparatively safe.

But Reno did not believe he would be as safe there as he might be on the high bluffs on the east side of the river.[26] He had not heard from Custer who had promised to support him, and he did not know the exact whereabouts of either Benteen or the pack train. A high point, such as the bluffs, offered an advantage in a matter of defense or observation. He thought it was time to move.

At the time he had made his decision to leave the timber only one man had been wounded, according to Dr. Porter, whose job it was to care for those who were.[27] This would be no real hindrance.

Oral orders were given by Reno to prepare to leave. Since they were oral rather than by trumpet calls some of the officers failed to hear the commands. One of the companies—G Company—was scattered through the timber. It had no word of the intended move until it was too late to accompany the other two companies.[28]

As Reno prepared to leave, his men ceased their fire. With this the Indians moved to within thirty feet of them and fired point blank. One of the men was hit while a scout, Bloody Knife, received a bullet between the eyes, scattering brains and blood in Reno's face. Shaken by this experience, Reno ordered his men to dismount, then to remount. In the noise and confusion many did not hear these commands. There were no trumpet calls and apparently Reno gave no further orders but demonstrated his wishes by heading off toward the river. In the wild ride toward the ford no attempt was made to deploy men to cover the retreat. The distance was about a mile. The width of the river at the ford was twenty-five to fifty feet, the water coming up to the saddles. The east bank was about eight feet, and the west bank about five feet above the water and perpendicular.[29]

In the wild scramble for the distant crossing Reno lost complete control. For the Indians it was a buffalo hunt. Riding alongside their retreating foe those with repeating rifles pumped them into the cavalrymen and their frenzied horses. Others during the pursuit clubbed the troopers, pulling many from their saddles. Indians on both banks of the crossing fired at the men in the water.

This does not mean that the troopers did not fire back. Though it was every man for himself the more seasoned officers and men tried to fight back and to protect the wounded. Others did their best. Some troopers were killed at the crossing while many others were killed along the line of retreat. Those bringing up the rear fought hand-to-hand all the way to the bluffs. Lieutenant Charles Varnum was one of the officers who tried to check the wild, leaderless retreat. From the rear he raced his horse to the front, shouting: "For God's sake men, don't run: we've got to go back and save the wounded."[30] Twenty-nine men were killed before the other side of the river was reached. No one would go back to aid the wounded.

Once all were across Reno led the ascent to the summit of the bluffs. The Indian firing had lessened somewhat for many were seen to withdraw and ride downstream. Word had reached them Custer was menacing their village from below.

After leaving Reno at the ford with orders to attack the village, Custer had continued along the bluffs on the east side of the river directly toward the upper end of the Indian camp. Several miles further on he sent Sergeant Dan Kanipe to Benteen with a message to hurry on toward him, and another to Captain McDougall to bring up the ammunition packs as rapidly as possible. At the time Kanipe was sent Custer could see that Reno's men had not fired a shot and he could also see the immense village just beyond Reno.

Soon after this he sent another message—and order—to Benteen. It was given orally to Trumpeter John Martin. But Custer's Adjutant, Lieutenant W.W. Cooke, not trusting the limited English vocabulary of the Italian immigrant, wrote: "Benteen. Come on. Big Village. Be quick. Bring packs. W.W. Cooke. P.S. Bring packs."

About 4 o'clock the message was placed in Benteen's hands. After reading it, Benteen showed it to two of his officers, Captain Tom Weir and Lieutenant W.S. Edgerly, then quickened his pace in the direction of the firing he could hear coming from the valley. He did not bother to hurry up the pack train for he had sent Kanipe to it earlier with Custer's first message to hurry.

Benteen had scouted to the left as ordered. After having traveled some distance and meeting only with a series of bluffs, the climbing of which had proved extremely hard on his men and horses, Benteen became convinced that nothing would be gained by riding further. Turning his command to the right he continued on until he rejoined Custer's trail some distance beyond the pack train.

Benteen reached the river near the spot Reno had first crossed. It was there he saw what he judged to be about 900 warriors on the valley bottom before him in an engagement along the river bank, and many of the troopers "running for the bluffs on the right bank of the stream."[32] It was obvious they were being repulsed and that his battalion, consisting mainly of recruits, would have little chance against them. He decided to move to the bluffs and report to Major Reno.

By this time Reno could count three officers and twenty-

View from Reno Hill to the southwest. The Little Big Horn crosses the center. The flat valley beyond is the area over which Reno led his inglorious retreat. Author's photo.

nine enlisted men dead. There were about eleven wounded. One officer, three scouts and fifteen men were missing; they had been left behind in the timber.

When Benteen reached the hill on which Reno's dismounted command rested, Reno ran out to meet him. Obviously beside himself, he shouted: "For God's sake, Benteen, halt your command and help me. I've lost half my men."[33] He had lost a third of his 112 men, almost all of them on his disastrous retreat.

A few Indians had occupied positions in ravines and on nearby hills. From these they received a light fire which did no damange. Most of the Indians had been seen earlier to be riding downstream. No one knew why. Some firing could be heard downstream, but it could not be determined who was doing it. It was now about 4:30 P.M.

Though the firing could be distinctly heard, Reno elected to remain where he was until the pack train arrived with the ammunition. In disgust over Reno's apparent timidity, Captain Weir told his Lieutenant Edgerly he proposed to move his company down river to assist Custer. Edgerly agreed to go along.

They moved out at the head of D Company for a little over a mile to a high point on the bluffs overlooking the Custer battlefield. The Custer battlefield was covered by a pall of dust and smoke. Indians were seen riding around shooting at objects on the ground. There was no fighting. There was no sign of Custer.[34]

When the pack train arrived, Reno and Benteen moved forward to Weir's position, reaching it around 6 o'clock. The Indians were now approaching that point in increasing numbers. Now aware that the position was untenable, orders were given to retire to Reno Hill, which was done in orderly fashion.

The Sioux followed them and immediately began to engage them. This continued until dark, after which they withdrew. That night while the troopers tended their wounded and dug in, the Indians in the village celebrated. At the first sign of dawn the Sioux began their fire, continuing it until shortly after noon. Then it suddenly stopped. Soon afterward the squaws began dismantling their tepees. Little by little they began moving out and by late afternoon the village site was completely deserted.

As they departed, various officers and men attempted to estimate the number of Indians occupying the village. They agreed that it was the largest gathering of Indians any white man had seen on the plains. The estimates varied from 3,000 to 5,000 warriors, exclusive of women, children and old men. It was later determined that there were more than 1,500 tepees in an area four miles in length and up to a half mile in width. And the number of ponies in their estimates varied from 15,000 to 25,000.

Though they might estimate the Indian losses they could count their own for on that hill eighteen more had died and fifty-two had been wounded. Those who survived were fortunate.

But what had happened to Custer? And why had the Indians left so suddenly on the 26th? The answers to these questions arrived on June 27 when Terry and Gibbon marched up the valley from the north. Custer and his 225 men had been found by Lieutenant James H. Bradley and Terry's Indian scouts that morning. All were dead, their bodies strewn upon that hillside now known as Custer Hill. Most of the bodies were stripped and mutilated to some degree. General Custer, though stripped, was not mutilated. A bullet hole in the left temple and another in the left breast near his heart caused his death. They were not self-inflicted as some claim for there were no powder burns. Tom Custer was mutilated beyond recognition. This provided the basis for the story that Rain-in-the-Face had carried out his vow to cut out the heart and eat it.

Mutilation was commonly seen on the dead in Reno's battalion for they were found in the valley close to the Indian camp and quite probably this work was that of squaws and children.

Captain Keogh's horse "Comanche" has been claimed to be the only living thing found upon the battlefield. This is not true, for there were several other wounded horses found that apparently were destroyed because of the severity of their wounds. Comanche's six wounds were so superficial it was decided to attempt to save the animal.

What must be the most prolific source of perplexing legends was that phase of the battle involving Custer and his battalion from which there were no survivors to tell what had happened to them after they were last seen alive.

Custer's column had turned to the right after Reno had received his orders to cross the river and charge the village. The column continued in a northerly direction just to the east of the bluffs that bordered the east side of the river for several miles. Though Custer and members of his staff were seen on this ridge at the beginning of Reno's attack, his command was never seen again alive.

It must be remembered that the last member of the Seventh destined to see Custer alive was John Martin, the trumpeter who carried the last communication. The last Indian scout to be with Custer was the Crow Curley. The only one who could provide an account of the fate of Custer and his command after they were last seen by Martin and Curley were those Indians who wiped out the five companies with Custer.

Unfortunately there are many conflicting Indian accounts of that portion of the battle. The eminent Custer battle historian, Charles Kuhlman,[35] has provided us with a superb analytical study of the various Indian accounts. From these he concluded that Custer's attack was a surprise to the Indians. They knew of the proximity of the troops but had no knowledge there was to be an attack or when and where it would come. Obviously the Indians had no battle plan; certainly none for setting a trap, as some claim.

Dr. Kuhlman logically and graphically details the steps and measures Custer took from the moment he saw the immensity of the two-mile long Indian village from his vista on the bluffs. Seeing Reno and his 112 men 300 feet below come to a stop and dismount rather than charge what Custer now knew to be overwhelming odds caused Custer to alter his plans.

Rather than announce his presence to the Indian village below by trumpet calls to Reno and then sending several companies to the river to cover Reno and his men as they crossed to the east side, he continued down river toward the next ford. Reno was safe for the protective cover of timber was near to him.

Dr. Kuhlman did not accept the theory that Custer left Reno in the lurch by rushing downstream to attack the village on the flank. It was after he had seen Reno safely established in the timber and had led his own battalion downstream a ways that he sent two orders in succession for the pack train to be hurried forward with the ammunition. The orders indicated he wanted the ammunition to come to him rather than to Reno so that it would be on the east side of the river where the action would be.

Custer had not fired a single shot at this point. Reno would soon be out of ammunition. Kuhlman assumes that the pack train ammunition was meant for Reno when he would rejoin Custer on the east side of the river. Custer would want the ammunition at a rallying point he was seeking for a time when Benteen would have rejoined him. Reno could join Custer later when the Indian pressure lessened. In the meantime Reno, while in the timber, would be an attractive nuisance, a menace at the edge of the village, forcing its occupants to maintain a large protective force nearby. Such a force would keep the pressure off Custer. It is interesting that the Custer battle researcher, W.M. Camp, learned from the Crow scout Curley that Custer "was seeking a high point to await the arrival of the other troops."[36]

And it is also of interest that Cheyenne participants in the Custer fight assert that Custer made no attempt to approach or cross the river.[37] They had seen the Gray Horse detachment ride down Medicine Tail Coulee toward the river as if threatening to attack the village while Custer rode off to the right toward the last high spot on the ridge of bluffs back from the river. The feint of the Gray Horse was a delaying tactic in an effort to buy time for the Seventh while it waited for Benteen and Reno to come up.[38]

This bluff on Custer's part worried the warriors into

believing they would be attacked. It pulled them down the valley and toward the river, decreasing the number in the way of any advance that might be made by Reno and Benteen.[38]

Custer and his battalion made it to the end of the ridge. There he prepared his defense or holding position, and it was there the first of the action began. As it developed, Custer found it necessary to send a detachment to hold another prominence, a hundred yards or so to the southeast, now known as Calhoun Hill. It was on these two hills the final action occurred.

Dr. Kuhlman reconstructed from Indian accounts and observations the final minutes of this engagement in a manner and fashion so logical none have been able to offer any generally acceptable substitute. There have been differences of opinion on minor points. Colonel Graham is quoted as having written to Dr. Kuhlman after having read his reconstruction of the battle on Custer Hill: "You and your damn logic!"

As indicated earlier, Custer and his men did not run into a trap. Once he had seen the immensity of the Indian village he had no choice but that of seeking a holding position and to await the arrival of Terry's reenforcements.[39] To attack on terrain that did not lend itself to a cavalry charge would have been foolhardy. Even so, the cavalrymen had no opportunity to use the mounted charge, a tactic in which they outmatched the Indians. They were forced to fight in the guerilla style of the Indians in which the latter were superior. For the Indians it was a matter of time. Lobbing arrows like mortar shells over the cavalry horses that were used as breast works inflicted considerable damage.

The horses were made to lie down and were then shot so they could serve as a shield or fortification as a protection against Indian arrows and bullets. There was no time or equipment to throw up earthworks.

The Indians drew cavalry fire and caused the cavalrymen to waste ammunition by bobbing up and down behind ridges and hillocks that peppered the terrain. Almost casually they picked off the troopers as they were forced to expose themselves in firing at the bobbing warriors before them.[40] There was no need for the Sioux and Cheyennes to risk their lives in a

Sitting Bull. The Sioux spiritual leader in their war against the whites in 1876-1877. National Archives photo.

headlong assault. Time and numbers were on their side.

When it was decided that the last soldier was dead a cry went out which brought hundreds of old men and boys onto the battlefield from the perimeter where they had been watching. The thick dust rose high into the air as they milled about in an effort to strike each dead cavalryman.

Custer's luck had deserted him, and so had the majority of his command. Over one-half of his regiment had failed to come to his aid when he had summoned them and when he had needed them most. Strange to say, no explanation has been requested of, nor disciplinary action leveled at, the officer whose duty it was to respond to Custer's last orders.

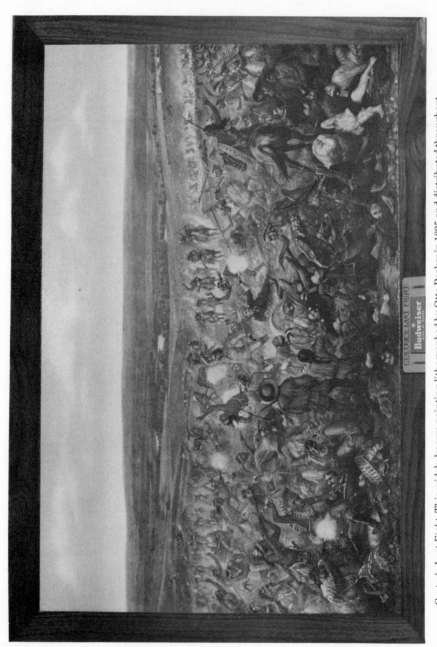

Custer's Last Fight. This widely known painting lithographed by Otto Becker in 1895 and distributed throughout the United States has been the source of many heated discussions. Though the terrain is correct, Custer and his men did not carry sabers, nor did he have long hair at the time of the battle. Courtesy of Anheuser-Busch, Inc.

Battle of the Little Big Horn. A pictograph by White Bird depicting the Indian version of the Custer battle. Courtesy of the West Point Museum Collections, U.S. Military Academy.

Custer's Flight by White Bird. Courtesy of the West Point Museums Collection. U.S. Military Academy.

Chapter Ten
Hostiles and Friendlies

NO DISCUSSION of Custer's Last Stand is complete without opposing sides. The beginning student of this epic battle soon finds that he has to wade through tomes of material, much of which is opinion and Monday morning quarterbacking, before he can reach any sort of conclusion. Once he reaches or nears a conclusion, his fate is sealed. No longer is he considered objective. He is labeled a Custerphobe or a Custerphil. To my way of thinking he is either hostile or friendly.

At this late date it still is difficult to determine just how the controversy started, or who started it. Some blame it on the first meeting of Custer and Benteen back in 1866. Benteen made it evident from the start he would have no part of Custer. He would obey orders and do his duty but there the association ended.

Others point back to Custer's jump in rank from a captain to a brigadier general on June 29, 1863, when men of equal or higher rank but with seniority in years of military service and age were by-passed. Recognizing that his youth—he was only 23—would create problems in commanding those older men, Custer quickly appointed a staff of young men he knew and had grown up with in Michigan.

As time passed he added his brother Tom to his staff—and what a choice that was, for Tom was one of the few to be awarded two Congressional Medals of Honor. Then, later on, he added his brother-in-law, James Calhoun. Others were added that had displayed abilities he admired. That was the origin of the Custer Clan Benteen and others spoke of disdainfully. All members of Custer's staff were qualified and friendly. What commanding officer worth his salt could ask for anything more?

With this background we'll try to unravel some of the legends that evolved from the battle of the Little Big Horn.

Custer, just prior to the campaign of 1876, had joined his regiment at Fort Lincoln under a cloud. He had been summoned to Washington by Representative Heister Clymer to testify before a House Committee investigating expenditures in the War Department. The committee had been informed that Secretary of War William W. Belknap was employing patronage by selling post traderships.[1] Custer first appeared before this committee on March 29, 1876.[2]

Custer was summoned to appear before this House Committee on Expenditures of the War Department, an order he dared not ignore. Though his interest in its activity was high, his "invitation" to appear before it came at a time he much preferred to devote to readying his troops for the coming campaign. There was no choice in the matter. To ignore the summons was tantamount to "contempt."

One author considered his testimony "incompetent, irrelevant and immaterial."[3] Some of Custer's testimony was, but all of it was in response to Clymer's questions. Clymer had been Secretary of War Belknap's roommate at Princeton College but this old friendship did not deter Clymer in what he considered his duty. And Custer, under oath, had to answer the questions presented, even though Clymer was on a fishing expedition. A careful evaluation of the testimony taken by this committee reveals Custer's testimony—both fact and opinion—as being of immense value in ferreting out the entire story of the scandalous sale of post traderships.

When the question of Belknap's malfeasance arose, Belknap hastened to Grant with his resignation. Grant, without any effort to investigate, immediately accepted the resignation Belknap offered. Blindly Grant had accepted Belknap's explanation and in doing so prevented the Congress from prosecuting the Secretary of War. By doing so, Grant convered himself with a film of suspicion.[4]

It was Senator Isaac P. Christiancy of Monroe who offered the opinion to the Senate that the impeachment proceedings against Belknap was unconstitutional since his resignation placed him outside the jurisdiction of Congress. Belknap was now a civilian and no longer an employee of the Senate— though most thought Belknap guilty—making it obvious an impeachment vote of two-thirds of the Senate could not be obtained.[5]

Just prior to Custer's appearance before the Clymer Committee, the Adjutant General of the Army, E.D. Townsend, testified. Townsend presented evidence that the office of sutler had been abolished, having been supplanted by post traders appointed by the Secretary of War. The post traders, according to the circulars issued by order of the Secretary of War, had the absolute and "exclusive privilege of trade upon the military reserve to which they are appointed, and no other person will be allowed to trade, peddle or sell goods" on that reserve.

Custer testified that a captain, desiring to obtain articles for his men at a lower rate, bought them in St. Paul for his men at cost. The trader at Ft. Lincoln protested to the Secretary of War who, in turn, directed Custer to abide by the orders in the circular. The captain and his men were compelled thereafter to pay the exorbitant prices of the post trader.[6]

In answer to other questions, Custer disclosed conversations he had had with the Fort Lincoln post trader as to the manner in which post traderships were obtained. The trader had indicated that he was paying a heavy "tax" to someone for the privilege of retaining the appointment. He estimated his annual profit at $15,000, one third of which went to General J.M. Hedrick of Iowa, another similar amount to General E.W. Rice, leaving trader Seip about $2,500 or $3.000.[7]

Clymer asked Custer if he had had any conversation with Orvil Grant—the President's brother—or his partner, A.L. Bonnafon. Custer replied that he had, on a train to Bismarck.

The conversation they carried on was of a general nature. Following that portion of the testimony Custer was questioned about the effectiveness and harmfulness of the post tradership system. His answers were honest and straightforward. He indicated his preference for the previous system, the sutlership, for its fair prices to the men and the right of the officers to select their own trader.

It was obvious that the chairman of the committee was trying to obtain information about the kickbacks from the post traders but on this subject Custer's testimony was of a hearsay nature.

Some of the newspapers expressed surprise that army officers had not reported these indiscretions. Clymer asked Custer why he and other army officers had not offered information of the abuses that existed at the posts. In replying, Custer quoted the Secretary of War's order of March 15, 1873, which required that:

no officer, either active or retired shall directly or indirectly, without being called upon by proper authority, solicit, suggest, or recommend action by members of Congress for or against military affairs. All petitions to Congress by offices relative to subjects of military character will be forwarded through the General of the Army and the Secretary of War for their action and transmittal. An officer visiting the seat of Government during a Congressional session will, upon his arrival, register his name at the Adjutant General's Office as now required and, in addition, address a letter to the Adjutant General of the Army reciting the purpose of, and the time that will be embraced by his visit, and the authority under which he is absent from his command or station. The purpose or object recited will be the strict guide of the officer during his stay.[8]

This order, according to Custer, "sealed the mouths and tied the hands of the officers of the Army about as effectually as could be done." It was apparent that officers had been treated disrespectfully by the Secretary of War in an effort "to discourage the visits of officers to Washington." Prior to this order an officer "could write to his member of Congress as freely as any other citizen."[9]

As an observer on the scene Custer could hardly be considered an incompetent witness. What he had to say certainly was relevant. It may not have been hard evidence but within its context were many leads and much background material of which Clymer's committee made extensive use.

Custer was anxious to return to his command at Fort Lincoln. Numerous telegrams from his brother Tom and other officers at the post emphasized the need for his presence there. Having completed his testimony he prepared to make the customary calls upon the Adjutant General and the General of the Army required before departing from the city.

Three times he called upon President Grant. On each occasion he was permitted to sit in the anteroom for hours and cool his heels while others arriving after him without appointments were given an audience. It was obvious the President did not intend to see Custer.

Custer was no pussywillow. An armchair general might enjoy sitting in an outer office of the Presidential suite while his troops were readying for a campaign against the hostiles, but not Custer. It was three times and out. And out he went, directly to General Sherman's office to report he was leaving town as he had previously agreed he would do when discharged from his Washington duties. Discovering that Sherman was in New York, he proceeded on a train west. He had a prior agreement with Sherman that he could leave town once he was released by the Committee.[10]

After a brief stop in Monroe to say goodbye to his parents he arrived in Chicago only to find himself under arrest under Grant's orders because he had failed to obtain an official authorization from the President or the War Department to leave Washington. He was ordered not to accompany the expedition against the Sioux.

The Adjutant General, E.D. Townsend, and both Generals Sherman and Alfred Terry requested executive clemency. There was no response. Then Custer wired the President: "I appeal to you as a soldier to spare me the humiliation of seeing my regiment march to meet the enemy and I not share its dangers."

This was an election year and Grant had visions of a third term. His first reaction to Custer's testimony against his friend

and appointee Belknap, and to the involvement of his brother
Orvil in the post tradership scandal, was one of vindictiveness.
He had struck Custer down at a vulnerable point but now this
thoughtless act was beginning to boomerang.

Custer had ever been popular with the press. He was
colorful and he had a charisma that appealed to the public. The
opposition press struck out at Grant where he was most
vulnerable—his thin skin. The New York *World* of May 2nd
charged Grant with misusing his presidential power in
relieving Custer from his command because Custer "gave
important testimony ... relative to the post tradership
frauds." Following an account under the heading *"Grant's
Revenge"* came an editorial stating that Custer's testimony
was not voluntary and was not disrespectful to the President,
that his removal would deter others who might testify in the
future. Other papers followed suit.

On May 8th General Terry received word from General
Sherman that the President had withdrawn his objections.
Grant had relented as far as permitting Custer to accompany
General Terry on the expedition, but Custer could go only in
command of his own regiment.

Then a strange thing happened. On May 29, 1976, Grant
announced he would not be a candidate for a third term.[11] If
Grant thought withdrawing from a race for reelection would
discourage the gadflies he was mistaken. The Whiskey Ring
scandal, the sale of post traderships ending in his acceptance
of Belknap's resignation, the involvement of his brother Orvil
and, to a lesser extent, his attempt to humiliate Custer, all
played a part in his final decision. The gadflies of the press had
taken all of this into account in their efforts to display him as
an incompetent chief executive. Under ordinary circumstances
the gadflies would have left him alone after his announcement.
If Grant now had even the remotest thought he might be
drafted for a third term it was erased when the story of the
Custer massacre hit the front pages of the nation's
newspapers.

"Who Slew Custer?" the New York *Herald* asked in its July
16 issue, then went on to declare that "the celebrated peace

policy of General Grant which feeds, clothes and takes care of their non-combatant force while the men are killing our troops—that is what killed Custer.... That nest of thieves, the Indian Bureau, with its thieving agents and favorites as Indian Traders, and its mock humanity and pretence of piety— that is what killed Custer."

On the day following, the *Herald* rubbed more salt into Grant's thin skin by stating: "Had Sheridan been killed by the Indians instead of Custer, President Grant would have published an address on the subject. But for Custer, who made Sheridan, and did more than any one man to make Grant President, the Sitting Bull of the White House has never a word to offer."

Grant had been selected by the Republican Party through no impulse to honor or reward him because of his record in the Civil War. He was selected because the party had no one popular enough to win an election at that time. As a result Grant served two terms. It is difficult to determine which of the two terms was the worse. Greed and dishonesty prevailed in both.[12] Personally honest, Grant seemed unable to detect dishonesty in those he considered to have been his friends. When men like Custer displayed honesty or offered honest opinions contrary to his own, Grant showed them no quarter.

There has been some question as to the responsibility for the overall planning of the campaign. General Sherman, in his annual report,[13] stated that Sioux under Sitting Bull were off their reservation and had not complied with the Secretary of Interior's order that "they must come in to their reservations by or before the 31st of January, 1876, or a military force would be sent to compel them." They had not complied so the matter was turned over to the Secretary of War for action on his part.

In March, Colonel J.J. Reynolds, leading ten companies of cavalry, struck the camp of Crazy Horse and destroyed it but its occupants fled to the hills. Sheridan then decided upon a strategy of encirclement such as he had used against the Comanches, Kiowas and Cheyennes so successfully in 1874 and 1875. A concurrent movement of three columns was to be used so that the Indians, in attempting to avoid one column might be confronted by another. Since the Indians were expected to be near the mouth of the Little Big Horn, General Terry would command a column from Montana and another from Dakota Territory. General Crook would command one from the Platte. The Indian Bureau estimated the number of hostile warriors to be about 500. Sherman emphasizes this by writing that: "Up to this moment, there was nothing official or private to justify an officer to expect that any detachment could encounter more than 500, or, at the maximum, 800 hostile warriors."[14]

At a conference on June 21, which included Terry, Gibbon and Custer, Terry disclosed his plan.

This plan was founded on the belief that at some point on the Little Big Horn a body of hostile Sioux would be found and that although it was impossible to make movements in perfect concert, as might have been done had there been a known fixed objective point to be reached, yet by the judicious use of the excellent guides and scouts which we possessed, the two columns might be brought within cooperating distance of each other, so that either of them which should be first engaged might be a 'waiting fight'—give time for the other to come up.... It was believed impracticable to join Col. Gibbon's to Lt. Col. Custer's force, for more than one-half of Col. Gibbon's troops were infantry, who would be unable to keep up with the cavalry in rapid movements.[15]

On the following day, June 22, Terry gave Custer written instructions which, among other things, stated that "he [Terry] desires that you should conform to them unless you shall see sufficient reason for departing from them."[16] No matter what was said in the instructions—and they were instructions—Custer was the one who had the authority to decide whether or not he had *sufficient reason* to depart from them.

Much ink has been used in printing various answers to the question Did Custer disobey Terry's orders? With permission from Terry to depart from the instructions it would be unreasonable to charge Custer with disobedience.

If one questioned whether or not Benteen had disobeyed Custer's orders to come to him with the ammunition packs,

Benteen could be considered vulnerable. It was his duty to go to Custer. His and Reno's excuse was that they did not know Custer's whereabouts; so Benteen testified at the Reno Court of Inquiry in 1879. A trail made by the hundreds of shod horses in Custer's detachment leading away from Reno Hill was easily visible. Anyone could have found Custer. His brother Boston, a civilian Easterner, had no difficulty in finding him by following this trail.

Benteen knew the direction Custer had taken. The great trail left by the shod horses was there for all to see. Benteen could have gone on to find Custer if he was prepared to face the consequences of disobedience. Once he had shown Custer's last orders to Reno, who was the ranking officer, he should have taken command and moved on when Reno failed to do what Custer had ordered. Had Benteen gone to Custer, Custer probably would have supported him. But if Custer had been wiped out, Benteen would have had to face Reno for disobedience.

Benteen, in his testimony at the Court of Inquiry, would have you think that he couldn't hear any firing from Custer's direction when his own command reached Reno Hill. Many of his men did, and Lieutenant Godfrey, who was hard of hearing, testified that he heard it quite clearly.

Did Reno have acceptible reasons for not obeying Custer's last orders? Was he cowardly as some have charged? Godfrey, who was there, spoke of Reno as having exhibited "nervous timidity."[17] The truth of the matter was that Reno was in over his head. He had never before fought an Indian. His experience in the past had been mostly as a staff officer rather than as a line officer. He certainly exhibited his inexperience when he lead the retreat from the woods and failed to post a rear guard to cover it. There is little doubt that his state of mind on reaching the crest of the hill after crossing the river was such that he prayed for help—and his prayers were answered by the timely arrival of Benteen and his three troops.

Reno's duty clearly was to go forward and see what had happened to Custer. There were not many wounded at this point for those troopers who had been left in the valley were dead. He could have gone, but chose not to. He must have known that by sitting on that hilltop he was disobeying Custer's orders, but his state of mind was such that he too was willing to face the consequences.

Benteen led many to believe that Custer's horses and men were played out from too much marching. Col. Gibbon's men, all of whom were infantrymen and had walked all the distance, weren't tired out. Custer's command had marched barely thirty miles each day.[18]

The statement is often made that Custer should have waited until the next day, June 26, as instructed, but wanted the glory of defeating the Sioux single-handed by charging their camp a day earlier. Had Custer waited another day, it still wouldn't have made a bit of difference, for Terry and Gibbon did not arrive until June 27th, a day too late.

Why did Custer charge the village a day earlier than had been generally planned, and why had he launched his attack at noon rather than at dawn as it was thought he would? Two things happened that compelled him to give up his plan to rest his command for one day. During the march of the night before the battle, a box of hard tack had dropped from the back of a pack animal along the trail. One of the men sent back to recover it discovered a small party of Sioux opening the box. They quickly moved in the direction of the valley. This incident was reported to Custer.

Then four Sioux scouts were seen watching the cavalry column. They too hurried toward the valley. Custer reasoned that concealment was no longer possible for it now was near noon of the 25th. He and the officers believed that once the Sioux scouts reached the village the Indians would scatter to every point of the compass.[19] They had experienced this kind of retreat in previous campaigns and knew the impossibility of rounding them up. That was why Custer sent Benteen to the left at this time in the hope that he could prevent Indians from escaping up the valley. There was still some chance of surprising the village, but that would require tactics they ordinarily were not accustomed to. Indians customarily ran when attacked, and so they did when Reno first charged the end of the village. But when Reno faltered and halted instead of hitting the village as ordered, the retreating Indians regrouped and countercharged when they sensed that Reno's charge had gone wrong and no longer carried any weight.

Reno later was charged by some of the civilians attached to the pack train with being drunk while his command was engaged after it had reached the top of the bluffs. This charge was discounted at the Court of Inquiry though several post traders were said to have sold Reno eight gallons of whiskey at the beginning of the campaign as compared to the ten gallons they sold to the entire regiment.

There are as many reasons as there are individuals offering them for the cause of Custer's overwhelming defeat. Godfrey believed there were three reasons: "The overwhelming numbers of the enemy and their unexpected cohesion; Reno's panic rout from the valley; the defective extraction of the empty cartridge shells from the carbines."[20]

Reno, in his report to General Sherman, expressed his belief that Custer was defeated because of "his rapid marching for two days and one night before the fight; attacking in the daytime at noon... instead of early in the morning; and lastly, his unfortunate division of the regiment into three commands."[21]

Everyone from Terry on down was concerned about the Indians getting away from them and escaping the three-pronged net that had been planned to contain them. No one, from Terry on down, thought they would encounter more than 1500 warriors. A reconnaissance of the village was thought unnecessary because the village had been discovered by Custer's scouts and the trail the Seventh Cavalry had been following led directly to it. To prevent the Indians from escaping once Custer was aware that his command had been discovered by the Sioux, he terminated the bivouac he expected to maintain for another twenty-four hours before engaging an attack. Then he instituted the division of his regiment into three parts, a division that Reno criticized.

If Custer can be criticized for dividing his command he certainly should be for having placed Reno and Benteen in command of his supporting columns. As the commanding officer, Custer assumed total responsibility for the actions of his subordinates. Reno had displayed his lack of ability on his scout of the Rosebud when he disregarded Terry's express orders. Benteen's dislike and disrespect for Custer had been exhibited previously. Yet Custer had to assign ranking officers to the command of each column unless there was good and sufficient reason to assign others.

The 45/70 breech-loading Springfield was blamed mostly because the cartridge cases tended to stick once the weapon was warm from repeated use. The weapon had been thoroughly tested prior to the time it was first issued to the Seventh Cavalry for use in the Black Hills expedition in 1874. It was found to be superior to all other weapons except it was not a rapid fire weapon.

About 11 per cent of the Seventh were raw recruits with less than six months experience and it is quite probable these were the ones who had such difficulty primarily because they did not follow instructions as to keeping their weapons and ammunition clean and well-oiled. Reno reported that of 380 guns in his establishment only six were found unserviceable.

Much has been made of Custer's refusal to take along the Gatling guns. The Gatling guns were drawn by condemned horses which certainly could not have kept up with any cavalry moving rapidly. Their rigid mounts prevented a necessary freedom against a scattered foe. In fact, on June 25th the three Gatlings Custer rejected had considerable difficulty traversing bad roads while approaching the Little Big Horn River.[22]

Some wonder why Custer selected Custer Hill as a defense position. Dr. Kuhlman did not think of it as a defense position but rather as a holding position, one that could be defended and held until the other seven companies of Custer's regiment could join the five companies with him and then await the arrival of Terry and Gibbon. His initial plan was that of holding a larger area than that of Custer Hill for his plan included Calhoun Hill. By encompassing the two hills and the intervening ridge he was lengthening his perimeter and thereby spreading out his adversaries. When Calhoun Hill was seized by the Indians

Custer was forced to contract and concentrate upon a smaller area. No longer spread out he became more vulnerable. He was forced to make his stand on a hillside that provided no cover.

Sitting Bull became known as the chief of the hostile Indian camp. This stocky forty-two year old man was not a war chief but was best known as a medicine man. Though not considered very brave, he was quite a politician, and wise in council. He took no active part in the battle, having spent his time in the village making medicine while the warriors were fighting, a custom he seemed to resort to in time of danger.

The war chiefs principally credited with leading the victorious Indians were Gall, Crazy Horse, Crow King and Two Moon. Other chiefs who played principal roles were Low Dog, Hump, He Dog, Spotted Eagle, Lame Deer, Big Road, Black Moon, White Bull and Little Horse.

Estimates of the number of warriors facing the Seventh vary from 1,000 to 10,000. Major James McLaughlin, former Sioux Indian agent at the Standing Rock Agency, was able to obtain a reasonably accurate estimate. Considering every male over fourteen as a warrior in a fight of this kind, he concluded that the minimum Indian warrior force was between 2,500 and 3,000.[23]

Nearly one hundred years of irrepressible controversy has raged over General Terry's last instructions to Custer. Some persist in declaring that they were orders, specific orders, Custer should not have deviated from. Others call it a letter of advice that gave Custer complete freedom of choice. At this time it is known that there were verbal as well as written statements issued by Terry. The question hovers over content and interpretation.

The argument was triggered by the comments Colonel James Fry made in an article published in the January, 1892 issue of *Century Magazine* in conjunction with Gen. E.S. Godfrey's authoritative and eye-witness account of the Custer battle. Fry drew attention to a statement in Terry's annual report for 1876 in which Terry implied that the Custer disaster was the result of not employing Terry's plan.

Fry maintained that "the plan when Custer moved had neither the force nor importance which it frequently acquired in Terry's mind." He stated that Terry's letters of instructions contained no mention of a plan though there were many other suggestions. It was not until July 2, six days after the battle, that Terry made mention of any plan.

Fry's comments had been animated by a funeral oration. On December 29, 1890, the Rev. Dr. T. T. Munger, in a sermon at General Terry's funeral stated:

> Custer's fatal movement was in direct violation of both verbal and written orders. When rashness and disobedience ended in the total destruction of his command, General Terry withheld the fact of the disobeyed orders....

This indiscrete accusation aroused widespread comment and question. When challenged as to the source of such a statement, Rev. Munger offered the name of General Terry's brother-in-law, Col. R. P. Hughes. Hughes admitted he was Munger's source but denied authorizing him permission to make the derogatory statement.

Hughes, who had been Terry's aid-de-camp at the time the instructions were given, was repeatedly asked to produce a copy of the "order." He never complied. It was not until some years later that the original copy was discovered in the Custer family files. It varied in an important way from a copy that had been supplied by a Custer detractor, Major James Brisbin, who had been on the expedition.

Brisbin offered the entire letter, but in it he had inserted "It is desired that you conform as nearly as possible to these instructions and that you do not depart from them unless you shall see *absolute necessity for doing so.*"[24] (italics are mine)

Why Brisbin inserted this fraudulent extra paragraph is unknown. He had evidenced his jealousy of Custer on occasion so perhaps that was basis enough. In any event it tended to nullify, if true, a previous paragraph of Terry's letter which stated "he desires that you conform to them (Terry's views) *unless you see sufficient reason from departing from them." (italics are mine)*

Colonel W.A. Graham began a search for Terry's Headquarters records in 1876 and finally found them at Ft. Snelling, Minnesota. His examination proved to his satisfaction that Terry's Headquarters records "showed his letter of instructions to Custer to have been exactly and precisely identical with the instructions as set out in Terry's official report" and identical to the copy in the Custer family files that had originally been issued to General Custer.[25] This was more than enough proof that Brisbin's additional paragraph was an effort to besmirch Custer's reputation with the charge that Custer had disobeyed Terry's orders.[26]

Brisbin died soon after this but the matter did not end. Clergymen seem to have the last word when presiding over the body of the deceased. Contrary to a prevailing opinion that nothing was said against General Custer while Mrs. Custer lived—and what has been related thus far is proof to the contrary for neither Colonel Brisbin, Hughes or Rev. Munger hesitated in attacking the deceased Custer—*Pearson's Magazine* began a series of articles authored by Rev. Cyrus Townsend Brady early in the summer of 1904. Each of the Brady's articles dealt with one of Custer's western Indian engagements, the last one covering Custer's last battle. In this last issue of the magazine it was announced that Brady's soon to be released book *Indian Fights and Fighters,* would contain an appendix presenting the story of Custer's alleged disobedience of orders as discussed by various military authorities. This was extremely disturbing to Mrs. Custer for she had the original copy of Terry's letter of instructions her husband had sent to her for safe keeping and was well informed as to its interpretation.

Brady then asked Mrs. Custer to respond to these opinions by writing a reply for publication in the appendix of the book. Libbie, as her friends called her, was apprehensive. She asked advice of her old friend Jacob Greene, president of the Connecticut Mutual Life Insurance Co. Greene questioned the propriety of an answer from her. He thought she was "right in thinking it would be just advertising to his (Brady's) book."[27] He suggested that she let the matter rest. Wisely she refrained from taking an active part.

With Greene it was a different matter for he had served on Custer's staff during the Civil War. He had read Brady's appendix and he decided upon a mode of action. His letter to Brady began:

Let me say that General Custer was my intimate friend....I know his virtues and his defects, which were the defects of virtues. He was born a soldier, and specifically a born cavalryman. The true end of warfare was to him not only a professional theory, it was an instinct. When he set out to destroy an enemy, he laid hand on him as soon as possible, and never took it off. He knew the whole art of war.

Did this man, this soldier, whose service throughout the Civil War and a long career of frontier warfare as for 18 years unequaled for efficiency and brilliancy within the range of its opportunities and responsibilities, who never failed his commanders, who never disobeyed an order, nor disappointed an expectation, nor deceived a friend, did this man, at the last, deny his whole life history, his whole mental and moral habit, his whole character, and wilfully disobey an understood order, or all of its right execution according to his best judgment, within the limits of his ability under the conditions of the event...?

To charge disobedience is to say that he wilfully and with a strong motive and intent did that which his own military judgement forbade; for it was his own military judgment, right or wrong, that was to govern his own actions under the terms of that order. The quality of his judgment does not touch the question of disobedience. If he disobeyed that order, it was by going contrary to his own judgment. That was the only way he could disobey it. If men differ as to whether he did then, they will differ.[28]

Brady's book caused Libbie no little pain. She thought that Miles, Godfrey and Fry had buried the charge of "disobedience of orders," but Brady had dug it up again for the obvious purpose of selling his book. He had little interest in truth.

Shortly after it reached the bookstores Libbie received a consoling letter from R. W. Barkley, who had been an Annapolis classmate of Brady's, saying: "He (Brady) is not a deep water sailor. He is not always accurate, even where his knowledge is firsthand....Getting down to the bottom of a thing is not Dr. Brady's forte...."[29]

The battle of the Little Big Horn did not end when the last of Custer's gallant Seventh went down. The battle continues to rage—on the screen, in print, over the air, on the lecture platform, and wherever men meet to discuss events present and past. Much is made of the alleged disobedience of orders and most of the comment is based on Hughes' charges that he had committed to writing in 1896.[30] Few have read the article. As a result there have been many misrepresentations, gross distortions, falsifications and innuendos applied to the original letter of instructions and Custer's response to it.

In substance, Hughes' article stated:

1. "On June 22, Custer believed he would be facing about 2,400 warriors." This is false. He anticipated meeting, at most, 1,500 warriors.

2. "Custer was 40 miles from the Little Big Horn on the evening of June 24." This is false. He was 23 miles by Terry's own map.

3. "Custer did not know the location of the Indian camp on the evening of June 24 other than what Terry had indicated in the letter of instructions." False. Custer knew the exact location.

4. "Terry, when preparing Custer's letter of advice, believed the Indians were where they were finally found." False. Terry did not know and had no way of knowing.

5. "On the evening of June 24 Custer was 'not nearly in the contact with the enemy'. " This is false. He was practically on their backs.

6. "On the evening of June 24 Custer decided to attack on June 25." This is false. Custer had planned to rest until June 26. On the morning of June 25 he was notified of the discovery of Indians observing his command. Experience had taught him that a surprise attack was essential. Indians just did not stand and fight a pitched battle.

7. "Custer could have marched up the Rosebud on June 25 and would have been in a good attack position at dawn of June 26." False. They would have been about a day's march away.

8. "In no way do I intend to assail General Custer, but it has been forced upon me that his error in disobeying the orders of his superior must be made plain. What reason he had—what justification he might have shown— are known to no one living."[31] Hughes didn't assail Custer; he just ran a bulldozer

over him. Since Hughes admits there is doubt as to Custer's reason, Custer, as the commander on the scene, should be entitled to the benefit of the doubt.

At this point the charge of disobedience—and the charge involves four instances—had become so involved and even intertwined that it has reached legendary proportions. It can be said that Reno disobeyed orders on his scout for Terry, causing the latter to abandon his plans. Then again, Reno disobeyed his orders in not attacking the Indian camp, a matter in which he was given no choice. Benteen disobeyed orders to bring up the packs and unite with Custer thereby abandoning 225 troopers when they sorely needed support. In Custer's instance it should be said that he was in contact with the enemy which, according to Terry's instructions, permitted him to depart from Terry's views since he had "sufficient reason for departure from them."

Chapter Eleven
You May Be The Judge

Terry had sent official reports of the Custer tragedy to Sheridan on June 27 and 28 and on July 2. None of these contained any mention of a plan of operation, nor did they suggest that Custer or anyone else had disobeyed orders.

A second message was sent to Sheridan on July 2 which Terry labeled "confidential." This had all the marks of a Little Big Horn coverup. Intended only for the eyes of General Sheridan, who was attending the Centennial Exposition in Philadelphia, he showed it to General Sherman who was with him. Sherman, wishing to hurry it on to the Secretary of War, entrusted it to a newspaperman, passing himself off as a War Department messenger. He sent the message on to Washington but only after he had arranged to publish it in the July 7 issue of the Philadelphia *Inquirer*.[1]

Such startling news on the heels of the Custer battle story amazed the readers. This "secret" communication indicated that while at the mouth of the Rosebud River on June 21, Terry had held a conference with Gibbon and Custer. Terry's plan, so he stated, was to move Custer and his regiment up the Rosebud "till he should meet a trail which Reno had discovered a few days before."[2] The main force was to be kept further to the south to keep the Indians from slipping between it and the mountains and getting away. It was expected that Gibbon's column would not reach the mouth of the Little Big Horn until June 26 and that Custer's simultaneous wide movement to the south would use up enough time. Gibbon would be close enough to cooperate with Custer's final move against the Indians. Custer, according to Terry, said he would be traveling about thirty miles each day.

Terry also suggested that Gibbon's cavalry should combine with Custer's. Custer indicted his preference for using his regiment alone, maintaining that they would be adequate for his purposes. Terry "shared his confidence." And it was at this time that Terry offered him the Gatling guns which Custer refused for fear they would interfere with his movements. Terry went on to say that Gibbon's movements went exactly according to those plans and that had Custer waited to attack, Terry had no "doubt that we should have been successful."[3]

Benteen had told Terry that Custer's column had marched twelve miles on June 22; thirty-five miles on June 23; fifty-five miles on June 24; then twenty-three miles to the battlefield on June 25. (Lieutenant George W. Wallace who, as the engineering officer, kept the record of the march, testifed at the Reno Court of Inquiry that they marched thirty-three to thirty-five miles on June 23; thirty during the day of June 24 and another eight or ten miles that night; and on June 25 from twenty-five to thirty-five miles.)

Terry concluded this portion of his confidential report saying:

> I do not tell you this to cast any reflection upon Custer. For whatever errors he may have committed he has paid the penalty and you cannot regret his loss more than I do, but I feel that our plan must have been successful had it been carried out, and I desire you to now the facts. In the action itself, so far as I can make out, Custer acted under a misapprehension. He thought, I am confident, that the Indians were running. For fear that they might get away he attacked....

These lines give the impression that there was a plan for the columns to meet on the morning of June 26. There was none. Had Custer followed Terry's nebulous suggestions, the Seventh Cavalry would have been on the Rosebud and Gibbon would have been at the mouth of the Little Big Horn.

Lieutenant James H. Bradley, who was chief of scouts with

Gibbon's infantry column, wrote in his journal under date of June 21: "it is understood that if Custer arrives first, he is at liberty to attack at once if he deems prudent. We have little hope of being in at the death, as Custer will undoubtedly exert himself to the utmost to get there first and win all the laurels for himself and his regiment.[4]

There is no evidence that Terry or anyone else knew of the exact location of the Indian village. Had there been, he would not have suggested that Custer stay on the Rosebud. In a dispatch to Sheridan sent on the morning of June 21 Terry said: "I only hope that one of the two columns will find the Indians. I go personally with Gibbon."[5] This indicates he did not know where the Indians were. So then, how could he have had a plan to attack them? Made to realize that his previous reports gave an impression of inadequate leadership on his part, the confidential communication was prepared as a cover up. In all probability the matter was pressed by his brother-in-law and chief-of-staff Col. Robert Hughes who, at a later date, went out of his way to trump up charges that Custer disobeyed Terry's orders.[6]

The uproar that followed the release of the coverup communication in the *Inquirer* came from the Custer partisans. Charges were made against Terry, Benteen and Reno, then finally settled upon an effort to prove that Terry had given Custer complete freedom of decision.

Mary Adams, who was called Maria by the Custers, was their Negro cook and housekeeper. She had taken Eliza's place in 1873 at a time Custer needed someone to do his cooking that summer on the Yellowstone expedition. Maria quickly became the family and regimental favorite. She readily adapted to the rough living on the trail along the proposed route of the Northern Pacific Railroad.[7]

In response to the charge that Custer had disobeyed orders several unidentified officers brought Mary Adams before George P. Flannery, a notary public in Bismarck, to certify her statement that she was present in General Custer's tent on the Rosebud when General Terry came in and said to Custer: "Custer, I don't know what to say for the last." Custer replied:

"Say whatever you want to say." Terry then said: "Use your own judgment and do what you think best if you strike the trial." The affadavit was signed January 16, 1878.[8]

According to Col. Graham, Generals Godfrey and Edgerly, and Col. Varnum, had told him that "Mary Adams did not accompany the expedition from Fort Lincoln in 1876." Then Graham reproduced an article by W.A. Falconer in the Bismarck *Capital*, June 25, 1925, in which Falconer called the affadavit a "frameup." Falconer repeated a story told by Lieut. C.L. Gurley, Sixth Infantry, how Gurley assisted in the task of breaking the sad news to the widows by going to the back door of the Custer residence at Ft. Lincoln before 7 A.M. of July 6 where he awakened Mary Adams, who let him in. Falconer talked to Flannery, the former notary public, during 1925 and Flannery "believed that Captain (John) Carland was the one who drew up the affadavit for Mary Adams to sign." Two years earlier, Flannery, who was president of the Northwestern Trust Company of St. Paul, wrote to Col. Graham—on August 12, 1922—"I know Mary Adams by sight, having seen her in General Custer's home, and later in the home of J.W. Raymond in Bismarck, but I have no recollection about the affadavit referred to by you." In his final paragraph of the lengthy letter he repeated: "I am sorry I am unable to recall anything in connection with the affadavit."

Doesn't it seem strange that Flannery, forty-seven years after the affadavit was signed in his presence the circumstances of which he could not recall in 1922 had in 1925 a sudden revival of memory? It is obvious that Falconer was no Custer partisan.

Another side to the story has been supplied by letters recently discovered in the Custer family files. On June 6, 1876, Tom Custer wrote to his niece Emma Reed, who was then at Fort Lincoln, telling her of catching a dozen young sage hens that had been turned over to Mary who was going to try to raise them.

Then on June 21, 1876, Autie Reed, the brother of Emma Reed, wrote to his mother and father, Mr. and Mrs. David Reed, that he was now in camp on the Yellowstone at the mouth of the Rosebud. Autie was excited with the news that a heavy Indian trail had been struck just thirty miles from camp and, though the trail was twelve days old, the Indians by moving only four or five miles a day made everyone feel certain of success. Autie wrote of a tame jack rabbit "which Mary thinks all the world of, Mary is staying on the boat." Mary is none other than Custer's cook, Mary Adams. How does one reconcile the statement that Mary was met at the door of the Custer residence at Ft. Lincoln by Lieut. Gurley when the two letters above prove that Mary was with Custer? Godfrey, Edgerly and Varnum told Col. Graham that Mary Adams did not accompany the expedition. They made this statement in the early 1920s, almost fifty years after the battle. Could their memories have been that faulty? Could Mary have returned to Fort Lincoln with the six Ree Indians who, on June 22, took the mail down to the Powder River where a small boat carried it down to Fort Buford and from there by steamboat to Fort Lincoln? This may be the answer to the dilemma, for by returning home just as the going appeared as though it would be rough, Mary would be able to open the back door for Lieut. Gurley on July 6. Gurley could have been right. Godfrey, Edgerly and Varnum could have been right too, for Mary left the boat and did not continue on the balance of the expedition. Tom Custer and Autie Reed had no reason to mention Mary in their letters unless she was with them as both indicted. Doesn't it follow that Mary Adams was in a position to overhear Terry's remark to Custer as he was about to lead out the Seventh: "Use your own judgment and do what you think best if you strike the trail"?

Many years after the Custer battle a story was introduced that Custer had disobeyed orders and attacked the Indian village a day early in an effort to further a political ambition to become president. There were others who espoused this accusation but the principal author of the charge was the historical writer Mari Sandoz. Sandoz outlined a plan—ludicrous to anyone familiar with convention protocol and political technique, which Custer purportedly had made that would thrust him into the limelight during the Democratic Convention in St. Louis.

Sandoz would have the reader believe that news of Custer's victory over the Sioux would have James Gordon Bennett of the New York *Herald* stampeding the convention in an all out effort to get Custer nominated for President. She would have one believe that the financier Jay Gould of the New York *World* would lend his weight.[9] All Custer would have had to do was "to defeat the warring Sioux." The victory would be relayed to a telegraph in Bozeman in two days by the scout Charlie Reynolds. Additional insurance could be added by having George Herendeen and a few other scouts such as Mitch Bouyer head out in other directions with similar messages. Custer, of course, would take the correspondent Mark Kellogg and "make the run to the Missouri River." To insure his nomination the victory telegram would have to reach the floor of the Convention by the morning of the 28th of June, so he was forced to finish off the Sioux by the evening of the 25th. Thus the need to attack Sitting Bull's camp at noon of the 25th, says Sandoz.

Now how could such an imaginative story originate? The only known source is the narrative of the Arikara scout Red Star.[10] Red Star relates the story in which Custer had told the Ree scouts that if they had a victory he would return to Washington and remain there as the Great Father, and that all of them would benefit thereafter.

Through the interpreter Red Start, old O.G. Libby, the editor of *The Arikara Narrative,* that with Fred Gerard as the interpreter, Custer had said: "When we return, I will go back to Washington and I shall take my brother here, Bloody Knife, with me. I shall remain at Washington and be (*with*) the Great Father. But my brother Bloody Knife will return, and when he arrives home he shall have a fine house built for him, and those of you present will be the ones appointed to look after the work that will be placed in charge of Bloody Knife."

Red Star related this incident in 1912, thirty-six years after it had occurred. To remember Custer's words verbatim after that period of time would be a near impossibility. Even so, I have inserted the word *with* in the quotation to give it a practical application for Custer obviously was exhorting the Ree scouts by making them promises of reward for services he was expecting of them. Then, too, the quotation had been made through two interpreters, Fred Gerard and O.G. Libby's, and from the time weakened memory of Red Star.

Custer may have had political aspirations at one time but bitter experience had dissipated any such thoughts. He had taken an active part in politics in 1866 by attending the National Union Convention as a delegate. The Convention was held to adopt a doctrine asserting the supremacy of representative government which they claimed Congress was failing to do. Custer firmly and even vehemently opposed the election of any individual to office who had supported the Rebellion. In one instance he publicly opposed a Michigan man because of his efforts to support the South during the Civil War. It was during this period that Custer was asked to run for Congress, and it was suggested that he become a candidate for Governor. He flatly refused.

As a guest of President Johnson in his "Swing Around the Circle" Custer had every opportunity of observing the professional politician in action and the response to him by inhospitable and radical mobs at some of the stops.

Custer had been exposed to the workup a candidate must undergo to obtain a nomination, the incumbent being no exception. Sandoz surely knew that any aspirant for this office must corral delegates long before a convention. There was no other way. And there is not one shred of evidence that anyone had introduced Custer's name prior to or during the Democratic Convention in St. Louis. A search of the records and of the St. Louis newspapers indicates as much.

When the St. Louis convention opened on June 27, Thomas F. Bayard of Delaware, Allen G. Thurman of Ohio, Winfield S. Hancock of Pennsylvania, Thomas A. Hendricks of Indiana and Governor Samuel J. Tilden of New York sought the nomination. Gov. Tilden was named on the first ballot. Hendricks was nominated for the Vice-presidency.[11] It is interesting that the Michigan delegates met in caucus several days prior to the convention after which they declared themselves in Tilden's corner.[12] There was no mention of Custer.

When one considers that news of the Custer disaster did not reach civilization until July 3 and was not publicized until the next day,[13] it follows that word of the event could not have reached St. Louis in time to be useful in securing the nomination. And one student of the battle aftermath maintains that Custer's supposed backers, Bennett and Gould, "were violent enemies" and hardly likely to join forces in his behalf.[14]

It has been stated by many that Custer was a Democrat. Apparently he had given that impression because of his father's strong feelings and because of his own ardent defense of Gen. McClellan when the latter was removed from command. McClellan had a charisma that drew men to him. He had recognized Custer, after an act of gallantry, by appointing him as one of his staff aides. As he said: "I became much attached to him. In the later days of the war, when he commanded cavalry troops, he displayed a degree of prudence and good sense, in conducting the most dangerous expeditions, that surprised many who thought they knew him well. In the battle ... against the Sioux ...those who accuse him of reckless rashness would, perhaps, have been the first to accuse him of timidity if he had not attacked, and thus allowed the enemy to escape unhurt. He died as he lived, a gallant soldier; and his whole career was such as to force me to believe that he had good reasons for acting as he did."[15] If Custer had supported him politically it would not have been because of McClellan's politics but because of his deep regard for his mentor.

Libbie did not know her husband's political sentiments. He never told her, but he did tell her this much: "My doctrine has ever been that a soldier should not meddle in politics."[16]

Over seventy-five years had passed before it was discovered there had been a hoax on Reno Hill. One week after

Gibbon and Terry had joined Reno a petition was circulated among the surviving enlisted men of the Seventh Cavalry appealing to the President for the promotion of Major Reno and the other officers of the regiment. The Reno Hill Hoax, though not recognized as such at the time, was first given public recognition at the Reno Court of Inquiry in 1879 where it was introduced as Exhibit No. 10. It read as follows:

Camp Near Big Horn On Yellowstone River.
July 4, 1876

To His
>   Excellency the President
>   And the Honorable Representatives
>   of the United States

Gentlemen:

We the enlisted men the survivors of the battle on the Heights of the Little Big Horn, on the 25th and 26th of June 1876, of the 7th Regiment of Cavalry who subscribe our names to this petition, most earnestly solicit the President and Representatives of our Country, that the vacancies among the Commissioned Officers of our Regiment, made by the slaughter of our brave, heroic, now lamented Lieutenant Colonel George A. Custer, and the other noble dead Commissioned Officers of our Regiment who fell close by him on the bloody field, daring the savage demons to the last, be filled by the Officers of the Regiment only. That Major M.A. Reno, be our Lieutenant Colonel vice Custer, killed; Captain F.W. Benteen our Major vice Reno, promoted. The other vacancies to be filled by Officers of the Regiment by seniority. Your petitioners know this to be contrary to the established rule of promotion, but prayerfully solicit a deviation from the usual rule in this case, as it will be conferring a bravely fought for and a justly merited promotion on Officers who by their bravery, coolness and decision on the 25th and 26th of June 1876, saved the lives of every man now living of the 7th Cavalry who participated in the battle, one of the most bloody on record and one that would have ended with the loss of life of every Officer and enlisted man on the field; only for the position taken by Major Reno, which we held with bitter tenacity against fearful odds to the last.

To support this assertion—had our position been taken 100 yards back from the brink of the heights overlooking the river we would have been entirely cut off from the water; and from behind those heights the Indian demons would have swarmed in hundreds picking off our men by detail, and before midday June 26th not an Officer or enlisted man of our Regiment would have been left to tell of our dreadful fate as we then would have been completely surrounded.

With the prayerful hope that out petition be granted, we have the honor to forward it through our Commanding Officer.

According to the Adjutant General in 1878, there wre 235 signatures under this petition. This was about eighty per cent of the survivors of the combined commands of Reno and Benteen. The petition never reached President Grant. Instead it went to the General of the Army, W.T. Sherman, who indorsed it as follows:

> Headquarters Army of the United States,
> Washington, D.C., August 5, 1876.

> The judicious and skilful conduct of Major Reno and Captain Beenteen is appreciated, but the promotions caused by General Custer's death have been made by the President and confirmed by the Senate; therefore this petition can not be granted. When the Sioux campaign is over I shall be most happy to recognize the valuable services of both officers and men by granting favors or recommending actual promotion.
> Promotion on the field of battle was Napoleon's favorite method of stimulating his officers and soldiers to deeds of heroism, but it is impossible in our service because commissions can only be granted by the President on the advice and consent of the Senate, and except in original vacancies, promotion in a regiment is generally if not always made on the rule of seniority.

General Sherman's letter above became a part of the record in the Reno Court of Inquiry and as such was Exhibit No. 11. Who would benefit the most from such a petition—Reno and Benteen? Of course! And who would draft such a petition? Someone closely associated with either of them and who had an equal relationship with the enlisted men. The man for that job would be either the sergeant major of the regiment or the first sergeant of a company. Since Reno was a field officer not commanding a company, and since the sergeant major was killed with Custer, we are left with the first sergeant of Benteen's company, Joseph McCurry.[17]

It was Major Edward S. Luce, former superintendent of the Custer Battlefield National Monument, who detected something highly irregular in the signatures on the petition. Comparing them to those on the company payrolls he discerned that in certain instances cavalrymen would sign for their pay with an X whereas on the Enlisted Men's Petition they had signed with a full signature. Major Luce had carefully examined the signatures on the petition and had concluded that many of the signatures that had been introduced to replace those who had exhibited their inability to sign with other than an X displayed characteristics intimately associated with the handwriting of First Sergeant Joseph McCurry of Benteen's "H" Company. It was obvious to Major Luce that someone—Luce had little doubt it was McCurry—had forged the names of those in the Seventh who were illiterate.

And Custer Battle student Rev. Charles DuBois perceived that three signatures on the petition were those of men who were on detached service at the Powder River Base nearly 150 miles from the mouth of the Little Big Horn River on July 4 when the petition was being signed. In addition to these three he discovered the signatures of three men whose names do not appear on the regimental records or on the Roster of Survivors![18]

Of those who regularly signed company payrolls with an X witnessed by an officer whose signature indicated that he had, seventeen had signed the petition with full signatures. Is it coincidence that each of the seventeen had learned to write in a matter of less than thirty days on the trail?

There were some who questioned the purpose of the Enlisted Men's Petition since it appeared obvious that those signing it and those promoting it knew that promotion on the field of battle—as General Sherman stated in his reply—"is impossible in our service." Could it be that a sense of guilt had begun to permeate those still in command of the Seventh and that in any possible inquiry to follow the revelation of any Reno-Benteen deficiences would be depreciated by a "white paper" signed by men who were there? By presenting such a petition for the record—for when it was signed on July 4, Reno and Benteen were above suspicion—it was acknowledged by its author that the request to promote Reno and Benteen was "contrary to the established rule of promotion." Any investigation of their conduct would bring to light that each had failed to obey orders, among other things. The weight of a statement of their conduct signed by the men who survived would aid considerably in nullifying their wrong-doing. Such a petition would not obtain a promotion, as all obviously knew, but it might prevent a few heads from rolling. Who knew at the time but what a courtmartial or a Court of Inquiry would be the outcome of what they had just undergone once the true story was made public?

About twenty-five years before the Reno Hill Hoax was discovered to have been associated with forgery, General Godfrey advised Capt. R.G. Carter as to the circumstances in which the Enlisted Men's Petition was signed. "We were so stunned, overcome as it were, from the fatigue and strain of the several days before, during and after the battle, and its results," he wrote, "that we did not *sense* its real importance, nor did we fully coordinate the events. The men were grateful that we escaped the disaster and the petitions were put before them at the psychological time to gain their signatures."[19]

Godfrey went on to relate how a number of men of the Seventh Cavalry, when asked if they had signed the petition denied it, yet their signatures proved genuine. None, it seems, could recall seeing or signing the petition. Du Bois wondered if it could be blamed on faulty memories or fraud.

Curiosity is a healthy thing. Major Luce's caused him to place the matter in the hands of the Federal Bureau of Investigation with the request that they determine which names on the petition were forged and whether First Sergeant McCurry wrote the majority of the names.

On November 5, 1954, Acting Director Hillory A. Tolson advised Luce that of the seventy-nine signatures they were listing "variations were noted in the signatures...and the corresponding signatures which suggest in all probability that the signatures on the petition are forgeries." It is noted that seventeen had fully signed their names appearing on the petition but had also signed their payroll with a witnessed X." The FBI concluded that "There is insufficient comparable handwriting of any individual available in the known specimens to determine whether or not any of these individuals wrote the petition...."[20]

There is no question that the petition contained seventy-nine forged signatures. It has not been determined that McCurry was the forger of the questionable signatures or the perpetrator of the hoax. Yet it seems very unlikely that he would have circulated a petition without the knowledge and approval of his company commander. He had served too long not to observe what would be considered proper military etiquette and politics.

One may wonder who authored the petition, who initially thought of it. Perhaps that can be determined by deciding who would gain the most through it. Reno and Benteen certainly head the list. DuBois singled out Benteen as the culprit, with his man McCurry as the only person having the trust and the association with the enlisted men to be able to obtain their signatures. Benteen needed someone to front the plea who would appear to receive no personal benefit. None but Sergeant McCurry could have filled the position. An unsolicited statement signed by the enlisted men lauding their commanding officers could have nothing but a beneficial effect against those questions that might arise at a later date. And that it did. It fooled the members of the Reno Court of Inquiry in 1879 by being accepted as evidence in the defense of Major Reno.

Chapter Twelve
Legend Into History

ALMOST EVERY school child knows that the only survivor found on the Custer battlefield was Captain Myles Keogh's horse "Comanche." During the last hundred years there have been over eighty individuals claiming to have been survivors of this greatest of all Western battles. None has been able to prove his claim.

E.A. Brininstool of Los Angeles, whose collection of over seventy such accounts is now in the files of the Thomas Gilcrease Institute of Tulsa, rejected all as fraudulent. In each case the "survivor" left a clue that proved him a liar or a cheat. Not all claimants are humbugs. The Indians asserted that none of the troopers escaped. This is not a fact, for over the years, a number of skeletal remains have been found on the periphery of the battle area each of which has been identified as a Seventh Cavalry trooper.

The War Department reported "about 225 officers and enlisted men" in the Custer battalion; obviously they were unsure about the exact number. A thorough search of official records indicates that there were at least 225. The number in the body count on Custer Hill varies from 202 to 212. There were civilians there like Boston Custer, Autie Reed, Mark Kellogg, and Mitch Bouyer, which has made some difference in the count. Any way the count was made, some twelve or thirteen were unaccounted for.

The muster rolls caused this confusion. They were in good order and were accurate up to the time of the battle. After that there was confusion. Some of the dead were discovered in the following years. Nobody can positively state that none escaped. Kuhlman believed that there was one survivor and went to great trouble to prove it.

Kuhlman referred to Private Frank Finkel of "C" Company commanded by Captain Tom Custer. After considerable research Kuhlman said: "I believe Finkel participated in the fight and escaped from the battlefield." This is how it happened.[1]

Finkel had enlisted in the army in October, 1874, under the name of Frank Hall. While mounted and surrounded by unmounted Indians on a ridge south of the Hill where Custer was engaged, it appeared that he and "C" Company were trapped like rats. At the height of the fight a bullet struck the butt of his gun splintering off a piece which struck him between the eyes. While wiping away the blood from his eyes another bullet struck the flank of his horse causing it to rear and plunge wildly. The horse bolted through a line of Sioux Indians circling to the south of the troopers just as his reins broke. It was all he could do to hold on to the animal and flatten himself as it broke into a wild gallop. A bullet struck Finkel in the side as he passed through the Indian line and another tore through his foot. The Indians gave chase to the frightened animal but were soon outdistanced. Finkel finally managed to regain the reins of the frightened animal and bring it to a halt.

Using a strip from his saddle blanket as a tourniquet on his profusely bleeding foot he pushed on in search of water. After several traumatic experiences he came upon a settler in a remote area in the hills. Nursed back to health by him, Finkel moved on to Fort Benton. There the officer in charge refused to believe his story unless he could produce two witnesses to vouch for him. Deciding this was a hopeless task to obtain a discharge he headed for the Northwest.

Finkel was a man of few words. It was not until 1930 that he told his story, and then it came out under the pressure of hearing his companions during a horseshoe game argue about the Custer Battle. Finally, unable to stand their misinformation he blurted out: "A hell of a lot you know about it!" Pressed for the reason of his outburst, he replied: "I was there."

Finkel had no solid reason for holding back any longer. He knew he would be unable to obtain a pension and he did not need one. If he had desired notoriety it was rather late to seek it. The wound in his foot had caused a permanent limp and when his first wife had questioned its cause he had told her that an Indian had shot him.

I happen to have known the mayor of Dayton, Washington back in 1963 when he told me that Finkel was a solid citizen there, very honest, proud and truthful. His word could be relied on.

Dr. Kuhlman went over the story with a magnifying glass, even visiting the points of reference in Finkel's account. He concluded: "The Finkel story does not contain any of the usual ear-marks of fraud. There is nothing in it that cannot be either verified or explained in a plausible manner."[22]

Fame or gain has been the drive behind a series of wondrous accounts of "sole survivors" of Custer's last battle. By this time the list of "sole survivors" must have passed the 200 mark. The aspirants for the title have shown little regard for the truth and have grown to such numbers that they could have replaced all of Custer's five troops on Custer Hill. Many seem plausible up to a certain point, then display the flaw that is easily discerned.

Mrs. Custer was the recipient of numerous accounts from individuals claiming they were witnesses to her husband's demise. Their observations hardly adhered to known facts. Custer had been "observed" to die by a tomahawk, an arrow, by bullets, and by a lance. Some saw him killed down by the river and carried up to Custer Hill while others saw him die at the top of the hill. He has been the last to die and the first. These stories have been picked up by newspapermen and embellished.[3]

Charles Windolph of Company H, who died in Lead, South Dakota on March 11, 1950, was the last survivor of the Seventh Cavalry who had participated in the Custer Battle. He was in the Reno Hill engagement at the other end of the battlefield. For the part he played he was presented with a Purple Heart and the Congressional Medal of Honor.

The last survivor of the Yellowstone Campaign was Jacob Horner of Bismarck, North Dakota. A member of Company K, he died on September 21, 1951. Horner, who consequently was at the Powder River camp at the time of the battle, is considered the last survivor of the Seventh Cavalry in that campaign, but not of the battle.

The earliest press accounts of the Custer Battle would have you believe that "only one Crow scout remained to tell the tale." The Indian scout referred to was a 17-year old lad named Curley. Curley, according to the Helena *Herald* Custer Battle account of July 15, 1876 introduced the information that he had provided them with "the only story of the fight ever to be looked for from one who was an actual participant on Custer's side— Curley being, in all human probability, the only survivor of his command."

Curley's account of the battle was lengthy and pretty much in accord with a version accepted by most authorities. He observed that the Sioux loss exceeded 300, that they engaged in a final charge when they were certain the troopers' ammunition was about exhausted, and that the termination of the fight was at such close quarters many of Custer's men were killed with arrows.

Curley claimed he escaped "by drawing a blanket about him in the manner of the Sioux, and passing through an interval in their line as they scattered over the field in their final charge." He believed he was probably mistaken for a Sioux or one of the Arapahoe or Cheyenne allies.

The blanket story was embellished in the numerous rewrites that followed. The Sioux blanket, probably taken off a dead Indian pony as a spoil of war, was later reported to have been wrapped about Curley to disguise himself. In another account he was supposed to have offered another such blanket to Custer, pleading with him to use it so he could escape. No conclusion was drawn that Custer refused only because there were not enough blankets for his entire command.

Indians commonly stripped for combat, wearing no more than a breech clout, war paint, and perhaps some feathers or fetich. This provided complete physical freedom and also prevented clothing from being carried into a wound with its resultant problems in wound healing. Then too, the reader should know that on this June day the early afternoon was boiling hot, probably over 100 degrees. The Indians were practical warriors and knew from long experience how to undress for a battle.

In this kind of atmosphere, an Indian appearing clothed in a blanket would have been as obvious as a knight in armor at a nudist camp. So, if that story isn't acceptable, perhaps one told in 1948 in *Life Magazine* might hold water. In its account of Curley, it was claimed that he crawled within the carcase of a disemboweled horse, remaining there safely for the duration.

At noon of June 28, Curley appeared at the mouth of the Little Big Horn River where the steamer *Far West* was moored. This is mentioned by Sergeant James E. Wilson in his diary. Wilson reported that Curley arrived at noon but gave little information about the battle, there being no interpreter on board. Curley was able, by drawing a crude sketch, to indicate that Custer had been defeated.

A short time later he was interviewed by Lt. James H. Bradley through interpreter Thomas LaForge. Curley said: "I was not in the fight. I did nothing wonderful; I was not in it." This was not colorful enough for the reporters or for Whittaker. Curley was truthful; they were not. Curley could not read and only learned to speak a little English in later years. He denied the wild tales he heard but no one would believe him. In time he gave up trying.

There is only one survivor of the fight on Custer Hill that rises above all contention—*Comanche*. This buckskin horse carried Capt. Myles W. Keogh into the battle. He was the only living object found on the battlfield when burial parties began their grisly assignment on the morning of June 27. It was Lieut. Henry J. Nowlan, Keogh's comrade in arms in the Pontifical Zouaves and the Civil War, who saw and recognized the animal. Covered with blood from numerous bullet and arrow wounds, *Comanche* neighed softly as if seeking some friend. Nowlan's first thought was to put the weakened animal out of its misery, but after a careful examination of the wounds he decided there was hope. The pitful mount was slowly led the fifteen miles to the steamer *Far West* where he was carefully bedded down on grass at the extreme stern of the boat. He became the special concern of the entire crew. The horse responded rapidly to these attentions. After arriving at Fort Lincoln, orders were issued by Col. Samuel D. Sturgis that no one was to ride *Comanche* under any circumstances, nor was he permitted to do any work, and that he was to be saddled and bridled and led by a trooper of I Company on every ceremonial occasion.[2]

According to Maj. Luce, Keogh and *Comanche* historian, *Comanche* became intemperate. During the year of convalescence he was given a whiskey bran mash about every other day. Convalescence soon became a pleasure. *Comanche* became a regular visitor at the enlisted men's canteen on pay day where the boys, willingly enough, treated their favorite to a bucket of beer. When the boys ran out of funds, he would visit the officers' quarters to panhandle.

Comanche became quite attached to blacksmith Gustave Korn, who had given him such devoted care during the convalescent period. He followed the trooper everywhere, even trotting down to Junction City and neighing in front of the house where Korn's lady friend lived until Korn appeared and led him to his garrison stall. It may have been jealousy.

Gustave Korn was killed at Wounded Knee. *Comanche*, as the "second commanding officer" of the Seventh Cavalry, as he was affectionately called, began to fail with the passing of his old comrade. He seemed to lose interest in everything except panhandling the beer. On November 6, 1891, he died at the age of nineteen.[3]

Of all the phony "survivors" one such character manages to stand out. Self-styled Man Mountain Ed Ryan staked his claim in the early 1950s in, of all places, Custer, South Dakota. Ryan, not to be outdone by the earliest settlers there, staked his claim for gold, only it was the tourists' gold he was after. The heavily bearded and long-haired Ryan claimed to have served with Custer's Seventh Cavalry during the Black Hills gold discovery expedition of 1874. Ryan told how he was left behind near the present city of Custer with orders from General Custer to care for a sick comrade, then to rejoin the outfit when he could.

Ryan's sick buddy, according to Ryan, died a few months later. The winter snows prevented his returning to his company. He went on to tell his enthralled listeners that by going AWOL he was saved from the awful fate that befell his comrades two years later at the Little Big Horn. Even so, he claimed that they had inscribed his name on the monument at the top of Custer Hill as one of those who had died in the battle.

Anyone hearing this story for the first time might be taken in by this "98" year-old fraud. He asserted that he had joined the Seventh Cavalry in June, 1874, after enlisting in St. Louis at the age of seventeen, using the name George Ryan because he was under age. An examination of the roster on the Custer Hill monument reveals the name of Daniel Ryan—but no Edward or George Ryan, but that didn't stop his story.

He explained that Custer had decided to break up camp near the present site of Custer, S.D. on July 1, and leave Ryan with his sick tentmate. This spoils his story since the Seventh Cavalry was still in camp at Fort Abraham Lincoln on that date and did not leave there until July 2, with nearly a month of travel to the point Ryan claimed he was left with his buddy. To add to the implausibility of the story one should be aware that the expeditionary force had over 100 wagons and ambulances and several surgeons with it, and no illness in the command at that time, so that there was ample space in all the ambulances. And it would be incredible to believe that Custer would leave a sick man in hostile Indian country in the hands of a mere youth who had neither military nor medical experience.

Ryan was not interested in facts. He was interested in getting tourists to buy his booklet, "Me And The Black Hills." He had a theory as to what had befallen Custer's men. "We had an Indian, Bloody Knife, that I never trusted. This is only a theory, mind you, but I can't help thinking that Bloody Knife double-crossed Custer." He wanted to simplify matters for historians.

When he was reminded that he had been AWOL from the Army for almost eighty years he came forth with a stock reply: "Gen. Custer's last orders to me were to rejoin the regiment. That would be pretty hard, considering it was wiped out by the Sioux."

The old fraud became the source of much irritation and discomfort to Maj. Edward S. Luce while he was Superintendent of the Custer Battlefield National Monument. Hardly a day passed but what someone asked him if he had heard of this man Ryan at Custer, South Dakota. After his affirmative reply they usually asked why he didn't employ him around the Custer Museum. In utter disgust Maj. Luce would push a file toward the naive questioner. In it was one of Hal Boyle's columns some four years old in which he emphatically stated that Ryan was "65—not 95 years old, and Custer died 10 years before Old Ed's birth. And the gentle bewhiskered fraud never was a real prospector. He used to run a gas station." On another page was a copy of a letter from the Adjutant General of the Army stating that in the years from 1874 to 1876 the name of Ed Ryan does not appear in Army records.

Ryan must have done well. At one time he was featured on a national television show. Before that publicity some of his townspeople had marked him as the biggest liar in all of South Dakota. Since then it has been said that Montana and North Dakota should be included.

Hollywood and television, not to be outdone, have added their hosts of inaccuracies to the ever increasing myths and legends. Producers and script writers, recognizing the glow and attraction of a man who was made a major general at age 25, have portrayed him as a symbol of frontier Indian fighters. In doing so they provided action packed entertainment for seven-year-old boys of all ages, sacrificing truth in every episode.

The results of one of their efforts was labeled *They Died With Their Boots On*. With typical Hollywood ingenuity Custer was jumped from a second lieutenant to a major general when General Winfield S. Scott absentmindedly wrote the name of the new West Point graduate on the wrong commission. The fact that commissions were always signed by the President after approval by the Senate was completely disregarded. Each of Custer's commissions may be seen at the Custer Battlefield Museum. None is signed by General Scott. All are signed by Presidents.

Another scene in this movie shows a palatial hallway in Judge Bacon's home with its winding staircase to the second floor. The hallway shown is larger than the original house. The most incongruous scene in the entire picture though is that showing Gen. Custer at a Monroe railway station before a towering mountain in the background. Monroe, situated between Detroit and Toledo on the shore of Lake Erie, is as flat as a tortilla.

This does not mean that the movie is not good entertainment. It just means that it is not accurate history. Of the many actors who have played the part of Custer none, in my opinion, has quite filled the role like Errol Flynn. And none has taken the part of Libbie like Olivia De Havilland. Of all the Custer movies, none has captured the popular imagination as this 1941 version has, for it is repeatedly seen on late hour television.

Even poets have used the Custer story to advantage. Henry Wadsworth Longfellow in "The Revenge of Rain-in-the-Face" perpetuated the story of Gen. Custer's death by telling how his heart was cut out in an act of revenge. The story began in 1873 when Gen. Custer and the Seventh Cavalry were acting as a protective escort for the surveying party of the Northern Pacific Railroad. While along the Yellowstone River, John Honsinger, the veterinary surgeon of the Seventh Cavalry, and Augustus Baliran, the regimental sutler, were captured by the Sioux and killed.

During the winter of 1874-75, the scout Lonesome Charles Reynolds overheard a young Sioux warrior relate how Rain-in-the-Face had boasted of killing two white men. The details left no room for doubt. Rain was responsible for the Honsinger and

Errol Flynn at the "Last Stand." Unquestionably Flynn's portrayal of Custer in Warner Brothers' "They Died With Their boots On" gave an impetus to the Custer story and its many legends.

Baliran deaths.

Lonesome Charlie immediately reported the facts to Gen. Custer who ordered Capt. Tom Custer and six soldiers to the Standing Rock Indian Agency to arrest Rain. This mission was successfully accomplished by Tom.

After Rain was placed in the Fort Lincoln guardhouse, he swore that some day he would cut Tom's heart out. Rain managed to escape when other prisoners cut a hole in the stockade wall. Two years later he took a prominent role in the Custer fight. An imaginative newspaperman conjured up a story describing how "Rain-in-the-Face cut the heart from Gen. Custer's body, put it on a pole and held a grand war dance about it."[6] This was thrilling stuff. The story quickly made the rounds of newspapers throughout the country. Gruesome details were given in the various versions. Most of the sensational early stories seemed to miss the point that Rain had threatened to cut out the heart of Tom Custer and had not mentioned that of the General.

Tom Custer was mutilated, horribly mutilated. As a matter of fact he was unrecognizable but for the close examination of Lieut. Edward Godfrey who found the tattooed letters T.W.C. on the arm of a body mutilated beyond recognition. The skull was crushed and most of the scalp removed. A number of arrows had been shot into the body. Capt. Benteen and Dr. Porter stated that the heart had not been removed. Godfrey was uncertain about that. Everyone agreed that the body was extensively mutilated, a condition that undoubtedly gave rise to the story that Rain-in-the-Face had carried out his threat.

Some claim Gen. Custer committed suicide yet there were no powder burns around the wound in his left breast, or the one in his left temple, either of which would have been fatal. Neither could have been made by a right-handed man, and Custer was that.

Robert M. Utley—a very thorough Custer battle historian and scholar—in discussing some of the accounts of those Indians who claim to have killed Custer, observed that: "So rapidly have the claims multiplied, that the number of "Indians who killed Custer" is now exceeded only by the number of 'sole white survivors' of the battle."[7]

It was some days after the battle the Indians learned that Custer had participated in it. They had been of the opinion they were fighting the soldiers they had defeated at the Rosebud one week earlier. At a distance they were unable to identify the leader of the battalion they were fighting. In all probability he would have been identified had he not had his hair cut short just before he had left Fort Lincoln. The Indians commonly had called him "Long Hair."

As Utley indicated, quite a number of Indians claimed the honor of firing the shot that killed Custer. It would have been impossible in the dust, confusion, and distance that prevailed, to determine who they were fighting. Sitting Bull admitted this while in exile in Canada.

It should be remembered that the day was extremely hot. The officers and men would have removed their outer clothing with its insignia. Prespiring, and covered with dust from that sandy soil, identification at even short distances would have been an impossibility. Both Sitting Bull and Curley observed that Custer was one of the very last to die, but his is in contrast with other Indian stories that claim he died early in the fight. The Indians were the only ones who would have known, and their stories were at variance.

Though Longfellow gave Rain-in-the-Face lasting and undeserved credit for finishing off Custer, an historian of note—Stanley Vestal—attempted to fasten all credit on a Sioux protege, White Bull. In the February, 1957 issue of *American Heritage Magazine,*[8] Vestal gave White Bull's verbatim account of his hand-to-hand account with Gen. Custer. As their affair of honor began, Custer threw his rifle at the charging chief without having first fired it, though he had aimed it as a bluff. Then grabbing the Indian's rifle, he tried to wrest it from him. This attempt was thwarted, according to White Bull, because he lashed Custer across the face several times with his quirt.

This part of the story is a bit difficult to accept when one considers that Custer, who was admittedly the stronger of the two, had grasped White Bull's rifle with both hands, yet the Indian was able to retain it with one hand while he used the other to wield his quirt. It sounds just a bit like one of Ned Buntline's Buffalo Bill yarns and more so when White Bull went on to say that Custer then drew his pistol, adding: "I wrenched it out of his hand and struck him with it three or four times on the head, knocked him over, shot him in the head and fired at his heart."[9] Yet none of the many who saw Custer just before he was buried made any mention of any violence done his body other than the two bullet holes that killed him. Lieut. Bradley, who was on the burial detail and gave a careful description of Custer as he appeared when found, stated that "Even the wounds that caused his death were scarcely discernable." It is difficult to believe that anyone struck across the face several times with a quirt, then pistol whipped three or four times, would not show evidence of abrasions or contusions.

It is even more diffficult to believe that Custer entered into any hand-to-hand fighting even though most Custer Battle art and motion pictures portray it. Hand-to-hand fighting on Custer Hill was extremely unlikely. The Indians greatly outnumbered the troopers. They had only to keep firing from a distance until the last soldier was accounted for.

Capt. Benteen counted the dead cavalry horses and the dead Indian ponies on the battlefield. It was his observation that there were only two dead Indian ponies. If there had been a mounted charge the defending troopers would have brought down a greater number of them.

Dr. Thomas B. Marquis, who had served as agency physician for the Northern Cheyennes in the early twenties, became well-acquainted with a number of Cheyennes who had participated in the Custer Battle. During his earliest association with them these old warriors, in answer to his query, would say: "Me see Custer—shoot—kill." At first he was overwhelmed with the discovery but after a number of these claims were made it was obvious there were just too many claimants. He concluded they were bragging or falsifying. It was not until he became proficient in communicating directly with them, for he had used interpreters previously, that he learned each one was saying to him: "Yes, I was at the battle. I saw the Custer soldiers, shot at them, helped in the killing of them. None of the Indians pretended to have seen Custer or to have recognized him.[10]

What Dr. Marquis did learn was that the Cheyennes had conferred upon a Cheyenne warrior the honor of representing all of those who had fought in the battle as the one who had killed Custer. By election this honorary status was conferred upon Brave Bear. After the old men of the tribe had dreamed and counciled they concluded that Brave Bear was the only warrior in the Custer Battle who had been in the Cheyenne camp on the Washita when Custer raided it in 1868, and had also been present in the spring of 1869 when Custer smoked the peace pipe and swore he would ever be friendly to the Cheyennes. It was ruled that Brave Bear's missile was the one that killed Custer. It could not be otherwise.

When confronted with the question, Brave Bear and a number of Cheyennes with him laughed when they learned that the whites were taking this information literally. They told Marquis: "None of the Indians ever knew who killed Custer. None of them even knew until long afterward that he was there."[11]

Many ask why General Custer ws not scalped or mutilated. As previosuly mentioned, a story had gone the rounds of the press that the Sioux had removed Custer's heart from his body and danced around it. The story made particular reference to Rain-in-the-Face. At this point there is doubt whether he even participated in the battle.[12]

Lieut. James H. Bradley, chief of scouts accompanying Col. Gibbon's column, was one of the first to see the appalling sight on Custer Hill. This occurred on the morning of June 27th. Later that day he guided Capt. Benteen to the scene. Benteen and two other officers of the Seventh Cavalry identified General Custer's body at that time. A short time later Bradley gave an eyewitness account.

In a letter published in the Helena (M.T.) *Herald,* July 25, 1876, Bradley said:

"Even the wounds that caused his death were scarcely discoverable, (though the body was entirely naked), so much so that when I afterwards asked the gentlemen whom I accompanied whether they had observed his wounds they were forced to say that they had not."

"Probably never did a hero who had fallen upon the field of battle appear so much to have died a natural death. His expression was rather that of a man who had fallen asleep and enjoyed peaceful dreams than that of one who had met his death amid such fearful scenes as that field had witnessed, the features being wholly without ghastliness or any impress of fear, horror or despair. He died as he lived—a hero—and excited the remark of those who had known him and saw him there, 'You could almost imagine him standing before you!' Such was Custer at the time of his burial, on the 28th of June, three days after the fighting which he had fallen, and I hope this assurance will dispose of the horrible tale of the mutilation and desecration of his remains."[13]

Fifty years later a story was told of a form of mutilation to Custer that Bradley could have missed. The story was told to Dr. Thomas B. Marquis by a Cheyenne woman, Kate Bighead, who had observed the Custer Hill fight. After informing her interrogator, Dr. Marquis, that neither she nor any of the Cheyenne warriors recognized Custer on the battlefield nor did they know he was there until they learned of it afterward at the forts and the Indian agencies, she went on to tell him:

"I learned something more about him from our people in Oklahoma. Two of those Southern Cheyenne women who had been in our camp at the Little Bighorn told of having been on the battlefield soon after the fighting ended. They saw Custer lying dead there. They had known him in the South. While they were looking at him some Sioux men came up and were about to cut up his body. The Cheyenne women, thinking of Me-o-tzi (Mon-ah-se-tah), made signs, 'He is a dead relative of ours,' but telling nothing more about him. So the Sioux cut off only one joint of a finger. The women then pushed the point of a sewing awl into each of his ears, into his head. This was done to improve his hearing, as it seemed he had not heard what our chiefs in the South said when he smoked the pipe with them. They told him then that if ever afterward he should break that peace promise and should fight the Cheyennes, the Everwhere Spirit would cause him to be killed."[14]

General Custer was not scalped. He was frequently called Long Hair by the Indians, but on this campaign his hair was short. Prior to leaving Fort Abraham Lincoln May 17, Libbie cut his hair. A practical soldier, he knew the value of a GI haircut while in the field. Photographs of him at this time evidence a balding at the temples. The short hair of a balding man would hardly tempt a scalping Indian.

Quite a number of Custer battle paintings and sketches show Custer or some of his officers wielding sabers in the throes of hand-to-hand combat. Trooper William C. Slaper of M Company, Seventh Cavalry, observed that "Attached to the expedition were four companies of the Second Cavalry, some artillery (Gatling guns) and some infantry. At the Power River, our wagons were all sent back. *Our sabers were also here boxed and returned; no one, not even an officer, retaining this weapon* (italics mine). The regimental band also was sent back.... On June 22d, we left our Powder River camp."[15]

You will observe the comment above regarding the wagons with the expedition. Some years ago while visiting Lincoln's New Salem, Illinois, I was quite impressed with a fine example of a Conestoga wagon drawn through the village by a team of oxen. The guide to our party explained that this wagon had been built by General Custer's father, Emanuel Custer, and that the wagon had been used by the General in his Western campaigns and that it had been with him in his last one.

The story was a little too big to swallow. Afterward, I took the young lady to one side and asked her for the source of her information. She remarked that her source for her comments was the printed manual provided by the State historian. A response to a letter of request to the State historian some years later mentioned that the wagon had been built in New Rumley, Ohio, by Emanuel Custer, in 1821—but apparently no copy of the manual was available. And so, another legend was born.

Emanuel Custer was born in 1806. He would have been 15 at the time he had completed the Consetoga wagon, rather youthful for such complex carpentry, blacksmithing and wheelwrithing. Also a rather useless task if it was intended to transport his family since he was not married for some years after that date. He married Matilida Viers in 1828.

The postcard photograph of the wagon that was sold at New Salem stated on the back that "This wagon was used a number of times by the Custer family crossing the continent." The Custer family left New Rumley, Ohio, only to travel to Tontogany, Ohio, near Toledo, and to Monroe, Michigan. No one in the Custer family had any recollection of any such wagon. The trip to either of these locations could hardly be considered "crossing the continent."

In the Columbus (Ohio) *Dispatch* of November 18, 1951, Laura Fenner provided some additional background on the wagon though she too had accepted the story that General Custer had used it in his Western campaigns as a supply wagon. It seems that Mr. F.P. McIntyre had purchased it to place in front of his Darrowville, Ohio, antique shop as an attention getter. Earlier it had been used in an Akron pioneer celebration then stored away in that city. He willed it to his brother, C.W. McIntyre, who had an antique shop in Jacksontown, 25 miles east of Columbus, and it was from him that the State of Illinois purchased it in 1945.

The McIntyres told Ms Fenner that "the old covered wagon carried the Custer family belongings across Ohio from new Rumley to Tontogany, and was used when the family moved to Monroe, Michigan, after the Civil War." As I mentioned previously, the Custer family in Monroe had no recollections of it. There were railroads not far from New Rumley going to Toledo, and to Detroit via Monroe.

Ms Fenner stated that "General Custer himself used the vehicle as a supply wagon in his various early Western campaigns, but it is believed that it was not taken the entire distance to Montana at the time of the massacre." It must be remarked that there is no evidence to substantiate this statement. Custer frequently did take along a cookstove and a Negro cook. This has been mentioned in the literature, but none had been made about taking his own wagon with him. There was no necessity for the army provided plenty for each of his campaigns.

Many stories have been circulated that General Custer's

Looking Down on the Dead. In the foreground are stone markers indicating where each trooper feel on Custer Hill. In the distance is the Custer Battlefield museum maintained by the National Park Service. Author's photo.

Custer Hill. Ca 1881 to 1886. The granite monument at top of hill displays the names of those who died there. The wooden stakes were the first indications where troopers fell. Courtesy of the Custer Battlefield National Monument.

death benefitted his wife through the payment of huge life insurance benefits to her. It has been determined that Custer had three insurance policies: one of $3,000 with the Equitable Assurance Company naming his parents as the beneficiaries;[16] one of an undisclosed amount with the Michigan Department of the Life Association of America with Libbie as beneficiary;[17] and another with the New York Life Insurance Company for $5,000 which was paid five months after the disaster to the sum of $4,750. On this last claim the company policy provided that if death occurred from "engaging in hostilities" the company would deduct 5% of the face of the policy.[18]

How many men were killed with Custer? How were they buried? Where were they buried? These are the questions most frequently asked about the officers and men who served with Custer that June 25th.

One of the first features to be seen as the visitor approaches the Custer Battlefield is the large number of marble headstones scattered individually and in groups. Each stone indicates the position of a soldier who has fallen in the battle.

On the crest of Custer Hill is an imposing pyramidal granite stone shaft on which is carved the names of all the known dead. It was erected in 1881 to replace a cordwood shaft that had been raised in 1879 over some of the human bones gathered from the battlefield. The cordwood memorial was capped with a small flag at the top. Once the granite memorial was in place a trench ten feet wide was dug around its base and in it were buried the bones and skeletons of Custer's men. Two years later an iron fence was erected around this area to prevent vandals from chipping away the stone shaft.[19]

Pamphlets prepared by the National Park Service and issued at the Custer Battlefield indicate that "Among the dead were Lt. Col. George A. Custer and every member of his immediate command of about 225 men." That, however, does not make it official for many others differ as to the number of dead. Robert M. Utley[20] offers a figure of 215. Capt. F.W. Benteen gave a body count of 203. Gen. A.H. Terry noted that there were 204. Lt. James Bradley counted 206. Sgt. John M.

Ryan said there were 207, while Lt. Edward S. Godfrey reported 212.

These variations weren't intended to confuse anyone. They were honest counts taken under very trying conditions. The wounded had to be taken care of first. It was several days before the dead could be disposed of.

Captain Myles Moylan, in a letter to Maggie Calhoun,[21] told her how each company of men were fanned out to sweep over the battle area in a search for the dead cavalrymen and that "positive orders were given that officers should not leave their respective companies unless special permission was granted them to do so in order that none of the bodies should be overlooked." It can be seen that every effort was made to arrive at a correct total though the figures quoted excluded (or included, as the case may be) some of the civilians and scouts found wiht the cavalrymen.

Gen. Terry used figures he received from Major Reno which were incomplete when he first obtained them. Capt. Benteen did not include a number found some distance to the north of the field. Sgt. Ryan and Lt. Bradley reported the finds made early on June 28. Lt. Godfrey seems to have included those found and buried in the Indian village. From time to time and over the years, skeletons of cavalrymen have been found at the periphery of the battle area—some at quite a distance. It appears that both Robert Utley and the Park Service have updated the earlier counts. These figures do not include the 55 men killed in the Reno Battle area. [22]

To identify all was an impossible task. The only attempt made to do so was that of identifying the officers. When this was done his name was placed in a cartridge shell which was pounded into a wooden stake driven into the ground at the head of the grave. The mutilation of the stripped bodies made identification extremely difficult.

In accounting for the numbers of men in each troop a check list had to be made from memory since the troop muster rolls had been taken by the Indians. All this was done on June 29, four days after the battle. According to Lt. Godfrey "there were only three or four spades in the whole command; axes, knives, table forks, tin cups, halves of canteens, were brought into use." The officers' bodies were the only ones given any sort of burial and that amounted only to covering each one with a thin layer of earth.

Just one year later Lt. Col. Michael V. Sheridan arrived at the Custer Battlefield with Capt. Henry J. Nowlan of the Seventh Cavalry and a company of his men ordered there by Gen. Phil Sheridan to return the dead officers to civilization, and to give the bodies of the enlisted men a proper burial. The remains of the officers were placed in pine boxes then transferred to Fort Keogh. The steamer *Fletcher* brought them down to Fort Lincoln for temporary interral await the arrival of caskets from Chicago after which they were shipped to their final destinations.[23]

General Custer's remains were reintered in the cemetery of the United States Military Academy, West Point, N.Y. Capt. Myles Keogh was reburied in the Martin Plot, Fort Hill Cemetery, Auburn, N.Y. Lt. W. W. Cooke was reburied in the Winer Plot, Hamilton, Ontario, Canada. Lt. H. G. Hodgson was reintered in the Laurel Hill Cemetery, Philadelphia, Pa. Surgeon J. M. DeWolfe was transferred to Norwalk, Ohio. Lt. W. Van W. Reilly was sent to Washington, D. C., cemetery unknown. Capt. Tom Custer, Capt. George W. Yates, Lt. A. E. Smith and Lt. James Calhoun were reintered in the Fort Leavenworth National Cemetery, Leavenworth, Kans. Lt. Donald McIntosh was also reintered with his fellow officers at Ft. Leavenworth, but was removed to the Arlington National Cemetery in 1909.

In the latter part of the summer of 1877, David Reed, the father of Harry (Autie) Armstrong Reed, left Monroe for the Custer Battlefield to exhume the bodies of young Autie Reed and Boston Custer. The remains were returned to Monroe and buried in the Woodland Cemetery. Lt. John J. Crittenden, at the request of his parents, was buried where he fell, remainng there until on Sept. 11, 1931, the Adjutant General's office ordered it exhumed and reburied in the Custer Battlefield National Cemetery. The bodies of Dr. Porter and Lieutenants H. M. Harrington and J. G. Sturgis never were found.[24]

From time to time human bones have been found in the area. In almost every instance they have been identified as cavalrymen. In 1926 a skeleton "of what was presumed to have

been one of Major Reno's troops, killed in the opening phase of the
battle in the river valley, was unearthed by a road construction
crew," about three miles from the Custer Battlefield near the
Garryowen store. On June 26, 1926, at the time of the fiftieth
anniversary, a ceremony was conducted over the grave of this
unknown soldier located near the site his remains were found.[25]
Erosion and other factors such as construction projects have
revealed skeletal remains from time to time, and as late as
1958.[26] Since all the missing men have not been recovered it is
reasonable to assume that others may be discovered in time.

As one views the scattered marble slabs on Custer Hill the
isolation of Custer's small battalion is very apparent. Though
each marble marker states that a soldier "fell here" there is no
certainty as to where he originally fell. All of the dead
cavalrymen were stripped and could have been moved in the
process. Indians often dragged wounded or dead enemies behind
their running horses, a lariat being used for that purpose. When
tired of the game the warrior would release the body with no
thought of returning it to the point of origin.[27]

Over the years there has been controversy among students of
the battle as to the location of the marble markers. Though there
are some inaccuracies in their placement most of them have been
placed on the best knowledge available. Even so, they serve
admirably in the study and contemplations of that appalling
disaster on the Little Big Horn. One may be certain they are
remarkably close to the spot each man was killed.[28]

Standing above the headstones on Custer Hill for the first
time, after having read the accounts of the Last Stand, a mental
vision of the action unrolls as if in replay. If you haven't visited
the Custer Battlefield you haven't had this experience. Beware
then, when you make your first visit, for you too may become a
victim of this dread disease—Custeritis. There is no known cure.

Notes

Chapter One

[1]Frederick Van De Water:*Glory-Hunter,* N.Y., 1934. Indians did not scalp the heroic dead.

[2]Nelson A. Miles: *Serving The Republic,* N.Y., 1911, p. 192.

[3]Talcott E. Wing: *History of Monroe County, Michigan,* N.Y., 1890, p. 318.

[4]Monroe *Commercial,* June 8, 1871.

[5]*Ibid.,* June 15, 1871.

[6]This amount would not have been considered huge.

[7]Libbie Bacon's Journal, Col. B.C.W. Custer collection.

[8]Marguerite Merington: *The Custer Story,* N.Y., 1950, p. 49.

[9]The source was Libbie Bacon's Journal, Col. B.C.W. Custer collection.

[10]Col. George G. Briggs to Mrs. G.A. Custer, July 2, 1906, letter in author's collection.

[11]Michigan Custer Memorial Association minutes. Ed Greening collection.

[12]*Ibid.,* January 16, 1907.

[13]William O. Lee to Mrs. G.A. Custer, February 5, 1907. BCWC collection.

[14]Frederic A. Nims to Mrs. G.A. Custer, June 19, 1907. BCWC collection.

[15]Gov. Fred M. Warner to Mrs. Custer, August 8, 1907. BCWC collection.

[16]George G. Briggs to Mrs. G.A. Custer, October 28, 1907. BCWC collection.

[17]George G. Briggs to Mrs. G.A. Custer, November 20, 1907. BCWC collection.

[18]George G. Briggs to Mrs. G.A. Custer, December 2, 1907. BCWC collection.

[19]*Unveiling Ceremonies, Custer Equestrian Monument,* Monroe, Mich., June 4, 1910, p. 5.

[20]Elizabeth B. Custer: *Account of the Monument Unveiling,* June 8, 1910. Original manuscript in author's collection.

[21]*Unveiling Ceremonies,* pp. 25-26.

[22]Monroe *Evening News,* June 16, 1923.

[23]*Ibid.,* The Hogarth and Phinney homes were just across the street from the track.

[24]Monroe *Evening News,* June 18, 1923.

[25]*Ibid,* June 22, 1923.

Chapter Two

[1]Chicago *Daily News*, July 1, 1938.

[2]Lawrence A. Frost: *The Custer Album*, Seattle, 1964, pp. 61, 67.

[3]Frederick Whittaker: *A Complete Life of Gen. George A. Custer*, N.Y., 1876, pp. 307-308.

[4]Charles J. Brill: *Conquest of the Southern Plains*, Oklahoma City, 1938, pp. 44-45.

[5]See illustrations in *The Custer Album*.

[6]James H. Kidd: *Personal Recollections of a Cavalryman*, Ionia, Mich. 1908, pp. 129-30.

[7]*Official Records*, War of the Rebellion, Washington, D.C., 1893, Vol. XLIII, Pt II, pp. 909-10, letter of October 29, 1864.

[8]*Ibid*, p. 910.

[9]O.R., Vol. XLIII, Pt. II, p. 920.

[10]Charles Russell (editor): *The Memoirs of Colonel John S. Mosby*, Bloomington, 1959, pp. 300-302.

[11]*Ibid*, pp. 368, 372.

[12]O.R. Series I, Vol. XLIII, Pt. I, p. 811.

[13]*Ibid*, p. 822.

[14]See Jay Monaghan: *The Life of General George Armstrong Custer*, Boston, 1959, pp. 220-223.

[15]J. J. Williamson: *Mosby's Rangers*, N.Y., 1909, p. 240.

[16]*Ibid*, p. 241; O.R., Vol. XLIII, Pt. II, p. 920.

[17]Williamson, pp. 240, 242.

[18]*Ibid*, pp. 239-40.

[19]O.R., Series I, Vol. XLIII, Pt. I, pp. 99, 463.

[20]Jubal Early: *A Memoir of the Last Year of the War for Independence*, Lynchburg, 1867, pp. 94-95.

[21]P. H. Sheridan: *Personal Memoirs*, N.Y., 1888, Vol. II, pp. 40-45.

[22]*Ibid*, p. 47.

[23]*Ibid*, p. 51.

[24]Williamson, p. 289.

[25]*Ibid*.

[26]New York *Times*, November 10, 12, 1864.

[27]Williamson, pp. 290-91.

[28]*Ibid*, p. 293.

[29]*Ibid*, p. 293.

[30]*Ibid*, p. 277.

[31]*Ibid*, p. 288.

[32]*op. cit.* p. 303.

[33]O.R. I, Vol. XLIII, Pt. II, p. 682.

[34]*Ibid*, p. 679.

[35]*Ibid*, pp. 671-72.

Chapter Three

[1]George A. Forsyth: *Thrilling Days in Army Life,* N.Y., 1900, p. 6.

[2]Robert G. Athearn: *Sherman and the Settlement of the West,* Norman, 1956, p. 223.

[3]*Ibid,* p. 224.

[4]*Ibid.*

[5]*Ibid,* p. 225.

[6]Brill, pp. 156-161.

[7]Brill, pp. 156-161.

[7]40th Cong., 3rd Sess., *Senate Exec. Doc.* 18, 9t. 2, P.H. Sheridan to W. A. Nichols, Jan. 1, 1869.

[8]*The Benteen-Goldin Letters on Custer*—Edited by J. M. Carroll, N.Y., 1974, pp. 100, 229, 252; W. A. Graham: *Custer Myths,* Harrisburg, 1953, pp. 212-13.

[9]P. H. Sheridan: *Record of Engagements with Hostile Indians,* Chicago, 1882, p. 18.

[10]40th Cong., 3rd Sess., *Senate Exec. Doc.* No. 18. P. H. Sheridan to W. T. Sherman, November 29, 1868.

[11]Charles F. Bates: *Custer's Indian Battles,* Bronxville, 1936, p. 15.

[12]*Ibid.*

[13]*Ibid,* p. 16.

[14]Mari Sandoz: *Cheyenee Autumn,* N.Y., 1953, p. xvii.

[15]Brill, p. 46.

[16]Elizabeth B. Custer: *Following the Guidion,* N.Y., 1890, p. 96.

[17]*Ibid,* p. 49.

[18]*Benteen-Goldin Letters.*

[19]Brill, p. 45.

[20]*Ibid,* p. 14.

[21]Brill, p. 41.

[22]*Proceedings of a General Court-Martial Which Convened At West Point,* N.Y., June 29, 1861, *Special Orders* No. 167, National Archives, Record Group No. 153.

[23]Brill, p. 44.

[24]*Annie Jones File;* a sworn statement of March 14, 1864, National Archives.

[25]*Annie Jones File,* RG 109, National Archives.

[26]*Ibid.*

[27]*Ibid.*

[28]*Ibid.*

Chapter Four

[1]G.A. Custer: "War Memoirs," *Galaxy Magazine,* Vol. 21, No. 4 (April 1876), p. 454.

[2]John M. Carroll: "Was Custer Really The Goat of His Class?" An unpublished manuscript.

[3]Custer: "War Memoirs," April 1876, p. 455.

[4]Court-Martial proceedings under Special Orders No. 167, National Archives, Record Group No. 153.

[5]Robert G. Athearn: *William Tecumseh Sherman* and the *Settlement of the West*, Norman, 1956, pp. 130-131.

[6]*Difficulties with the Indian Tribes*, 41st Cong., 2 sess., H. R. Exec. Doc. No. 240, p. 132, Nov. 28, 1864.

[7]*Ibid*, pp. 68-69.

[8]*Ibid*, p. 132.

[9]G.A. Custer: *My Life on the Plains, 1874*, N.Y., p. 22.

[10]*Difficulties with Indian Tribes*, p. 60.

[11]40th Cong., 2 Sess., House Exec. Doc. 1, p. 35.

[12]Custer: *My Life*, pp. 70-71; Theo. R. Davis: "A Summer on the Plains," *Harper's Monthly Magazine*, Vol. XXXVI (February, 1868), loc. cit., p. 306; Mrs. Frank Montgomery: "Fort Wallace and its Relation to the Frontier," *Kansas Historical Collections*, Vol. XVII (1928), loc. cit., p. 217.

[13]L. A. Frost: *The Court-Martial of General George Armstrong Custer*, Norman, 1968, pp. 69-70.

[14]Custer: *My Life*, p. 77.

[15]*Fort Wallace, Record of Deceased Citizens*, pp. 110-111; *Fort Wallace, Record of Deceased Soldiers*, pp. 48-51. Captain Myles W. Keogh, 7th U.S. Cavalry, in the *Post Return of Fort Wallace, Kansas* for the month of July, wrote: "Bvt. Maj. Genl. Custer arrived at this Post on the 13th of July with his command and encamped 3 miles above the Post; Cholera has made its appearance in the camp causing a considerable number of deaths daily; no cases have as yet occurred at this Post and it is expected that the disease will abate."

[16]Desertions in the 7th Cavalry from April 19 to July 13, 1867 were 156. See Frost: *Court-Martial*, pp. 210-211.

[17]Martha L. Sternberg: *George Miller Sternberg*, Chicago, 1920, pp. 11-12. Dr. Sternberg reported that at Fort Harker "there were, from June 28 to August 1, 47 cases (of cholera) with 32 deaths among the troops, besides a number of cases among civilizan employees." Dr. Sternberg's wife was among the first civilian victims. She died July 15, 1867. A study of the epidemic revealed that cholera was introduced by black troops who had arrived from Jefferson Barracks, Mo., where there were 256 cases with 134 deaths.

[18]*Harper's Weekly*, August 3, 1867, p. 481.

[19]*General Court-Martial of Captain Robert M. West at Fort Leavenworth, Kansas*, December 23, 1867. National Archives.

[20]Frost: *Court-Martial*, p. 156.

[21]*Ibid*, pp. 191-93.

[22]Marguerite Merrington: *The Custer Story*, N.Y., 1950, pp. 211-12.

[23]Frost: *Court-Martial*, pp. 235-236.

[24]*Ibid*, p. 246.

Chapter Five

[1]Wing, p. 318.

[2]All of General Custer's commissions listed are in the files of the Custer Battlefield National Monument. Also in the files is a letter from Maj. Gen. Phil Sheridan to Secretary of War Stanton, dated April 6, 1866, requesting that General Custer be appointed "Colonel of Cavalry upon the reorganization of the Army." He added to the request that "The record of this officer is so conspicuous as to render its recital by me unnecesary. I ask this appointment as a reward to one of the most gallant and efficient officers that ever served under me." It is obvious this request was written well before Pres. Johnson's "swing around the circle."

[3]Custer was dropped in rank from that of a Major General to that of a regular army Captain.

[4]Robert M. Utley: *Frontier Regulars,* N.Y., 1973, p. 13, 37.

[5]*Ibid.*

[6]J. M. Lee to Mrs. Eliz. B. Custer, Madison Barracks, Sackett's Harbor, N.Y., June 27, 1897. E.B. Custer collection, CBNM.

[7]E.B. Custer collection, CBNM.

[8]*Ibid.*

[9]*Ibid.*

[10]John M. Bulkley: "As a Classmate Saw Custer," N.Y. *POST,* May 28, 1910.

[11]*Ibid.*

[12]Eliz. B. Custer: "Account of the Monument Unveiling," June 8, 1910.

[13]*Ibid.*

[14]*Ibid.*

Chapter Six

[1]O.R., Vol. XXVII, Part III, p. 923.

[2]Gen. James H. Kidd, "Address," *Michigan at Gettysburg,* Detroit, 1889, p. 143.

[3]*Ibid.*

[4]*Ibid,* pp. 144-145.

[5]*Ibid,* p. 145.

[6]Burke Davis: *Jeb Stuart; The Last Cavalier,* N.Y., 1957, p. 337.

[7]George B. Davis, "Operations of the Cavalry in the Gettysburg Campaign," *Cavalry Studies From Two Great Wars,* Kansas City, Mo., 1896, p. 264.

[8]James H. Kidd: *Personal Recollections of a Cavalryman,* Ionia, Mich., 1908, p. 153.

[9]*Ibid,* pp. 154-155.

[10]Gen. L. S. Trowbridge, "Address," *Michigan at Gettysburg,* p. 38; William Brooke—Rawle: *Gregg's Cavalry Fight at Gettysburg,* Phila., 1884, pp. 15-16.

[11]John Robertson: *Michigan in the War,* Lansing, 1880, p. 410.

[12]O.R., Series I, Vol. XLVI, Part I, p. 1109; Sheridan: *Memoirs,* Vol. II, p. 188, states that one of his scouts informed him there were four trains of cars; F.C. Newhall: *With General Sheridan in Lee's Last Campaign,* Phila., 1866, pp. 203-204.

[13]Col. A.M. Randol, Philadelphia *Weekly Times,* July 26, 1879, cited by Dr. Frank P. Cauble: *The Battle of Appomattox Station,* April 8, 1865, National

Park Service, Appomattox, Va., p. 3. Randol was of the opinion that Custer, if successful, "expected to add to his reknown and glory, and if not, Merritt would soon be up to help him out of the scrape."

[14]Cauble: *Battle of Appomatox Station*, p. 3.

[15]Morris Schaff: *The Sunset of the Confederacy*, Boston, 1912, p. 192.

[16]H. E. Tremain: *Last Hours of Sheridan's Cavalry*, N.Y., 1904, p. 217. "It is a doubtful principle, but one held by some of our most successful cavalry leaders, that it is the province of cavalry never to hesitate in making an attack; that no time should be lost in cautious reconnoitering. If anything is to be gained, the more precipitate and unexpected the attack, the greater its probable success. The changes in its favor greatly overbalance the risks of serious disaster incurred by attacking an enemy with a position and force uncertainly ascertained, and should the movement prove injudicious, a skillful general will usually discover it in time to prevent any great misfortune to a well-disciplined cavalry. It was in strict accordance with views of this character that Sheridan and his generals pursued this stirring campaign." pp. 220-221.

[17]Newhall: *With Gen. Sheridan*, p. 201.

[18]*Ibid*, p. 200.

[19]Schaff, p. 194.

[20]Tremain, p. 230

[21]*Ibid*

Chapter Seven

[1]John Carroll: *Custer in Texas*, N.Y., 1975.

[2]Frederic F. Van De Water: *Glory Hunter*, N.Y., 1934, p. 126.

[3]Whittaker, p. 313.

[4]Tremain: *Last Hours*, p. 319; O. L. Hein: *Memories of Long Ago*, N.Y., 1925, pp. 36-38.

[5]Sheridan: *Personal Memoirs*, Vol. II, pp. 209-228.

[6]Charles H. Lothrop: *History of First Regiment Iowa Cavalry*, Lyons, Iowa, 1890, p. 230.

[7]*Ibid*, p. 219.

[8]*Ibid*, pp. 243-293.

[9]Elizabeth B. Custer: *Tenting on the Plains*, N.Y., 1887, pp. 100-106.

[10]*Ibid*, p. 114.

[11]Carroll: *The Benteen-Golden Letters on Custer and His Last Battle*, N.Y., 1974.

[12]Charles F. Bates: *Custer's Indian Battles*, N.Y., 1936, p. 16.

[13]*Ibid*.

[14]*Ibid*, Benteen stated that he had written the letter to William J. DeGresse of St. Louis, from Fort Cobb, I.T. DeGresse had been a captain in Benteen's regiment, the 6th Missouri Cavalry, during the Civil War. Benteen reported that both Tom Custer and W. W. Cooke heard him admit he had written it, if so, neither reported that to Gen. Custer. See *Benteen Goldin Letters:* Edited by John Carroll, pp. 266-67. It is a fact that Custer knew nothing of Elliott's leaving the battlefield

until well after the engagement had concluded. Custer sent out search parties for Elliott all that afternoon. The only conclusion that could be reached, if Elliott had not reached the wagon train, was that he and his command were dead. To continue a search for the dead would have endangered the entire command.

[15]Bates: *Custer's Indian Battles,* p. 16.

[16]*Ibid,* p. 22.

[17]*Ibid,* p. 8. Letter was written to Sr. Romero, Mexican Minister to U.S.

[18]G.A. Custer: "War Memoirs," *Galaxy Magazine,* Vol. 21, No. 4 (April, 1876) p. 454.

[19]Carroll: "Was Custer Really the Goat of His Class?" An address given before The Little Big Horn Associates at Louisville, Kentucky, October, 1974.

[20]Milton Ronsheim: *The Life of General Custer,* Cadiz, Ohio, 1929, p. 8.

[21]*Ibid,* p. 7; Morris Schaff: *The Spirit of Old West Point,* N.Y., 1907, p. 67.

[22]Letter of Brig. Gen. Evan A. Andruss to Mrs. Libbie Custer, Sept. 27, 1905. Mrs. E. B. Custer collection, CGNM.

[23]A. Noel Blakeman: *Personal Recollections of the War of the Rebellion,* N.Y., 1897, p. 194.

[24]Joseph P. Farley: *West Point in the Early Sixties,* Troy, N.Y., 1902, p. 21.

[25]James H. Wilson: *Under the Old Flag,* N.Y., 1912, Vol. 1, p. 101.

[26]Farley, p. 78.

[27]Merington, p. 8.

[28]Schaff, pp. 193-195.

[29]Letter of G.A. Custer to Minnie St. John, from West Point, August 7, 1857. Author's collection.

Chapter Eight

[1]Capt. Mike Koury: Address at annual meeting of Little Big Horn Associates, Louisville, Ky., Nov. 2, 1974.

[2]George E. Hyde: *Red Cloud's Folk,* Norman, 1937, p. 51.

[3]John Gibbon: "Hunting Sitting Bull," *American Catholic Quarterly,* Vol. 11, No. 3 (October, 1877) p. 69.

[4]Robert M. Utley: *Frontier Regulars, The United States Army and the Indian, 1866-1890,* N.Y., 1973, p. 241; *Annual Report of the General of the Army for 1876,* p. 8.

[5]General Sherman to General Sheridan, October 7, 1872, Library of Congress.

[6]General Sherman to General Sheridan, September 26, 1872, LC.

[7]*Annual Report, Commissioner of Indian Affairs, 1872,* Wash., 1872, p. 9.

[8]42 Cong., 3 sess., House Exec. Doc. 1.

[9]43 Cong., 2 sess., House Exec. Doc. 2, p. 24.

[10]G.A. Custer to P. H. Sheridan, April 27, 1874, *Calhoun Diary* (unpublished manuscript).

[11]Hyde, p. 217.

[12]Gen. Sherman's August 3, 1874 endorsement to Gen. Terry's letter of July 27, 1874. National Archives, Roll 152, Letters received, Adjutant General's Office.

[13]Telegram of Acting Assistant Adjutant General Smith to Capt. J. D. Poland, August 27, 1874, Bismarck. Author's collection.

[14]*Annual Report, General of the Army,* 1876. Wash., 1876, p. 146.

[15]Harry H. Anderson: "A Challenge to Brown's Sioux Indian Wars Thesis, *Montana Magazine of Western History,* Vol. 12, No. 1 (January, 1962), p. 44.

[16]J. Leonard Jennewein: *Black Hills Booktrails,* Mitchell, S.D., 1962, pp. 1, 5.

[17]Report of the Special Commission Appointed to Investigate the Affairs of the Red Cloud Agency, July, 1875, Wash., 1875.

[18]John G. Bourke: *On The Border With Crook,* N.Y., 1891, p. 244.

[19]Utley: *Frontier Regulars,* p. 247.

[20]*Ibid.*

[21]Anderson: *A Challenge,* p. 48.

[22]George W. Manypenny: *Our Indian Wards,* Cincinnati, 1880, pp. 308-309.

[23]*Annual Report, General of the Army,* (1876), pp. 9-10.

[24]*Ibid,* p. 9.

[25]Talcott E. Wing: *History of Monroe County, Michigan,* N.Y., 1890, p. 318.

[26]George A. Custer: *My Life on the Plains,* Norman, 1962, pp. 166-169. Custer presents an interesting insight of graft in the Indian Bureau.

[27]Hyde, pp. 253, 256-257.

[28]*Ibid,* p. 265.

[29]John Finerty: *Warpath and Bivouac,* Chicago, 1890, p. 181.

Chapter Nine

[1]Edward S. Godfrey: "Custer's Last Battle," *Century Magazine,* January, 1892, p. 362.

[2]Charles F. Bates: *Custer's Indian Battles,* Bronxville, 1936, p. 29.

[3]Alfred H. Terry: "Report of November 21, 1876." *Annual Report, General of the Army* (1876) Wash., 1876, p. 107.

[4]Robert P. Hughes: "The Campaign Against The Sioux in 1876," *Journal of the Military Institution of the U.S.,* January, 1896, p. 22.

[5]Bates, pp. 29-30.

[6]Jesse Brown and A. M. Williard: *The Black Hills Trails,* Rapid City, 1924, p. 143; Fred Dustin: *The Custer Tragedy,* Ann Arbor, 1939, pp. 62-63.

[7]Elizabeth B. Custer: *Boots and Saddles,* N.Y., 1885, pp. 311-12.

[8]Terry: Report of Nov. 21, 1876, p. 107.

[9]*Ibid.*

[10]John Gibbon: "Last Summer's Expedition Against The Sioux And Its Great Catastrophe," *American Catholic Quarterly Review,* April, 1877, p. 292.

[11]William A. Graham: *The Story of the Little Big Horn,* Harrisburg, 1945, p. 16.

[12]James H. Bradley: "Journal of Lieut. James H. Bradley," *Contributions to the Historical Society of Montana,* Vol. II, Helena, 1896, p. 215.

[13]Bates, p. 31.

[14]Godfrey, pp. 363-364.

[15]Bates, p. 31.

[16]"Diary of Matthew Carroll," *Contributions to the Historical Society of Montana,* Vol. II, Helena, 1896, p. 233.

[17]Edgar I. Stewart: *Custer's Luck,* Norman, 1955, pp. 249-50.

[18]Nelson A. Miles: *Serving The Republic,* N.Y., 1911, p. 186; Lawrence Frost: "Custer's Lost Orders—Found!" *Westerner Magazine,* March, 1971, pp. 20-25, 58-62; Bates, p. 31; Stewart, pp. 250-251.

[19]Miles, p. 188.

[20]Stewart, p. 249.

[21]Miles, p. 188.

[22]William A. Graham: *The Reno Court of Inquiry,* Pacific Palisades, 1951, Vol. I, p. 19.

[23]Godfrey, p. 369.

[24]Graham: *Court of Inquiry,* p. 75.

[25]Godfrey, p. 371.

[26]Stewart, p. 360.

[27]Graham: *Court of Inquiry,* p. 161.

[28]Stewart, p. 362. For details and comprehensive reference relating to Reno's fight, Stewart should be consulted, pp. 343-79.

[29]*Ibid,* p. 372.

[30]Graham: *Story,* p. 46.

[31]Bates, p. 32.

[32]*Annual Report of the General,* p. 126.

[33]Graham: *Story,* p. 58.

[34]*Ibid,* p. 64.

[35]Charles Kuhlman: *Legend Into History; The Custer Mystery,* Harrisburg, 1951.

[36]*Ibid,* p. 160.

[37]*Ibid,* pp. 166-169.

[38]*Ibid,* p. 171.

[39]*Ibid,* p. 172; James McLaughlin: *My Friend The Indian,* N.Y., 1910, p. 171.

[40]Kuhlman, p. 177.

Chapter Ten

[1]"Mangement of The War Department," 44th Cong., lst sess., H.R. Report No. 799, p. 1.

[2]*Ibid,* p. 152.

[3]Frederick F. Van de Water: *Glory Hunter,* N.Y., 1934, pp. 275-277.

[4]Lawrence A. Frost: U.S. *Grant Album,* Seattle, 1966, pp. 160-161.

[5]"Trial of William W. Belknap," 44th Cong., 1st sess., 1876, pp. 238-241.

[6]H.R. Report No. 799, pp. 153-154.

[7]*Ibid,* p. 154.

[8]*Ibid,* p. 162.

[9]*Ibid,* p. 163.

[10]Frost: *Grant Album,* pp. 161-162; Frost: *Custer Album,* Pp. 148-149.

[11]*Ibid.*

[12]Don C. Seitz: *The Dreadful Decade,* Indianapolis, 1926, p. 261.
[13]*Report of the General of the Army—1876,* Wash., 1875, pp. 8-9.
[14]*Ibid,* p. 10.
[15]*Ibid,* pp. 107-108.
[16]*Ibid,* p. 108.
[17]*Reno Court of Inquiry—1879.*
[18]E. S. Godfrey: "Custer's Last Battle," *Century Magazine,* January, 1892, pp. 365-366.
This eye-witness account unquestionably is the most accurate, the most complete, and the most authentic of Custer's last battle. Godfrey, as a lieutenant at the time, served under Major Reno.
[19]*Ibid,* p. 368.
[20]*Ibid,* p. 383.
[21]*Report, General of the Army—1876,* p. 125.
[22]*Contributions, Historical Society of Montana,* Vol. II. Helena, 1896, p. 233.
[23]James McLaughlin: *My Friend The Indian,* N.Y., 1910, pp. 133-134.
[24]Wm. A. Graham: *The Custer Myth,* Harrisburg, Pa., 1953, pp. 55-56; Frost: "Custer's Lost Orders," pp. 20-25.
[25]Wm. A. Graham: *The Story of The Little Big Horn,* Harrisburg, Pa., 1945, pp. 115-117; Graham: Myths, p. 156.
[26]E. A. Brininstool: *Troopers with Custer,* Harrisburg, Pa., 1952, pp. 275-286.
[27]Lawrence A. Frost: *General Custer's Libbie,* Seattle, 1976, pp. 709.
[28]Cyrus T. Brady: *Indian Fights and Fighters,* N.Y., 1904, pp. 391-395.
[29]R. W. Barkley to Mrs. E. B. Custer, Dec. 12, 1904, E. B. Custer collection, CGNM.
[30]Robert P. Hughes: "The Campaign Against The Sioux," *Journal of the Military Service Institution,* January, 1896.
[31]Frost: "Custer's Lost Orders," p. 60.

Chapter Eleven

[1]Graham: *Myths,* pp. 279-282, 312, 315.
[2]Lloyd J. Overfield II: *The Little Big Horn—1876,* Glendale, Col., 1971, p. 68.
[3]*Ibid,* p. 37.
[4]Edgar I. Stewart: Louis *Republican,* June 29-30, 1876.
[5]Ibid, p. 239.
[6]Charles Kuhlman: *Did Custer Disobey Orders,* Harrisburg, 1957.
[7]D. S. Stanley: *Personal Memoirs,* Cambridge, Mass., 1917, p. 239. Stanley refers to Custer's "old negro woman, and castiron cooking stove" which seemed to be the cause of delays each morning because of extensive packing.
[8]Graham: *Myths,* p. 280; Nelson A. Miles: *Personal Recollections,* N.Y., 1896, pp. 204-205.
[9]Mari Sandoz: *The Battle of the Little Big Horn,* N.Y., 1966, pp. 54-55.
[10]O. G. Libby: *The Arikara Narrative,* Bismarck, 1920, pp. 62-82.
[11]Wayne Andrews (editor): *Concise Dictionary of American History,* N.Y.

1962, p. 140; St. Louis *Republican*, June 29-30, 1876.

[12]St. Louis *Republican*, June 25, 1876.

[13]Graham: *Myths*, p. 8.

[14]John B. Lundstrom: "George Armstrong Custer; The Making of a Myth," *Lore*, Summer, 1973, p. 109.

[15]George B. McClellan: *McClellan's Own Story*, N.Y., 1887, p. 365.

[16]Marguerite Merington: *The Custer Story*, N.Y., 1950, pp. 118-119.

[17]Charles G. DuBois: *Kick The Dead Lion*, Billings, 1961, Section III.

[18]*Ibid.*

[19]Graham: *Myths*, E. S. Godfrey to R. G. Carter letter of April 14, 1925, pp. 318-319.

[20]Original Communication, CBNM.

Chapter Twelve

[1]Charles Kuhlman: *Massacre Survivor*, Fort Collins, Colo., 1982.

[2]*Ibid.*

[3]Graham: *Myths*, pp. 353-357.

[4]Edward S. Luce: *Keogh, Commanche and Custer*, Dedham, Mass., 1939, pp. 65-70; Joseph M. Hanson: *The Conquset of the Missouri*, N.Y., 1946, pp. 296-297.

[5]Luce: *Keogh*, p. 77.

[6]New York *Herald*, July 13, 1876.

[7]Robert M. Utley: *Custer and the Great Controversy*, Los Angeles, 1962, p. 132.

[8]Stanley Vestal: "The Man Who Killed Custer," *American Heritage*, (Feb. 1957), Vol. VIII, No. 2; Stanley Vestal: *Sitting Bull*, Norman, 1957, pp. 170-171.

[9]Vestal: *Sitting Bull*, p. 171.

[10]Thomas B. Marquis: *Which Indian Killed Custer?* Hardin, Mont., 1933, p. 1.

[11]*Ibid.*, p. 4-5.

[12]Edgar I. Stewart (editor): *The March of the Montana Column*, Norman, 1961, p. 172.

[13]*Ibid.*, p. 173.

[14]Thomas B. Marquis: *She Watched Custer's Last Battle*, Hardin, Montana, 1933, p. 8.

[15]E. A. Brininstool: *A Trooper with Custer*, Columbus, O., 1926, p. 25.

[16]Lawrence A. Frost: *General Custer's Libbie*, Seattle, 1976, p. 572-573.

[17]*Army & Navy Journal*, Dec. 23, 1876, L.B. Custer letter to Mr. F.O. Davenport.

[18]Bruce R. Liddic: "Life Insurance and the Seventh," *Little Big Horn Associates Newsletter*, Vol. III, No. 2b (Summer, 1969), pp. 14-15; "Insurance Salesmanship," *Montana Post*, Vol. 7, No. 3, (May, 1969), p. 3; letter of V. deKanel, March 5, 1969.

[19]Don Rickey Jr.: *History of Custer Battlefield*, Billings, 1967, pp. 65-66.

[20]Robert M. Utley: *Custer Battlefield Historical Handbook Series*, No. 1 Wash., 1969, p. 37.

[21]Letter of Capt. Myles Moylan to Mrs. Maggie Calhoun, Dec. 21, 1876. Col. Brice C. W. Custer collection.

[22]R. L. Nelson, Seattle, Wash., provided considerable assistance but is in no way responsible for my conclusions.

[23]Graham: *Myth*, p. 373-375.

[24]List of burial places, Sept. 16, 1945, E. S. Luce, Supt., Custer Battlefield National Monument, with some additions and corrections by R. L. Nelson, John S. Manion Jr., and the author.

[25]Rickey: *History*, p. 82.

[26]*Ibid*, p. 55.

[27]Thomas B. Marquis: *Custer Soldiers Not Buried*, Hardin, Mont., 1933, p. 7.

[28]Kuhlman: *Legend*, pp. XI-XVIII.

Index

Adams, Mary (Maria): 160, 199, 201
Alger, Col. Russell: 112
American Numismatic Society: 92
Andrew, Gov. John C.: 72, 135
Appomattox Court House (Va.): 40-41, 117-118, 120, 125, 237n
Arickaree Fork (Republican River): 58
Arkansas: 57
Arkansas River: 79
Armitage, Mrs. George: 33
Augur, Gen. Christopher C.: 88
Averell, William W.: 51

Bacon, Albert: 18
Bacon, Judge Daniel S.: 8, 16, 19, 219
Bacon, Libbie: see Mrs. G.A. Custer
Baker, Col. L.C.: 72, 73
Baliran, Augustus: 219, 221
Barker, K.C.: 103
Barkley, R.W.: 194
Barnitz, Capt. Alfred: 62
Bates, Col. Charles F.: 132
Bayard, Thomas F.: 203
Bear Butte (Dakota Territory): 143, 151
Beech Point School (Ohio): 92
Belknap, Sec. W.W.: 95, 104, 149, 180, 181, 184
Benet, Lt. Stephen: 3, 76, 77
Bennett, James Gordon: 202-203
Benteen, Capt. Frederick W.: 7, 60-61, 66, 69-70, 94, 129, 130-132, 162, 165-166, 171, 179, 187-188, 198-199, 205-

209, 221, 223, 224, 229-230
Bingham, Rep. John: 12, 92
Bismarck (D.T.): 145, 199, 200, 214
Black Hills (S.D.): 67, 142-143, 145, 146-147, 190, 217
Bloody Knife (Arickaree): 163, 217
Bonaparte, Napoleon: 94, 96, 125, 206
Bonnafon, A.L.: 181
Bouyer, Mitch: 202, 211
Boyle, Hal: 218
Bradley, Lt. James H.: 168, 215, 223, 224-225, 229, 230
Brady, Rev. C.T.: 193-194
Brewster, Lt. Charles: 53
Bridwell, Lowell K.: 69
Briggs, Col. Geroge G.: 21
Brill, Charles J.: 63, 66-68
Brininstool, E.A.: 211
Brisbin, Col. James: 159, 192-193
Buffalo Bill,see William Cody
Bulkley, John: 103, 105
Bull Run (Va.): 37
Buntline, Ned: 222

Calhoun, Lt. James: 93, 180, 231
Calhoun, Mrs. James (Margaret Custer): 93, 230
Cambridge (Mass.): 70
Camp, W.M.: 170
Carland, Capt. John: 200
Carlisle (Pa.): 108
Carroll, John M.: 134
Carter, Capt. R.G.: 208
Carter,Thomas W.: 50
Carver, George W.: 4

245